Level 2   **STUDENT** BOOK   Units 7–12

LANGUAGE!®Live

VOYAGER SOPRIS LEARNING®

Louisa Moats, Ed.D., Author

For a complete listing of copyright permission acknowledgements, please see p. 554.

Printed in the United States of America
Published and Distributed by

VOYAGER SOPRIS
LEARNING®

17855 Dallas Parkway, Suite 400 • Dallas, TX 75287 • 800-547-6747
www.voyagersopris.com

Unit 7

Lesson 1 1
Lesson 2 10
Lesson 3 14
Lesson 4 18
Lesson 5 22
Lesson 6 23
Lesson 7 28
Lesson 8 30
Lesson 9 32
Lesson 10 35

Unit 8

Lesson 1 39
Lesson 2 51
Lesson 3 55
Lesson 4 58
Lesson 5 68
Lesson 6 69
Lesson 7 88
Lesson 8 90
Lesson 9 93
Lesson 10 106

Unit 9

Lesson 1 111
Lesson 2 121
Lesson 3 126
Lesson 4 129
Lesson 5 136
Lesson 6 137
Lesson 7 201
Lesson 8 204
Lesson 9 207
Lesson 10 238

Unit 10

Lesson 1 243
Lesson 2 253
Lesson 3 257
Lesson 4 260
Lesson 5 266
Lesson 6 268
Lesson 7 274
Lesson 8 276
Lesson 9 278
Lesson 10 284

Unit 11

Lesson 1 289
Lesson 2 299
Lesson 3 305
Lesson 4 307
Lesson 5 315
Lesson 6 317
Lesson 7 325
Lesson 8 327
Lesson 9 330
Lesson 10 335

Unit 12

Lesson 1 339
Lesson 2 350
Lesson 3 358
Lesson 4 360
Lesson 5 368
Lesson 6 369
Lesson 7 376
Lesson 8 378
Lesson 9 381
Lesson 10 386

Progress

Let's Focus: Excerpt from *White Fang*

Content Focus	**Type of Text**
survival; conditioning	literature—fiction

Author's Name _____

Author's Purpose _____

Big Ideas
Consider the following Big Idea questions. Write your answer for each question.

Can good and evil be conditioned, or are people born that way?

_____

_____

Can a vicious beast be tamed in an environment of love and support?

_____

_____

Narrative Preview Checklist: The excerpt from *White Fang* on pages 5–9.

☐ Title: What clue does it provide about the passage?

☐ Pictures: What additional information is added here?

☐ Margin Information: What vocabulary is important to understand this story?

Enduring Understandings
After reading the text . . .

_____

_____

_____

_____

_____

Plot Summary Outline

Story Title: _____

Part 2—Born of the Wild

1. Kiche, known as she-wolf, mates with a wolf and gives birth to five pups.

2. All pups die of famine except one.

3. Surviving pup has a wolf's coloring and intelligence, as well as the stamina of a strong, wild wolf.

4. Kiche's pup learns the law of the wild: EAT OR BE EATEN.

Part 3—The Gods of the Wild

1. Kiche and her pup learn to live in civilization at an Indian camp with Gray Beaver as their master.

2. Pup is named White Fang due to his extremely white fangs.

3. Gray Beaver trades Kiche (the mom) to settle a debt.

4. White Fang is mistreated by other dogs. Because he fights back, he is hated by all people but Gray Beaver.

5. White Fang learns to become a ferocious fighter because of his environment.

6. White Fang becomes dog-like when he escapes but realizes that he prefers the camp to the wild and returns.

7. White Fang has loyalty and respect for Gray Beaver, but no love.

Plot Summary Outline (*cont.*)

Part 4—The Superior Gods

1. White Fang becomes violent toward all other dogs.

2. Gray Beaver settles a debt by giving White Fang to Beauty Smith, a cruel, evil, and ugly man.

3. Beauty Smith attempts to tame White Fang with beatings and force.

4. White Fang learns to take out his hostility and hatred for Smith on other dogs when he is entered in dogfights. He becomes known as "The Fighting Wolf."

5. Weedon Scott saves White Fang from near death during a fight with a dog.

6. Weedon Scott becomes White Fang's new master and tries to teach White Fang how to experience love.

Part 5—The Tame

1. Weedon Scott returns to California with White Fang to live on his ranch with his family (wife: Alice, mom, and dad: Judge Scott).

2. _____

_____

_____

3. _____

_____

_____

4. _____

_____

_____

5. _____

_____

_____

6. _____

_____

_____

Key Passage Vocabulary: Excerpt from *White Fang*

Read each word. Write the word in column 3. Then, circle a number to rate your knowledge of the word.

Vocabulary	Part of Speech	Write the Word	Knowledge Rating
restrain	(v)		0 1 2 3
encounter	(v)		0 1 2 3
pursue	(v)		0 1 2 3
vainly	(adv)		0 1 2 3
compel	(v)		0 1 2 3
vengeance	(n)		0 1 2 3
ignorant	(adj)		0 1 2 3
promotion	(n)		0 1 2 3
advantage	(n)		0 1 2 3
ascent	(n)		0 1 2 3

from
WHITE FANG
by Jack London

It was about this time that the newspapers were full of the daring escape of a convict from San Quentin prison. He was a ferocious man. He had been ill-made in the making. He had not been born right,
5 and he had not been helped any by the molding he had received at the hands of society. The hands of society are harsh, and this man was a striking sample of its handiwork. He was a beast—a human beast, it is true, but nevertheless so terrible a beast
10 that he can best be characterized as carnivorous. **1**

In San Quentin prison he had proved incorrigible. Punishment failed to break his spirit. He could die dumb-mad and fighting to the last, but he could not live and be beaten. The more fiercely he fought,
15 the more harshly society handled him, and the only effect of harshness was to make him fiercer. Straight-jackets to **restrain** him, starvation, and beatings and clubbings were the wrong treatment for Jim Hall; but it was the treatment he received. It
20 was the treatment he had received from the time he was a little pulpy, shapeable boy in a San Francisco slum—soft clay in the hands of society and ready to be formed into something. **2**

It was during Jim Hall's third term in prison that
25 he **encountered** a guard that was almost as great a beast as he. The guard treated him unfairly, lied about him to the warden, lost his credits, and persecuted him. The difference between them was that the guard carried a bunch of keys and a gun. Jim
30 Hall had only his naked hands and his teeth. But he sprang upon the guard one day and used his teeth on the other's throat just like any jungle animal.

restrain
to hold back

encounter
to meet; to come in contact with

1 What animal-like qualities does the prisoner have?

2 What kind of punishment did Jim Hall receive that did not lead to reform?

pursue
to chase; to go after

After this, Jim Hall went to live in the incorrigible cell. He lived there three years. The cell was of iron,
35 the floor, the walls, the roof. He never left this cell. He never saw the sky nor the sunshine. Day was a barely noticeable twilight and night was a black silence. He was in an iron tomb, buried alive. He saw no human face, spoke to no human thing. When his
40 food was shoved in to him, he growled like a wild animal. He hated all things. For days and nights he bellowed his rage loudly at the universe. Then, for weeks and months he never made a sound, in the black silence eating his very soul. He was a man
45 and a monstrosity, as fearful a thing of fear as ever imagined in the visions of a maddened brain. **3**

3 What was life like for Jim Hall before his attack on the prison guard and after his attack on the prison guard?

And then, one night, he escaped. The warders said it was impossible, but nevertheless the cell was empty, and half in half out of it lay the body of a
50 slain guard. Two other dead guards marked his trail through the prison to the outer walls, and he had killed with his hands to avoid noise.

He was armed with the weapons of the slain guards—a live arsenal that fled through the hills
55 **pursued** by the organized might of society. A heavy price of gold was upon his head. Greedy farmers hunted him with shotguns. His blood might pay off a loan or send a son to college. Public-spirited citizens took down their rifles and went out after
60 him. A pack of bloodhounds followed the way of his bleeding feet. And the sleuth-hounds of the law, the paid fighting animals of society, with telephone, and telegraph, and special train, clung to his trail night and day. **4**

4 Where did Jim Hall get his weapons?

65 Sometimes they came upon him, and men faced him like heroes, or stampeded through barbed-wire fences to the delight of the people reading the account at the breakfast table. It was after such encounters that the dead and wounded were carted
70 back to the towns, and their places filled by men eager for the manhunt.

And then Jim Hall disappeared. The bloodhounds **vainly** quested for him on the lost trail. Inoffensive, ordinary ranchers in remote valleys were held up by
75 armed men and **compelled** to identify themselves. While the remains of Jim Hall were discovered on a dozen mountainsides by greedy claimants for blood-money. **5**

In the meantime the newspapers were read at Sierra
80 Vista, not so much with interest as with anxiety, or worry. The women were afraid. Judge Scott pooh-poohed and laughed, but not with reason, for it was in his last days on the bench that Jim Hall had stood before him and received sentence. And in open
85 courtroom, before all men, Jim Hall had proclaimed that the day would come when he would wreak **vengeance** on the Judge that sentenced him.

For once, Jim Hall was right. He was innocent of the crime for which he was sentenced. It was a case, in
90 the language of thieves and police, of "railroading." Jim Hall was being "railroaded" to prison for a crime he had not committed. Because of the two prior convictions against him, Judge Scott imposed upon him a sentence of fifty years. **6**

95 Judge Scott did not know all things, and he did not know that he was party to a police conspiracy, that the evidence was hatched and falsified, that Jim Hall was guiltless of the crime charged. And Jim Hall, on the other hand, did not know that Judge Scott was
100 merely **ignorant**. Jim Hall believed that the judge knew all about it and was hand in glove with the police in the **promotion** of the monstrous injustice. So it was, when the doom of fifty years of living death was uttered by Judge Scott, that Jim Hall,
105 hating all things in the society that misused him, rose up and raged in the courtroom until dragged down by half a dozen of his blue-coated enemies. To him, Judge Scott was the keystone in the arch of injustice, and upon Judge Scott he emptied the
110 vials of his wrath and hurled the angry threats of his revenge yet to come. Then Jim Hall went to his living death . . . and escaped. **7**

vainly
without success; not achieving what one hoped to

compel
to make someone take a certain action

vengeance
the act of repaying one hurtful deed with another

ignorant
not knowing or having important information

promotion
an attempt to convince others that they should do, believe, or buy something

5 Why did so many men want to find Jim Hall?

6 What is Jim Hall's connection to Judge Scott?

7 In what ways are Jim Hall and Judge Scott both "falsely accused"?

advantage

something that puts you in a better position than others

ascent

an upward journey

8 Why do you think White Fang is introduced at this time?

9 Who is the strange god and the lovemaster?

Of all this White Fang knew nothing. But between him and Alice, the master's wife, there existed a
115 secret. Each night, after Sierra Vista had gone to bed, she rose and let in White Fang to sleep in the big hall. Now White Fang was not a house dog, nor was he permitted to sleep in the house; so each morning, early, she slipped down and let him out
120 before the family was awake. **8**

On one such night, while all the house slept, White Fang awoke and lay very quietly. And very quietly he smelled the air and read the message it bore of a strange god's presence. And to his ears came
125 sounds of the strange god's movements. White Fang burst into no furious outcry. It was not his way. The strange god walked softly, but more softly walked White Fang, for he had no clothes to rub against the flesh of his body. He followed silently. In the Wild
130 he had hunted live meat that was infinitely timid, and he knew the **advantage** of surprise.

The strange god paused at the foot of the great staircase and listened, and White Fang was as dead, so without movement was he as he watched and waited.
135 Up that staircase the way led to the lovemaster and to the lovemaster's dearest possessions. White Fang bristled, but waited. The strange god's foot lifted. He was beginning the **ascent**. **9**

Then it was that White Fang struck. He gave no
140 warning, with no snarl anticipated his own action.
Into the air he lifted his body in the spring that
landed him on the strange god's back. White Fang
clung with his forepaws to the man's shoulders, at
the same time burying his fangs into the back of
145 the man's neck. He clung on for a moment, long
enough to drag the god over backward. Together
they crashed to the floor. White Fang leaped clear,
and, as the man struggled to rise, was in again with
the slashing fangs. **10**

> **10** How did White
> Fang complete
> the mission
> Alice had
> given him?

Jack London, born in 1876, was one of the first
famous fiction writers known worldwide for
his work. Early in his career, London wrote the
groundbreaking novel *The Call of the Wild*, which
featured a domesticated dog forced to revert back
to his wild instincts. Because of its success, London
felt it was necessary to write a companion novel,
White Fang, but he wanted to add a twist. "I'm going
to reverse the process. Instead of the devolution
or de-civilization of a dog, I'm going to give the
evolution, the civilization of a dog—development of
domesticity, faithfulness, love, morality, and all of
the amenities and virtues." This allows the readers
to see their society through the eyes of a being who
has never experienced it, all of the good qualities but
also the bad ones. In both of these novels, London's
exploration of the violent natures of man and beast
gives the audience a new insight into themselves.
London was heavily involved in the creative writing
world of his time and even helped jump-start
commercial magazine fiction.

*Wolf fang,
actual size*

Phrase vs. Clause

Read the following groups of words and place an X in the proper column to identify them as a phrase or a clause.

	Phrase	Clause
Ex: of the daring escape	X	
Ex: he was a ferocious man		X
1. had been helped		
2. punishment failed to break his spirit		
3. in the hands of society		
4. during Jim Hall's third term in prison		
5. the cell was of iron		
6. he saw no human face		
7. for weeks and months		
8. in the visions of a maddened brain		
9. he escaped		
10. Jim Hall disappeared		

Subordinating Conjunctions and Dependent Clauses

Subordinating Conjunctions				
• although	• as	• because	• how	• if
• since	• unless	• until	• while	• after
• when	• where	• why	• as if	• before
• than	• regardless			

Two jobs of a subordinating conjunction:

- Joins a dependent clause to a main clause
- Establishes a relationship between the two clauses

Read the sentences below. Circle the subordinating conjunctions and underline the dependent clauses.

Examples:

(As)the stranger crept through the house, White Fang watched his every move.

The guards patrolled the area carefully (because) Jim Hall threatened to escape.

1. When his food was shoved in to him, he growled like a wild animal.

2. Each night, after Sierra Vista had gone to bed, she rose and let in White Fang to sleep in the big hall.

3. She slipped down and let him out before the family was awake.

4. On one such night, while all the house slept, White Fang awoke and lay very quietly.

5. White Fang leaped clear, and, as the man struggled to rise, was in again with the slashing fangs.

Sentences with Subordinating Conjunctions

Part A

Finish each sentence by completing the dependent clause.

> **Example:**
>
> While **he was held in the incorrigible cell** ,
> Jim Hall spoke to no human being.

1. Jim Hall was considered incorrigible because _____

_____ .

2. Until _____ ,

Jim Hall lived in darkness.

3. Since _____ ,

the judge's wife was frightened by Jim Hall's escape.

4. Although _____ ,

Jim Hall was imprisoned for a crime he did not commit.

5. White Fang attacked the stranger when _____

_____ .

Part B

Reread the sentences above. Circle the commas and deduce the rule for
when commas are needed with dependent clauses.

_____

_____

Combining Dependent and Independent Clauses

Read the clauses and determine if they are dependent or independent clauses. Write them in the proper column in the chart. Then, create sentences by combining a dependent clause with an independent clause from the chart. Write the sentences on the lines below and remember to add commas when needed.

- while I waited for the bus
- when wolves returned to Yellowstone Park
- ranchers began to worry about their cattle and sheep
- she has not worked out regularly
- because the storm brought heavy rains
- the roads in the neighborhood were flooded
- I finished my homework
- birds darted up and down the beach
- as the young boy played in the sand
- since the gym closed

Dependent Clauses	Independent Clauses

_____

_____

_____

_____

_____

_____

_____

_____

Critical Understandings: Direction Words

Prompt	How to Respond	Model
If the prompt asks you to . . .	The response requires you to . . .	For example . . .
Analyze	break down and evaluate or draw conclusions about the information	**Analyze** the development of the text's central idea.
Assess	decide on the value, impact, or accuracy	**Assess** how the author's point of view affects the story.
Cite Evidence	support your answer by paraphrasing or using a direct quote	**Cite evidence** that supports your argument.
Clarify	make a statement or situation less confusing	**Clarify** the events leading up to the marriage.
Compare	state the similarities between two or more things	**Compare** Indian and Chinese marriage arrangements.
Connect	tie ideas together, relate	**Connect** each storm with its safety plan.
Contrast	state the differences between two or more things	**Contrast** Indian and Chinese marriage arrangements.
Demonstrate	show how to do it	**Demonstrate** your knowledge of wolves through poetry.
Develop an Argument	work on a case over a period of time, during which it grows or changes	Use evidence from both stories to **develop an argument** against arranged marriages.
Differentiate	tell apart or tell the difference between	**Differentiate** between the protagonist and the antagonist.
Distinguish	recognize something for a specific reason	**Distinguish** your claim from the opposing view by telling how it is different.

Critical Understandings: Direction Words (*cont.*)

Prompt	How to Respond	Model
If the prompt asks you to . . .	The response requires you to . . .	For example . . .
Evaluate	think carefully to make a judgment; form a critical opinion of	**Evaluate** the impact of the character's personality traits.
Illustrate	use examples to demonstrate or prove	**Illustrate** the internal battle between good and evil through Dr. Jekyll's research and explanations.
Integrate	combine different kinds of information to form a complete whole	**Integrate** information from several sources to write a report.
Present	deliver information	**Present** the benefits of wolf reintroduction.
Prove	give evidence to show that it is true	**Prove** that arranged marriages can work.
Relate	explain the connection between ideas or concepts	**Relate** Mr. Hyde to Jim Hall.
Summarize	tell the most important ideas or concepts	**Summarize** the passage.
Support	help it succeed	**Support** the statement that people have two selves.
Synthesize	combine information in a logical way	**Synthesize** information from both texts to explain the impact of anger.
Trace	follow information closely	**Trace** the boy's bad decisions.

Passage Comprehension

Reread the excerpt from *White Fang*. Respond to each prompt using complete sentences. Refer to the chart on pages 14 and 15 to determine how to respond to each prompt. Provide text evidence when requested.

1. Distinguish between the story's primary sequence of events and its flashback.

   _____

   _____

   _____

   _____

   _____

2. Assess society's treatment of Hall from childhood to adulthood.

   _____

   _____

   _____

   _____

   _____

   _____

3. Evaluate Hall's reaction to the harsh hands of society. Provide text evidence.

   _____

   _____

   _____

   _____

   _____

   Text Evidence: _____

   _____

   _____

   _____

   _____

   _____

Passage Comprehension (*cont.*)

4. Distinguish between Judge Scott's and Jim Hall's missing information and explain how it led to the prisoner's revenge.

_____

_____

_____

_____

_____

_____

_____

5. Use your summary plot outline to evaluate White Fang's perception of Weedon Scott.

_____

_____

_____

_____

_____

_____

6. Analyze Alice Scott's nightly routine.

_____

_____

_____

_____

_____

_____

_____

Close Reading

Read the text.

from *White Fang*

It was about this time that the newspapers were full of the daring escape of a convict from San Quentin prison. He was a ferocious man. He had been ill-made in the making. He had not been born right, and he had not been helped any by the molding he had received at the hands of society.
5 The hands of society are harsh, and this man was a striking sample of its handiwork. He was a beast—a human beast, it is true, but nevertheless so terrible a beast that he can best be characterized as carnivorous.

In San Quentin prison he had proved incorrigible. Punishment failed to break his spirit. He could die dumb-mad and fighting to the last,
10 but he could not live and be beaten. The more fiercely he fought, the more harshly society handled him, and the only effect of harshness was to make him fiercer. Straight-jackets to **restrain** him, starvation, and beatings and clubbings were the wrong treatment for Jim Hall; but it was the treatment he received. It was the treatment he had received from the
15 time he was a little pulpy, shapeable boy in a San Francisco slum—soft clay in the hands of society and ready to be formed into something.

It was during Jim Hall's third term in prison that he **encountered** a guard that was almost as great a beast as he. The guard treated him unfairly, lied about him to the warden, lost his credits, and persecuted him. The
20 difference between them was that the guard carried a bunch of keys and a gun. Jim Hall had only his naked hands and his teeth. But he sprang upon the guard one day and used his teeth on the other's throat just like any jungle animal.

After this, Jim Hall went to live in the incorrigible cell. He lived there
25 three years. The cell was of iron, the floor, the walls, the roof. He never left this cell. He never saw the sky nor the sunshine. Day was a barely noticeable twilight and night was a black silence. He was in an iron tomb, buried alive. He saw no human face, spoke to no human thing. When his food was shoved in to him, he growled like a wild animal. He hated all
30 things. For days and nights he bellowed his rage loudly at the universe. Then, for weeks and months he never made a sound, in the black silence eating his very soul. He was a man and a monstrosity, as fearful a thing of fear as ever imagined in the visions of a maddened brain.

Close Reading (*cont.*)

And then, one night, he escaped. The warders said it was impossible, but
35 nevertheless the cell was empty, and half in half out of it lay the body of
a slain guard. Two other dead guards marked his trail through the prison
to the outer walls, and he had killed with his hands to avoid noise.

He was armed with the weapons of the slain guards—a live arsenal that
fled through the hills **pursued** by the organized might of society. A
40 heavy price of gold was upon his head. Greedy farmers hunted him with
shotguns. His blood might pay off a loan or send a son to college. Public-
spirited citizens took down their rifles and went out after him. A pack
of bloodhounds followed the way of his bleeding feet. And the sleuth-
hounds of the law, the paid fighting animals of society, with telephone,
45 and telegraph, and special train, clung to his trail night and day.

Sometimes they came upon him, and men faced him like heroes, or
stampeded through barbed-wire fences to the delight of the people
reading the account at the breakfast table. It was after such encounters
that the dead and wounded were carted back to the towns, and their
50 places filled by men eager for the manhunt.

And then Jim Hall disappeared. The bloodhounds **vainly** quested for him
on the lost trail. Inoffensive, ordinary ranchers in remote valleys were
held up by armed men and **compelled** to identify themselves. While the
remains of Jim Hall were discovered on a dozen mountainsides by greedy
55 claimants for blood-money.

Close Reading (*cont.*)

In the meantime the newspapers were read at Sierra Vista, not so much with interest as with anxiety, or worry. The women were afraid. Judge Scott pooh-poohed and laughed, but not with reason, for it was in his last days on the bench that Jim Hall had stood before him and
60 received sentence. And in open courtroom, before all men, Jim Hall had proclaimed that the day would come when he would wreak **vengeance** on the Judge that sentenced him.

For once, Jim Hall was right. He was innocent of the crime for which he was sentenced. It was a case, in the language of thieves and police, of
65 "railroading." Jim Hall was being "railroaded" to prison for a crime he had not committed. Because of the two prior convictions against him, Judge Scott imposed upon him a sentence of fifty years.

Judge Scott did not know all things, and he did not know that he was party to a police conspiracy, that the evidence was hatched and falsified,
70 that Jim Hall was guiltless of the crime charged. And Jim Hall, on the other hand, did not know that Judge Scott was merely **ignorant**. Jim Hall believed that the judge knew all about it and was hand in glove with the police in the **promotion** of the monstrous injustice. So it was, when the doom of fifty years of living death was uttered by Judge Scott, that Jim
75 Hall, hating all things in the society that misused him, rose up and raged in the courtroom until dragged down by half a dozen of his blue-coated enemies. To him, Judge Scott was the keystone in the arch of injustice, and upon Judge Scott he emptied the vials of his wrath and hurled the angry threats of his revenge yet to come. Then Jim Hall went to his living
80 death . . . and escaped.

Of all this White Fang knew nothing. But between him and Alice, the master's wife, there existed a secret. Each night, after Sierra Vista had gone to bed, she rose and let in White Fang to sleep in the big hall. Now White Fang was not a house dog, nor was he permitted to sleep in the
85 house; so each morning, early, she slipped down and let him out before the family was awake.

Close Reading (*cont.*)

On one such night, while all the house slept, White Fang awoke and lay very quietly. And very quietly he smelled the air and read the message it bore of a strange god's presence. And to his ears came sounds of the
90 strange god's movements. White Fang burst into no furious outcry. It was not his way. The strange god walked softly, but more softly walked White Fang, for he had no clothes to rub against the flesh of his body. He followed silently. In the Wild he had hunted live meat that was infinitely timid, and he knew the **advantage** of surprise.

95 The strange god paused at the foot of the great staircase and listened, and White Fang was as dead, so without movement was he as he watched and waited. Up that staircase the way led to the lovemaster and to the lovemaster's dearest possessions. White Fang bristled, but waited. The strange god's foot lifted. He was beginning the **ascent**.

100 Then it was that White Fang struck. He gave no warning, with no snarl anticipated his own action. Into the air he lifted his body in the spring that landed him on the strange god's back. White Fang clung with his forepaws to the man's shoulders, at the same time burying his fangs into the back of the man's neck. He clung on for a moment, long enough to
105 drag the god over backward. Together they crashed to the floor. White Fang leaped clear, and, as the man struggled to rise, was in again with the slashing fangs.

Quick Write in Response to Reading

Review the plot summary on pages 2 and 3. Think about how dramatically White Fang's life changed when he left the Yukon and came to live with the Scotts. Write a narrative from White Fang's point of view that describes this turning point. Use evidence from the plot summary in your writing. Consider using foreshadowing in your opening sentence to alert the reader of the big change that is coming.

Let's Focus: "Return of the Wolves"

Content Focus
reintroduction of wolves; human involvement
in the environment

Type of Text
informational—nonfiction

Author's Name _____

Author's Purpose _____

Big Ideas
Consider the following Big Idea questions. Write your answer for each question.

How do stereotypes of wolves affect their image and perhaps even their existence?

_____

_____

Should humans interfere with nature? Explain.

_____

_____

Informational Preview Checklist: "Return of the Wolves" on pages 25–27.

☐ Title: What clue does it provide?

☐ Pictures: What additional information is added here?

☐ Margin Information: What vocabulary is important to understand this story?

☐ Features: What other features do you notice?

Enduring Understandings
After reading the text . . .

_____

_____

_____

_____

_____

Key Passage Vocabulary: "Return of the Wolves"

Read each word. Write the word in column 3. Then, circle a number to rate your knowledge of the word.

Vocabulary	Part of Speech	Write the Word	Knowledge Rating
persistence	(n)		0 1 2 3
insecurity	(n)		0 1 2 3
relocation	(n)		0 1 2 3
habitat	(n)		0 1 2 3
alter	(v)		0 1 2 3
competition	(n)		0 1 2 3
aspect	(n)		0 1 2 3
decline	(v)		0 1 2 3
economy	(n)		0 1 2 3
compromise	(n)		0 1 2 3

Return of the Wolves

The wolf has taken on many images over time. It has been known as both the noblest animal and the vilest animal. Native Americans respect the wolf for its bravery, intelligence, **persistence**, hunting skills, and love of family. However, authors and storytellers have made the wolf the villain of many stories like *Little Red Riding Hood* and *The Three Pigs*. And of course Hollywood has put its spin on the wolf by creating horror films to scare us. But the true image of the wolf in North America today is one of **insecurity**. It is trying to fit back into the land over which it once reigned king. **1**

The wolf once ruled the West. Its spot at the top of the food chain was unchallenged for centuries. By the 1930s, however, this had changed. The wolf fell victim to overhunting and trapping. Laws did not protect it. By the early 1970s, the gray wolf had mostly vanished from the western United States. It was placed on the endangered species list. The federal government began a **relocation** project. Several dozen wolves were captured in Canada and released in Yellowstone National Park. This project was a great success. However, it created a division between people in the area. Some were for it. Others were against it. **2**

persistence
the ability to keep doing something even though it is difficult

insecurity
the state of not feeling safe or steady

relocation
the act of moving to a different place

1 What is your image of wolves?

2 How did the federal government protect wolves?

habitat
the natural home of a plant or animal

alter
to change

competition
the struggle between two or more people or groups who are trying to get the same thing

3 How has the reintroduction been good for the area?

4 How has the wolf's return affected elk, beavers, birds, coyotes, and aspen trees?

There have been many good things about the relocation of
45 wolves to Yellowstone. For one, tourists love wolves. People who like seeing wildlife have come to the park to see the wolf in its **habitat** and to take
50 pictures. Naturalists have seen the relocation of the wolf as a victory in returning the West to the way it used to be. In addition, the people who visit
55 the park to see the wolves have boosted the economy greatly.

The reintroduction of wolves into Yellowstone has helped bring the elk population under
60 control. Wolves are natural carnivores. Because elk and deer are their favorite meal, the populations of these animals have decreased. This is a
65 positive change because the elk had overpopulated Yellowstone. **3**

Having too many elk had caused damage to aspen
70 tree forests. This **altered** the beaver and bird populations. The flow of streams and rivers were changed as a result. The presence of wolves in the elk
75 habitat creates what is called an "ecology of fear." Elk spend less time eating in one place. As a result, trees and shrubs grow back quicker. There's
80 more variety in the plant life. In Yellowstone, researchers saw that open fields became more vegetated when they brought back wolves.

85 Because the wolf has returned, coyotes have been able to return to their natural habit of scavenging. Without wolves, coyotes had jumped up in
90 the food chain. They could hunt animals without much **competition**. However, they struggled because they are not naturally good hunters. Having
95 wolves in the area has provided more food for the coyotes. They feed on the remains of the wolves' kills. **4**

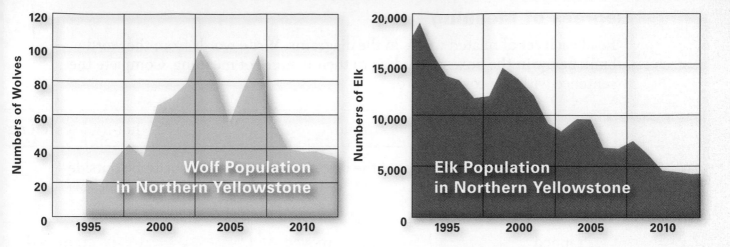

There have also been negative **aspects** to reintroducing
100 wolves. Ranchers believe that
wolves pose a threat to the
sheep and cattle industries
of the areas surrounding
105 Yellowstone. Wolves hunt as
a pack. This makes herds of
sheep and cattle surrounding
the park vulnerable to their
attacks. Ranchers have
110 struggled to deal with the
wolves' presence. According to
ranchers, predatory livestock
deaths have increased as the
wolf population has increased.
115 Because wolves are now
protected by law, ranchers
feel defenseless. However, the
federal government pays the
ranchers for the loss of their
120 animals, and the actual losses
of livestock to wolves have been
relatively small.

Hunters, too, have been
affected by the hunting
125 skills of the wolf pack. The
declining numbers of large-
game animals such as elk and
deer in the areas surrounding
the park have made hunting

130 tougher. It is estimated that
in the surrounding areas, the
elk population has been cut in
half since the wolf's return to
Yellowstone. Elk have fallen
135 prey to the wolves, and they
have moved to higher ground
for safety. Hunters now have
fewer animals for their own
hunting activities. This in turn
140 affects the **economy** of the
surrounding areas because
fewer hunters buy hunting
permits. **5**

The battle of the wolf will
145 rage on. Naturalists, ranchers,
hunters, and people who
want to see the wolf return
to its historical home all
have valuable viewpoints.
150 The outcome must be a
compromise. But for now, deep
in the heart of Yellowstone
National Park, there are wolves.
Their lonesome howls can be
155 heard on the darkest nights.
Their shadowy images can be
seen gliding through the aspen
forests as they do what they do
best—survive. **6**

aspect
one part, element,
or angle of
something

decline
to grow smaller in
size or strength

economy
the flow of
money, goods,
and services in a
community

compromise
the settlement
reached when
each side in an
argument gives up
a part of what it
wants

5 How has the
reintroduction
of wolves been
bad?

6 What is your
viewpoint on the
reintroduction
of wolves?

Degrees of Meaning

Read each set of related words in the diagrams. Write words from the word bank below in the boxes according to their degrees of meaning. Complete the sentence with the correct word.

freezing		mild		hot	scorching

1. The _____ heat of the desert makes it dangerous to be outside in the afternoon.

tapped		moved		rammed

2. Vern _____ his dirty clothes into the overflowing hamper.

	fling		pitch	

3. In this relay, you must gently _____ your partner the egg without dropping and breaking it.

		ran		

4. Even though the turtle _____ along, he beat the rabbit to the finish line.

		firmly		

5. Afraid he would never see her again, he _____ proclaimed his love and begged her not to go.

Word Bank

warm	cool	shoved	nudged	throw
toss	hurl	stampeded	jogged	plodded
dashed	fiercely	steadily	resolutely	gently

Critical Understandings

Reread lines 1–42 of "Return of the Wolves" and the graphs on page 27. Respond to each prompt using complete sentences. Refer to the chart on pages 14 and 15 to determine how to respond to each prompt. Provide text evidence when requested.

1. Synthesize the various images people have had of wolves over time and tell how these images have changed.

   _____

   _____

   _____

   _____

   _____

2. Clarify the meaning of *endangered* using context clues. List the context clues as text evidence.

   _____

   _____

   Text Evidence: _____

   _____

3. Present information from the Wolf and Elk Population graphs.

   _____

   _____

   _____

   _____

   _____

   _____

4. Prove that the reintroduction of wolves affected the elk population.

   _____

   _____

   _____

   _____

   _____

Passage Comprehension

Reread "Return of the Wolves." Respond to each prompt using complete sentences. Refer to the chart on pages 14 and 15 to determine how to respond to each prompt.

1. Clarify the author's basic claim or focus of information in "Return of the Wolves."

_____

_____

_____

2. Synthesize and explain the economic changes brought about by the wolf reintroduction.

_____

_____

_____

_____

_____

_____

_____

3. Prove the theory that the author supports wolf reintroduction.

_____

_____

_____

_____

_____

_____

_____

_____

Passage Comprehension (*cont.*)

4. Clarify the counterclaim of ranchers.

_____

_____

_____

_____

_____

5. Present data to prove that the ranchers' counterclaim is weak.

_____

_____

_____

_____

_____

_____

6. Synthesize and explain the author's recommendation regarding the reintroduction of wolves.

_____

_____

_____

_____

_____

Close Reading

Read the text.

"Return of the Wolves"

The wolf has taken on many images over time. It has been known as both the noblest animal and the vilest animal. Native Americans respect the wolf for its bravery, intelligence, **persistence**, hunting skills, and love of family. However, authors and storytellers have made the wolf the villain
5 of many stories like *Little Red Riding Hood* and *The Three Pigs*. And of course Hollywood has put its spin on the wolf by creating horror films to scare us. But the true image of the wolf in North America today is one of **insecurity**. It is trying to fit back into the land over which it once reigned king.

10 The wolf once ruled the West. Its spot at the top of the food chain was unchallenged for centuries. By the 1930s, however, this had changed. The wolf fell victim to overhunting and trapping. Laws did not protect it. By the early 1970s, the gray wolf had mostly vanished from the western United States. It was placed on the endangered species list. The federal government
15 began a **relocation** project. Several dozen wolves were captured in Canada and released in Yellowstone National Park. This project was a great success. However, it created a division between people in the area. Some were for it. Others were against it.

There have been many good things about the relocation of wolves to
20 Yellowstone. For one, tourists love wolves. People who like seeing wildlife have come to the park to see the wolf in its **habitat** and to take pictures. Naturalists have seen the relocation of the wolf as a victory in returning the West to the way it used to be. In addition, the people who visit the park to see the wolves have boosted the economy greatly.

Close Reading (*cont.*)

25 The reintroduction of wolves into Yellowstone has helped bring the elk population under control. Wolves are natural carnivores. Because elk and deer are their favorite meal, the populations of these animals have decreased. This is a positive change because the elk had overpopulated Yellowstone.

30 Having too many elk had caused damage to aspen tree forests. This **altered** the beaver and bird populations. The flow of streams and rivers were changed as a result. The presence of wolves in the elk habitat creates what is called an "ecology of fear." Elk spend less time eating in one place. As a result, trees and shrubs grow back quicker. There's more variety in
35 the plant life. In Yellowstone, researchers saw that open fields became more vegetated when they brought back wolves.

Because the wolf has returned, coyotes have been able to return to their natural habit of scavenging. Without wolves, coyotes had jumped up in the food chain. They could hunt animals without much **competition**.
40 However, they struggled because they are not naturally good hunters. Having wolves in the area has provided more food for the coyotes. They feed on the remains of the wolves' kills.

Close Reading (*cont.*)

There have also been negative **aspects** to reintroducing wolves. Ranchers believe that wolves pose a threat to the sheep and cattle industries of 45 the areas surrounding Yellowstone. Wolves hunt as a pack. This makes herds of sheep and cattle surrounding the park vulnerable to their attacks. Ranchers have struggled to deal with the wolves' presence. According to ranchers, predatory livestock deaths have increased as the wolf population has increased. Because wolves are now protected by 50 law, ranchers feel defenseless. However, the federal government pays the ranchers for the loss of their animals, and the actual losses of livestock to wolves have been relatively small.

Hunters, too, have been affected by the hunting skills of the wolf pack. The **declining** numbers of large-game animals such as elk and deer 55 in the areas surrounding the park have made hunting tougher. It is estimated that in the surrounding areas, the elk population has been cut in half since the wolf's return to Yellowstone. Elk have fallen prey to the wolves, and they have moved to higher ground for safety. Hunters now have fewer animals for their own hunting activities. This in turn 60 affects the **economy** of the surrounding areas because fewer hunters buy hunting permits.

The battle of the wolf will rage on. Naturalists, ranchers, hunters, and people who want to see the wolf return to its historical home all have valuable viewpoints. The outcome must be a **compromise**. But for now, 65 deep in the heart of Yellowstone National Park, there are wolves. Their lonesome howls can be heard on the darkest nights. Their shadowy images can be seen gliding through the aspen forests as they do what they do best—survive.

Six Traits of Effective Writing

	Trait	What does this mean?	Comments
	Ideas and Content	Focus on the main ideas or story line. Supporting details (expository) or images/events (narrative) build understanding.	
	Organization	Order of ideas and supporting details (expository) or clear beginning, middle, and end (narrative) make sense. Introduction, transitions, and conclusion help keep the reader hooked on the writing.	
	Voice and Audience Awareness	Style suits both the audience and purpose of the writing.	
	Word Choice	"Just right" words for the topic and audience	
	Sentence Fluency	Varied sentence use; no run-on sentences and sentence fragments	
	Conventions	Spelling, punctuation, grammar and usage, capitalization, and indenting paragraphs	

Editor's Marks
∧ add or change text
⟋ delete text
⟿ move text
P new paragraph
≡ capitalize
/ lowercase
⊙ insert period
◌ check spelling or spell out word

Prepare to Write: Argument Essay

Part A. Study the Prompt

Write an argument essay in which you take a position regarding the reintroduction of wolves into Yellowstone National Park. Present two reasons that support your position that are supported by evidence from the text.

Topic: _____

Directions: _____

_____

Purpose for writing: _____

_____

Part B. Write an Introduction

Write a topic sentence that clearly states your position. Incorporate attention-getting details into the introductory paragraph.

_____

_____

_____

_____

_____

_____

_____

_____

_____

Part C. Map Your Argument

Get the reader's attention with an example/situation:

_____

_____

Statement of Position:

_____

_____

Prepare to Write: Argument Essay (*cont.*)

First reason:

_____

Evidence:

_____

_____

_____

Second reason:

_____

Evidence:

_____

_____

_____

Anticipated objection:

_____

Response to objection:

_____

_____

_____

Restate position:

_____

_____

Part D. Write a Conclusion That Defends Your Position

Restate your topic sentence and defend your position.

_____

_____

_____

_____

_____

_____

The Persuasive Writer's Checklist

Trait	Yes	No	Did the writer . . .?
Ideas and Content			clearly state a position on an issue
			focus the content of each paragraph on the topic
			include examples, evidence, and/or explanations that are logically, emotionally, or ethically compelling
			when necessary, include recent, relevant, reliable research to validate the position
			create a title
Organization			write an introductory paragraph that captures the reader's interest and contains a clear thesis statement that serves as a "map" for the essay
			sequence body paragraphs logically and use transition sentences that make clear the relationship between ideas
			write a concluding paragraph that restates the position and issues a call to action
Voice and Audience Awareness			write in a voice that is confident and reasonable
			write in a tone of voice that suits the audience and purpose for writing
			demonstrate that the beliefs and opinions that others might have on the topic have been considered
			acknowledge one or more objections that others may make
Word Choice			use words that are lively, accurate, specific to the content, and convey authority
			vary the words so that the writing does not sound repetitive
Sentence Fluency			write complete sentences
			use the steps of Masterpiece Sentences
			use compound sentence elements and compound sentences
Conventions			capitalize words correctly:
			capitalize the first word of each sentence
			capitalize proper nouns, including people's names
			punctuate correctly:
			put a period or question mark at the end of each sentence
			put an apostrophe before the s for a singular possessive noun
			use a comma after a long adverb phrase at the beginning of a sentence
			use grammar correctly:
			use the correct verb tense
			make sure the verb agrees with the subject in number
			use correct spelling

Let's Focus: "The White Wolf of the Hartz Mountains"

Content Focus
werewolves

Type of Text
literature—short story

Author's Name _____

Author's Purpose _____

Big Ideas
Consider the following Big Idea questions. Write your answer for each question.

To what degree is the proverb "love is blind" true? Explain.

_____

_____

Do humans have the ability to know things that cannot be known by normal use of the senses? Do animals? Explain.

_____

_____

Narrative Preview Checklist: "The White Wolf of the Hartz Mountains" on pages 41–50.

☐ Title: What clue does it provide about the passage?

☐ Pictures: What additional information is added here?

☐ Margin Information: What vocabulary is important to understand this story?

Enduring Understandings
After reading the text . . .

_____

_____

_____

_____

_____

Key Passage Vocabulary: "The White Wolf of the Hartz Mountains"

Read each word. Write the word in column 3. Then, circle a number to rate your knowledge of the word.

Vocabulary	Part of Speech	Write the Word	Knowledge Rating
beckon	(v)		0 1 2 3
reside	(v)		0 1 2 3
converse	(v)		0 1 2 3
perish	(v)		0 1 2 3
resolve	(v)		0 1 2 3
seldom	(adv)		0 1 2 3
rashness	(n)		0 1 2 3
implicated	(v)		0 1 2 3
restore	(v)		0 1 2 3
penalty	(n)		0 1 2 3

The White Wolf of the Hartz Mountains

Adapted from a part of *The Phantom Ship*

By Captain Frederick Marryat

My oldest memories are of a simple, yet comfortable
cottage in the Hartz Mountains. I lived with my
father, brother, and sister. In summertime the
landscape was beautiful; but during the severe
5 winter, it was desolate. In the winter we remained
indoors, for the vicious wolves incessantly prowled
about in the cold. **1**

> **1** How many people lived in the cottage?

In the winter, my father hunted; every day he left us
and often locked the door to keep us inside. During
10 the short cold days of winter we would sit silent,
longing for the happy hours when the snow would
melt, and we should again be free.

One evening, the howl of a wolf, close under
the window of the cottage, fell on our ears. My
15 father jumped up, seized his gun, and hastily
left the cottage, locking the door after him. We
anxiously waited.

We waited for some time, but the sound of the gun
did not reach us. After several hours, my father
20 entered, with a young female and an old hunter. **2**

> **2** Who are the new arrivals in the cottage?

beckon

to signal to someone to come to you

reside

to live or stay in a place long-term

The female's features were very beautiful. Her hair was flaxen and bright as a mirror; her mouth, although somewhat large when it was open, showed the most brilliant teeth I have ever seen. But there

25 was something about her eyes which made us children afraid; they were so restless, so sly; I could not at that time tell why, but I felt as if there was cruelty in her eyes; and when she **beckoned** us to come to her, we approached her with fear and

30 trembling. Still she was beautiful, very beautiful. She spoke kindly to my brother and myself, patted our heads, and caressed us; but Marcella would not come near her; on the contrary, she slipped away and hid herself.

35 My father offered the young lady, whose name was Christina, his bed and he would remain at the fire, sitting up with her father. This arrangement was agreed to, and I and my brother crept into the other bed with Marcella, for we always slept together.

40 But we could not sleep; there was something so unusual, not only in seeing strange people, but in having those people sleep at the cottage, that we were bewildered. As for poor little Marcella, she was quiet, but trembled and sobbed the whole night.

45 My father and the hunter remained drinking and talking before the fire. Our curious ears were ready to catch the slightest whisper.

They filled their mugs to the brim and drank to one another in the German fashion. The conversation

50 was then carried on in a low tone; all that we could collect from it was that our new guest and his daughter were to **reside** in our cottage, at least for the present. After an hour, they both fell back in their chairs and slept.

55 When we awoke the next morning, we found that the hunter's daughter had risen before us. She came up to little Marcella and caressed her; the child burst into tears and sobbed as if her heart would break. **3**

3 Why didn't Marcella like Christina?

60 The hunter and his daughter stayed in the cottage.
My father and he went out hunting daily, leaving
Christina with us. She performed all the household
duties; was very kind to us children; and, gradually,
we grew to like her—even Marcella. But a great
65 change took place in my father; he was most
attentive to Christina. Often, after her father and we
were in bed, he would sit up with her, **conversing** in
a low tone by the fire. After three weeks of this, my
father asked for Christina's hand in marriage. Soon
70 after, the wedding took place.

My father repeated his vows after the hunter. "I
swear by all the spirits of the Hartz Mountains,
by all their power for good or for evil, that I take
Christina for my wedded wife; that I will protect
75 her, cherish her, and love her; that my hand shall
never be raised against her to harm her."

"And if I fail in this my vow, may all the vengeance
of the spirits fall upon me and upon my children;
may they **perish** by the vulture, by the wolf, or
80 by other beasts of the forest; may their flesh be
torn from their limbs, and their bones fade in the
wilderness; all this I swear."

My father hesitated, as he repeated the last words;
little Marcella could not restrain herself and burst
85 into tears. **4**

The next morning, the hunter mounted his horse
and rode away.

Things went on much as before the marriage, except
that our new stepmother did not show any kindness
90 towards us; indeed, during my father's absence, she
would often beat us, particularly little Marcella, and
her eyes would flash fire as she looked eagerly upon
the fair and lovely child.

converse
to talk with one or
more people

perish
to die

4 Why did Father
hesitate?

resolve

to make a firm decision to do something

seldom

rarely; not often

One night, my sister awoke me and my brother.

95 "What is the matter?" said Caesar.

"She has gone out," whispered Marcella.

"Gone out!"

"Yes, gone out the door, in her night-dress," replied the child. "I saw her."

100 What could bring her to leave the cottage, in such bitter wintry weather, was incomprehensible; we lay awake, and in about an hour we heard the growl of a wolf, close under the window.

"There is a wolf," said Caesar; "she will be torn
105 to pieces."

A few minutes afterwards, our stepmother appeared; she was in her night-dress, as Marcella had stated. She let down the latch of the door, so as to make no noise, went to a pail of water, and
110 washed her face and hands, and then slipped into the bed where my father lay.

We all three trembled, we hardly knew why, but we **resolved** to watch the next night. We did so—and many other nights as well, and always at about the
115 same hour, would our stepmother rise from her bed, and leave the cottage—and after she was gone, we invariably heard the growl of a wolf under our window, and always saw her, on her return, wash herself before she retired to bed. We observed, also,
120 that she **seldom** sat down to meals, and that when she did, she appeared to eat with dislike; but when the meat was being prepared, she would often put a raw piece into her mouth. **5**

5 What do you know about Christina so far?

My brother Caesar did not want to tell my father
125 until he knew more. He resolved to follow her out
and ascertain what she did. Marcella and I tried to
dissuade him; but he would not be deterred, and the
very next night he lay down in his clothes, and as
soon as our stepmother left the cottage, he jumped
130 up, took down my father's gun, and followed her.

Marcella and I waited in suspense. After a few
minutes, we heard the sound of a gun. It did not
awaken my father, and we lay trembling with
anxiety. In a minute afterwards, we saw our
135 stepmother enter the cottage—her dress was bloody.
I put my hand to Marcella's mouth to prevent her
crying out, although I was myself in great alarm.
Our stepmother looked to see if our father was
asleep, and then started a fire. **6**

> **6** Who was
> shot?

140 "Who is there?" said my father, waking up.

"Lie still, dearest," replied my stepmother, "it is only
me; I have lighted the fire to warm some water; I am
not quite well."

My father turned round and was soon asleep, but
145 we watched our stepmother. She changed her
clothes and threw the garments she had worn into
the fire; and we then perceived that her right leg
was bleeding, as if from a gun-shot wound. She
bandaged it up and dressed herself.

150 Poor little Marcella, her heart beat quick as she
pressed me to her side—so indeed did mine. Where
was our brother, Caesar? How did my stepmother
receive the wound unless from his gun? At last
my father rose, and then, for the first time I spoke,
155 saying, "Father, where is my brother, Caesar?"

"Your brother!" exclaimed he, "why, where can
he be?"

rashness

a tendency to act without thinking something through

7 What does Christina want her husband to believe?

"Merciful Heaven! I thought as I lay very restless last night," observed our stepmother, "that I heard
160 somebody open the latch of the door; and dear husband, what has become of your gun?" **7**

My father cast his eyes up above the chimney, and perceived that his gun was missing. For a moment he looked perplexed, then seizing an axe, he went
165 out of the cottage without saying another word.

He did not remain away from us long. In a few minutes he returned, bearing in his arms the mangled body of my poor brother; he laid it down and covered up his face.

170 My stepmother rose up and looked at the body, while Marcella and I threw ourselves by its side, wailing and sobbing bitterly.

"Go to bed again, children," said she sharply. "Husband, your boy must have taken the gun
175 down to shoot a wolf, and the animal has been too powerful for him. Poor boy! He has paid dearly for his **rashness**."

My father made no reply; I wished to tell all, but Marcella, who saw my intention, held my arm and
180 looked at me so imploringly that I stopped. **8**

8 Why didn't Marcella want him to tell what he knew?

My father, therefore, was deceived; but Marcella and I, although we could not comprehend it, knew that our stepmother was in some way connected with my brother's death.

185 That day, my father went out and dug a grave, and when he laid the body in the earth, he piled up stones over it, so that the villainous wolves should not be able to dig it up. The shock of this tragedy was severe for my father; for several days he did
190 not hunt but uttered bitter vengeance against the wolves.

During this time of mourning, my stepmother's nocturnal wanderings continued with the same regularity as before. **9**

9 What did Christina do on her nighttime wanderings?

195 At last, my father took down his gun, and went hunting; but he soon returned and appeared bothered.

"Would you believe it, Christina, that the wolves—most evil of all animals—have actually dug up the
200 body of my poor boy, and now there is nothing left of him but his bones?"

Marcella looked at me, and I saw in her intelligent eyes all she would have uttered.

"A wolf growls under our window every night,
205 father," said I.

"Really?—why did you not tell me, boy?—wake me the next time you hear it."

I saw my stepmother turn away; her eyes flashed fire, and she gnashed her teeth. **10**

10 Why is Christina upset?

210 The spring finally came. The snow disappeared, and we were permitted to leave the cottage; but never would I leave, for one moment, my dear little sister, to whom, since the death of my brother, I was more attached than ever. I was afraid to leave her
215 alone with my stepmother, who appeared to have a particular pleasure in ill-treating the child. My father was now working his little farm, and I was able to assist him.

Marcella used to sit by us while we were at work,
220 leaving my stepmother alone in the cottage. As spring advanced, my stepmother decreased her nocturnal rambles, and we never heard the growl of the wolf under the window after I had spoken of it to my father.

225 One day, when my father and I were in the field, Marcella being with us, my stepmother came out, saying that she was going into the forest to collect some herbs my father wanted, and that Marcella must go to the cottage and watch the dinner.

230 Marcella went, and my stepmother disappeared in the forest. **11**

11 Predict what will happen next.

About an hour afterwards, we were startled by shrieks from the cottage. "Marcella has burnt herself, father," said I, throwing down my spade. My

235 father threw down his, and we both hastened to the cottage. Before we arrived, out darted a large white wolf. We rushed into the cottage and there saw poor little Marcella. Her body was extremely mangled, and the blood pouring from it had formed a large

240 pool on the cottage floor. My father's first intention had been to seize his gun and pursue, but he was checked by this horrid spectacle; he knelt down by his dying child and burst into tears. Marcella looked kindly at us for a few seconds and then closed her

245 eyes in death.

My father and I were still hovering over my sister's body when my stepmother came in. At the dreadful sight, she expressed much concern, but she did not appear to recoil from the sight of blood, as most

250 women do.

"Poor child!" said she, "it must have been that great white wolf which passed me just now and frightened me so." **12**

12 Where was Christina?

My father cried in agony.

255 I thought my father would never recover from the effects of this second tragedy. He mourned over the body of his sweet daughter and for several days would not bury her. At last he dug a grave for her close by that of my poor brother and took

260 every precaution that the wolves should not violate her remains.

I was now really miserable, as I lay alone in the bed which I had formerly shared with my brother and sister. I could not help thinking that my stepmother was **implicated** in both their deaths, although I could not explain it. I no longer felt afraid of her; my heart was full of hatred and revenge.

The night after my sister was buried, as I lay awake, I saw my stepmother get up and go out of the cottage. I waited some time, then dressed myself, and looked out through the door. The moon shone bright, and I could see the spot where my brother and sister had been buried; and to my horror, I perceived my stepmother busily removing the stones from Marcella's grave. **13**

She was in her white night-dress, and the moon shone full upon her. She was digging with her hands and throwing away the stones behind her with all the ferocity of a wild beast. At last, she raised the body to the side of the grave. I could bear it no longer; I ran to my father and awoke him.

"Father! Father! Dress yourself, and get your gun."

"What!" cried my father, "Is it the wolves?" **14**

He jumped out of bed, threw on his clothes, and in his anxiety did not notice the absence of his wife. I opened the door, he went out, and I followed him.

Imagine his horror, when (unprepared as he was for such a sight) he beheld, as he advanced towards the grave, not a wolf, but his wife, in her night-dress, on her hands and knees, crouching by the body of my sister, and tearing off large pieces of the flesh and devouring them with the viciousness of a wolf. She was too busy to be aware of our approach. My father dropped his gun; he breathed heavily, and then his breath for a time stopped. I picked up the gun and put it into his hand. Suddenly he appeared as if rage had **restored** him to vigor; he leveled his piece, fired, and with a loud shriek, down fell the wretch whom he had married. **15**

implicated
thought to be involved in or guilty of something

restore
to bring back; to return something to its usual state

13 What is Christina going to do?

14 What does the narrator want to happen as indicated by the advice he has given his father?

15 Why did Father drop his gun? Why did his son put the gun back in his hand?

penalty

the price you pay for breaking a rule or doing something wrong

300 To our astonishment and horror, we found that instead of the dead body of my stepmother, we found the body of a large, white wolf.

For some time, my father remained in silence and deep thought. He then carefully lifted up the body
305 of my sister, replaced it in the grave, and covered it over as before. Raving like a madman, he then struck the head of the wolf with the heel of his boot. He walked back to the cottage, shut the door, and threw himself on the bed; I did the same.

310 Shortly after, we left the cottage forever and headed for Holland. We had not been many days in Amsterdam before my father was seized with a fever and died raving mad.

16 What is the narrator afraid of? Are his fears valid?

Now the question remains whether I am to pay the
315 **penalty** of the vow my father made on his wedding day? I am convinced that, in some way or another, I shall. **16**

As an English Royal Navy officer, Captain Frederick Marryat spent much of his literary career spinning tales about life at sea. One of his most famous collections of sea-faring stories is *The Phantom Ship* (published in 1839), where "The White Wolf of the Hartz Mountains" can be found. This short story was groundbreaking because it contained the first female werewolf in a short story.

Apostrophes: Contraction or Possessive

Circle words that contain apostrophes. Place a check mark in the proper column to identify its meaning. If it's a contraction, write the two words it represents. If it's a possessive, write what it possesses.

Sentence	Contraction	Possessive
Ex: (You're) not going on about the wolves again, are you?	✓ you are	
Ex: I believe that a (wolf's) life is important.		✓ life
I'm convinced I shall pay the penalty for his vow.		
I couldn't believe my eyes.		
When we awoke the next morning, we found that the hunter's daughter had risen before us.		
He's bound to believe me.		
My father and I were still hovering over my sister's body when my stepmother came in.		
The female's features were very beautiful.		
Lie still, dearest, it's only me.		

Relative Pronouns

Relative Pronoun	Function/Meaning	Example
who	subject or object pronoun for people	It was Marcella *who* feared Christina the most.
which	subject or object pronoun for animals and things; does not change the meaning of the sentence; set off with commas	The gun, *which* belonged to my father, was missing from the mantle.
whose	possessive pronoun for people, animals, and things	We wept for Caesar, *whose* death frightened us.
whom	object pronoun for people	It was Marcella for *whom* I felt the most responsible.
that	subject or object pronoun for people, animals, and things; changes the meaning of the sentence	Father grabbed the gun *that* hung above the fireplace.

All relative pronouns:

- Begin a relative clause—a type of dependent clause that modifies or describes a noun or noun phrase
- Follow the noun or noun phrase that it modifies
- Have a noun or pronoun as its antecedent

Circle the relative pronoun that correctly completes each sentence.

1. Christina is a woman _____ likes raw meat. (who, whom)

2. Christina removed the rocks _____ covered the body. (whose, that)

3. Christina, _____ mouth was large and filled with polished teeth, looked like a wolf. (whose, whom)

4. Christina, toward _____ I expressed my anger, showed no remorse. (whom, that)

5. Christina's clothes, _____ she burned, were covered in blood. (whom, which)

Relative Pronouns and Relative Clauses

Read the sentences. Circle the relative pronoun and underline the relative clause. Draw an arrow from the relative clause to the noun or noun phrase it is describing.

> **Example:**
> The curse, (which) had already claimed the lives of Marcella and Caesar, haunted my thoughts.

1. My father offered the young lady, whose name was Christina, his bed and he would remain at the fire, sitting up with her father.

2. My father, who feared for our safety, hastily grabbed his gun and left the cottage.

3. Never would I leave my dear little sister to whom I was more attached than ever.

4. The sound, which sounded remarkably like a wolf howl, kept us from sleeping.

5. He took every precaution that the wolves should not violate her remains.

6. Marcella, who had reason to be afraid, cried when touched by Christina.

7. My father regretted making the vow, which sentenced us to death, on his wedding day.

8. The wolf that passed us looked familiar somehow.

9. The hunter, whose daughter was a werewolf, had cursed our family.

10. It was my father for whom I cried.

Using Relative Clauses

Combine each pair of sentences using the relative pronoun provided in the parentheses. Make sure each sentence has an independent clause and a relative clause.

> **Example:**
> The wolf howled under our window. The wolf disappeared quickly. (that)
>
> ## The wolf that howled under our window disappeared quickly.

1. While in the woods, our father met a hunter. The hunter had a beautiful daughter. (who)

   _____

   _____

2. During the winter, we always stayed inside the cabin. The winter seemed to last forever. (which)

   _____

   _____

3. Christina treated us cruelly. Christina became our stepmother. (who)

   _____

   _____

4. Our new stepmother frightened us. Our stepmother's mouth was extremely large. (whose)

   _____

   _____

5. The hunter made our father repeat vows. The vows contained a curse. (that)

   _____

   _____

Passage Comprehension

Reread "The White Wolf of the Hartz Mountains." Respond to each prompt using complete sentences. Refer to the chart on pages 14 and 15 to determine how to respond to each prompt. Provide text evidence when requested.

1. Clarify the narrator's intuition about his siblings' deaths. Provide text evidence.

   _____

   _____

   _____

   Text Evidence: _____

   _____

   _____

2. Synthesize and present the information that leads to the narrator's intuition regarding his siblings' deaths.

   _____

   _____

   _____

   _____

   _____

   _____

   _____

3. Clarify Christina's counterclaims used to prevent her husband's suspicion.

   _____

   _____

   _____

   _____

   _____

   _____

   _____

Passage Comprehension (*cont.*)

4. Present evidence to prove Christina's likeness to wolves.

_____

_____

_____

_____

_____

_____

_____

_____

_____

_____

5. Use the text to prove that werewolves exist.

_____

_____

_____

_____

_____

_____

_____

_____

_____

_____

_____

_____

_____

Passage Comprehension (*cont.*)

6. Use the text to prove the narrator's fears at the end of the story are rational.

_____

_____

_____

_____

_____

_____

_____

_____

_____

_____

Close Reading

Read the text.

> ### "The White Wolf of the Hartz Mountains"
>
> My oldest memories are of a simple, yet comfortable cottage in the Hartz Mountains. I lived with my father, brother, and sister. In summertime the landscape was beautiful; but during the severe winter, it was desolate. In the winter we remained indoors, for the vicious wolves incessantly
> 5 prowled about in the cold.
>
> In the winter, my father hunted; every day he left us and often locked the door to keep us inside. During the short cold days of winter we would sit silent, longing for the happy hours when the snow would melt, and we should again be free.
>
> 10 One evening, the howl of a wolf, close under the window of the cottage, fell on our ears. My father jumped up, seized his gun, and hastily left the cottage, locking the door after him. We anxiously waited.

Close Reading (*cont.*)

We waited for some time, but the sound of the gun did not reach us.
After several hours, my father entered, with a young female and an
15 old hunter.

The female's features were very beautiful. Her hair was flaxen and bright
as a mirror; her mouth, although somewhat large when it was open,
showed the most brilliant teeth I have ever seen. But there was something
about her eyes which made us children afraid; they were so restless, so
20 sly; I could not at that time tell why, but I felt as if there was cruelty in
her eyes; and when she **beckoned** us to come to her, we approached her
with fear and trembling. Still she was beautiful, very beautiful. She spoke
kindly to my brother and myself, patted our heads, and caressed us; but
Marcella would not come near her; on the contrary, she slipped away and
25 hid herself.

My father offered the young lady, whose name was Christina, his bed and
he would remain at the fire, sitting up with her father. This arrangement
was agreed to, and I and my brother crept into the other bed with
Marcella, for we always slept together.

30 But we could not sleep; there was something so unusual, not only in
seeing strange people, but in having those people sleep at the cottage,
that we were bewildered. As for poor little Marcella, she was quiet but
trembled and sobbed the whole night. My father and the hunter remained
drinking and talking before the fire. Our curious ears were ready to catch
35 the slightest whisper.

They filled their mugs to the brim and drank to one another in the
German fashion. The conversation was then carried on in a low tone; all
that we could collect from it was that our new guest and his daughter
were to **reside** in our cottage, at least for the present. After an hour, they
40 both fell back in their chairs and slept.

Close Reading (*cont.*)

When we awoke the next morning, we found that the hunter's daughter had risen before us. She came up to little Marcella and caressed her; the child burst into tears and sobbed as if her heart would break.

45 The hunter and his daughter stayed in the cottage. My father and he went out hunting daily, leaving Christina with us. She performed all the household duties; was very kind to us children; and, gradually, we grew to like her—even Marcella. But a great change took place in my father; he was most attentive to Christina. Often, after her father and we were in bed, he would sit up with her, **conversing** in a low tone by the fire. After 50 three weeks of this, my father asked for Christina's hand in marriage. Soon after, the wedding took place.

My father repeated his vows after the hunter. "I swear by all the spirits of the Hartz Mountains, by all their power for good or for evil, that I take Christina for my wedded wife; that I will protect her, cherish her, and love 55 her; that my hand shall never be raised against her to harm her."

"And if I fail in this my vow, may all the vengeance of the spirits fall upon me and upon my children; may they **perish** by the vulture, by the wolf, or by other beasts of the forest; may their flesh be torn from their limbs, and their bones fade in the wilderness; all this I swear."

60 My father hesitated, as he repeated the last words; little Marcella could not restrain herself and burst into tears.

The next morning, the hunter mounted his horse, and rode away.

Close Reading (*cont.*)

Things went on much as before the marriage, except that our new stepmother did not show any kindness towards us; indeed, during my
65 father's absence, she would often beat us, particularly little Marcella, and her eyes would flash fire as she looked eagerly upon the fair and lovely child.

One night, my sister awoke me and my brother.

"What is the matter?" said Caesar.

70 "She has gone out," whispered Marcella.

"Gone out!"

"Yes, gone out the door, in her night-dress," replied the child. "I saw her."

What could bring her to leave the cottage, in such bitter wintry weather, was incomprehensible; we lay awake, and in about an hour we heard the
75 growl of a wolf, close under the window.

"There is a wolf," said Caesar; "she will be torn to pieces."

A few minutes afterwards, our stepmother appeared; she was in her night-dress, as Marcella had stated. She let down the latch of the door, so as to make no noise, went to a pail of water, and washed her face and
80 hands, and then slipped into the bed where my father lay.

We all three trembled, we hardly knew why, but we **resolved** to watch the next night. We did so—and many other nights as well, and always at about the same hour, would our stepmother rise from her bed, and leave the cottage—and after she was gone, we invariably heard the growl of a
85 wolf under our window, and always saw her, on her return, wash herself before she retired to bed. We observed, also, that she **seldom** sat down to meals, and that when she did, she appeared to eat with dislike; but when the meat was being prepared, she would often put a raw piece into her mouth.

Close Reading (*cont.*)

90 My brother Caesar did not want to tell my father until he knew more. He resolved to follow her out and ascertain what she did. Marcella and I tried to dissuade him; but he would not be deterred, and the very next night he lay down in his clothes, and as soon as our stepmother left the cottage, he jumped up, took down my father's gun, and followed her.

95 Marcella and I waited in suspense. After a few minutes, we heard the sound of a gun. It did not awaken my father, and we lay trembling with anxiety. In a minute afterwards, we saw our stepmother enter the cottage—her dress was bloody. I put my hand to Marcella's mouth to prevent her crying out, although I was myself in great alarm. Our 100 stepmother looked to see if our father was asleep, and then started a fire.

"Who is there?" said my father, waking up.

"Lie still, dearest," replied my stepmother, "it is only me; I have lighted the fire to warm some water; I am not quite well."

My father turned round and was soon asleep, but we watched our 105 stepmother. She changed her clothes and threw the garments she had worn into the fire; and we then perceived that her right leg was bleeding, as if from a gun-shot wound. She bandaged it up and dressed herself.

Poor little Marcella, her heart beat quick as she pressed me to her side—so indeed did mine. Where was our brother, Caesar? How did my 110 stepmother receive the wound unless from his gun? At last my father rose, and then, for the first time I spoke, saying, "Father, where is my brother, Caesar?"

"Your brother!" exclaimed he, "why, where can he be?"

"Merciful Heaven! I thought as I lay very restless last night," observed our 115 stepmother, "that I heard somebody open the latch of the door; and dear husband, what has become of your gun?"

My father cast his eyes up above the chimney, and perceived that his gun was missing. For a moment he looked perplexed, then seizing an axe, he went out of the cottage without saying another word.

Close Reading (*cont.*)

120 He did not remain away from us long. In a few minutes he returned, bearing in his arms the mangled body of my poor brother; he laid it down and covered up his face.

My stepmother rose up and looked at the body, while Marcella and I threw ourselves by its side, wailing and sobbing bitterly.

125 "Go to bed again, children," said she sharply. "Husband, your boy must have taken the gun down to shoot a wolf, and the animal has been too powerful for him. Poor boy! He has paid dearly for his **rashness**."

My father made no reply; I wished to tell all, but Marcella, who saw my intention, held my arm and looked at me so imploringly that I stopped.

130 My father, therefore, was deceived; but Marcella and I, although we could not comprehend it, knew that our stepmother was in some way connected with my brother's death.

That day, my father went out and dug a grave, and when he laid the body in the earth, he piled up stones over it, so that the villainous wolves 135 should not be able to dig it up. The shock of this tragedy was severe for my father; for several days he did not hunt but uttered bitter vengeance against the wolves.

During this time of mourning, my stepmother's nocturnal wanderings continued with the same regularity as before.

140 At last, my father took down his gun, and went hunting; but he soon returned and appeared bothered.

Close Reading (*cont.*)

"Would you believe it, Christina, that the wolves—most evil of all animals—have actually dug up the body of my poor boy, and now there is nothing left of him but his bones?"

145 Marcella looked at me, and I saw in her intelligent eyes all she would have uttered.

"A wolf growls under our window every night, father," said I.

"Really?—why did you not tell me, boy?—wake me the next time you hear it."

150 I saw my stepmother turn away; her eyes flashed fire, and she gnashed her teeth.

The spring finally came. The snow disappeared, and we were permitted to leave the cottage; but never would I leave, for one moment, my dear little sister, to whom, since the death of my brother, I was more attached than 155 ever. I was afraid to leave her alone with my stepmother, who appeared to have a particular pleasure in ill-treating the child. My father was now working his little farm, and I was able to assist him.

Marcella used to sit by us while we were at work, leaving my stepmother alone in the cottage. As spring advanced, my stepmother decreased her 160 nocturnal rambles, and we never heard the growl of the wolf under the window after I had spoken of it to my father.

Close Reading (*cont.*)

One day, when my father and I were in the field, Marcella being with us, my stepmother came out, saying that she was going into the forest to collect some herbs my father wanted, and that Marcella must go to
165 the cottage and watch the dinner. Marcella went, and my stepmother disappeared in the forest.

About an hour afterwards, we were startled by shrieks from the cottage. "Marcella has burnt herself, father," said I, throwing down my spade. My father threw down his, and we both hastened to the cottage. Before we
170 arrived, out darted a large white wolf. We rushed into the cottage and there saw poor little Marcella. Her body was extremely mangled, and the blood pouring from it had formed a large pool on the cottage floor. My father's first intention had been to seize his gun and pursue, but he was checked by this horrid spectacle; he knelt down by his dying child and
175 burst into tears. Marcella looked kindly at us for a few seconds, and then closed her eyes in death.

My father and I were still hovering over my sister's body when my stepmother came in. At the dreadful sight, she expressed much concern, but she did not appear to recoil from the sight of blood, as most
180 women do.

"Poor child!" said she, "it must have been that great white wolf which passed me just now and frightened me so."

My father cried in agony.

I thought my father would never recover from the effects of this second
185 tragedy. He mourned over the body of his sweet daughter and for several days would not bury her. At last, he dug a grave for her close by that of my poor brother and took every precaution that the wolves should not violate her remains.

I was now really miserable, as I lay alone in the bed which I had formerly
190 shared with my brother and sister. I could not help thinking that my stepmother was **implicated** in both their deaths, although I could not explain it. I no longer felt afraid of her; my heart was full of hatred and revenge.

Close Reading (*cont.*)

195 The night after my sister was buried, as I lay awake, I saw my stepmother get up and go out of the cottage. I waited some time, then dressed myself, and looked out through the door. The moon shone bright, and I could see the spot where my brother and sister had been buried; and to my horror, I perceived my stepmother busily removing the stones from Marcella's grave.

200 She was in her white night-dress, and the moon shone full upon her. She was digging with her hands and throwing away the stones behind her with all the ferocity of a wild beast. At last, she raised the body to the side of the grave. I could bear it no longer; I ran to my father and awoke him.

"Father! Father! Dress yourself, and get your gun."

205 "What!" cried my father, "Is it the wolves?"

He jumped out of bed, threw on his clothes, and in his anxiety did not notice the absence of his wife. I opened the door, he went out, and I followed him.

Imagine his horror, when (unprepared as he was for such a sight) he
210 beheld, as he advanced towards the grave, not a wolf, but his wife, in her night-dress, on her hands and knees, crouching by the body of my sister, and tearing off large pieces of the flesh and devouring them with the viciousness of a wolf. She was too busy to be aware of our approach. My father dropped his gun; he breathed heavily, and then his breath for
215 a time stopped. I picked up the gun and put it into his hand. Suddenly he appeared as if rage had **restored** him to vigor; he leveled his piece, fired, and with a loud shriek, down fell the wretch whom he had married.

Close Reading (*cont.*)

To our astonishment and horror, we found that instead of the dead body of my stepmother, we found the body of a large, white wolf.

220 For some time, my father remained in silence and deep thought. He then carefully lifted up the body of my sister, replaced it in the grave, and covered it over as before. Raving like a madman, he then struck the head of the wolf with the heel of his boot. He walked back to the cottage, shut the door, and threw himself on the bed; I did the same.

225 Shortly after, we left the cottage forever and headed for Holland. We had not been many days in Amsterdam before my father was seized with a fever and died raving mad.

Now the question remains whether I am to pay the **penalty** of the vow my father made on his wedding day? I am convinced that, in some way or 230 another, I shall.

Quick Write in Response to Reading

Authors often include clues about how the story will unfold and how characters will develop. In this text, the details provided by the narrator cause the reader to distrust Christina and suspect her true identity. Write a paragraph that describes three examples of foreshadowing and how that helped you determine Christina's true nature.

Let's Focus: *Who Speaks for Wolf: A Native American Learning Story*

Content Focus
man's impact on the environment
learning from nature, others, mistakes

Type of Text
literature—fiction: legend, learning story

Author's Name _____

Author's Purpose _____

Big Ideas
Consider the following Big Idea questions. Write your answer for each question.

What impact do humans have on the environment?

_____

_____

What does "Just because you can, doesn't mean you should" mean to you?

_____

_____

Narrative Preview Checklist: *Who Speaks for Wolf* on pages 71–87.

☐ Title: What clue does it provide?

☐ Pictures: What additional information is added here?

☐ Margin Information: What vocabulary is important to understand this story?

☐ Features: What other text features do you notice?

☐ Form: What do you notice about the text's shape, layout, font, and punctuation?

Enduring Understandings
After reading the text . . .

_____

_____

_____

_____

Key Passage Vocabulary: *Who Speaks for Wolf*

Read each word. Write the word in column 3. Then, circle a number to rate your knowledge of the word.

Vocabulary	Part of Speech	Write the Word	Knowledge Rating
immobile	(adj)		0 1 2 3
sought	(v)		0 1 2 3
counsel	(v)		0 1 2 3
reconsider	(v)		0 1 2 3
apparent	(adj)		0 1 2 3
devise	(v)		0 1 2 3
course	(n)		0 1 2 3
maintain	(v)		0 1 2 3
cherish	(v)		0 1 2 3
omission	(n)		0 1 2 3

WHO SPEAKS FOR WOLF

A Native American Learning Story
by Paula Underwood

immobile
completely still

$\mathbf{A}$lmost at the edge of the circle of light cast by Central Fire—Wolf was standing. His eyes reflected the fire's warmth with a colder light. Wolf stood there, staring at the fire.

5 A boy of eight winters was watching Wolf—as **immobile** as Wolf—as fascinated. Finally, the boy turned to Grandfather, warming his old bones from winter's first chill.

"Why does Wolf stand there and only watch
10 the fire?"

"Why do you?" Grandfather replied.

And then the boy remembered that he had sat there, ever since the fire was lit, watching the flames— until Wolf came. Now, instead, he watched Wolf.
15 He saw that it was because Wolf was so different from him, yet also watched the fire, and that there seemed no fear in Wolf. It was this the boy did not understand.

Beyond where Wolf was standing there was a hill—
20 still so close to the Central Fire that the boy was surprised to see the dim outline of another Wolf face. This one was looking at the moon.

Moon-Looking-Wolf began to sing her song. More and more joined her until at last even Wolf-Looks-
25 at-Fire chortled in his throat the beginnings of a song. They sang for the Moon, and for each other, and for any who might listen. They sang of how Earth was a good place to be, of how much beauty surrounds us, and of how all this is sometimes most
30 easily seen in Moon and Fire. **1**

1 Why do the wolves sing?

The boy listened and—and wanted to do nothing else with his life but listen to Wolf singing.

After a long and particularly beautiful song, Moon-Looking-Wolf quieted, and one by one her brothers
35 joined her in silence, until even the most distant—crying "I am here! Don't forget me!"—made space for the night and watched—and waited. Wolf-Looks-at-Fire turned and left the clearing, joining his brothers near the hill.

40 "But I still don't understand," the boy continued. "Why does Wolf look at Fire? Why does he feel at home so close to our living space? Why does Wolf Woman begin her song on a hill so close to us who are not Wolf?"

45 "We have known each other for a long time," the old man answered. "We have learned to live with one another."

The boy still looked puzzled. Within himself he saw only the edges of understanding.

50 Grandfather was silent for a time—and then began at last the slow cadences of a chant. The boy knew with satisfaction that soon he would understand—would know Wolf better than before—would learn how it had been between us. **2**

55 *LONG AGO . . . LONG AGO . . . LONG AGO . . .*

Grandfather chanted, the rhythm taking its place with Wolf's song as something appropriate for the forest.

2 What is the boy hoping that his grandfather will teach him? How will the grandfather teach him?

LONG AGO

60 *Our People grew in number so that where we were*

was no longer enough

Many young men

were sent out from among us

to seek a new place

65 *where the People might be who-they-were*

They searched

and they returned

each with a place selected

each determined his place was best **3**

3 Why did the
People need to
move?

70 *AND SO IT WAS*

That the People had a decision to make:

which of the many was most appropriate

NOW, AT THAT TIME

    There was one among the People

75   *to whom Wolf was brother*

    He was so much Wolf's brother

        that he would sing their song to them

          and they would answer him

    He was so much Wolf's brother

80   *that their young*

        would sometimes follow him through the forest

        and it seemed they meant to learn from him

SO IT WAS, AT THIS TIME

    That the People gave That One a special name

85   *They called him WOLF'S BROTHER*

    *and if any **sought** to learn about Wolf*

    if any were curious

        or wanted to learn to sing Wolf's song

        they would sit beside him

90   *and describe their curiosity*

          hoping for a reply **4**

> **sought**
> tried to do, find, or get something

> **4** Why was Wolf's Brother important?

"Has it been since that time that we sing to Wolf?" the boy asked eagerly. "Was it he who taught us how?" He clapped his hands over his mouth to stop
95 the tumble of words. He knew he had interrupted Grandfather's Song.

The old man smiled, and the crinkles around his eyes spoke of other boys—and other times.

"Yes, even he!" he answered. "For since that time it
100 has pleased many of our people to sing to Wolf and to learn to understand him."

Encouraged, the boy asked, "And ever since our hunters go to learn to sing to Wolf?"

"Many people go, not only hunters. Many people go,
105 not only men," Grandfather chided. "For was it not Wolf Woman who began the song tonight? Would it then be appropriate if only the men among us replied?"

The boy looked crestfallen. He wanted so much
110 to be a hunter—to learn Wolf's song, but he knew there was wisdom in Grandfather's words. Not only hunters learn from Wolf.

5 Why was the boy disappointed? What gave the boy hope?

"But you have led me down a different path," the Old One was saying. "It would please me to finish
115 my first song."

The boy settled back and waited to learn. **5**

AS I HAVE SAID

The people sought a new place in the forest

They listened closely to each of the young men

120   *as they spoke of hills and trees*

        of clearings and running water

        of deer and squirrels and berries

They listened to hear which place

    might be drier in rain

125   *more protected in winter*

    and where our Three Sisters

        Corn, Beans, and Squash

        might find a place to their liking **6**

They listened

130   *and they chose*

Before they chose

    they listened to each young man

Before they chose

    they listened to each among them

135   *he who understood the flow of waters*

    she who understood Long House construction

    he who understood the storms of winter

    she who understood Three Sisters

to each of these they listened

140   *until they reached agreement*

and the Eldest among them

    finally rose and said:

        "SO BE IT—

        FOR SO IT IS"

> **6** Who are the Three Sisters? Why are crops referred to in familial terms?

counsel
to give advice or
support to someone

7 Explain the
attributes of the
land they were
seeking.

145 *"BUT WAIT"*

Someone cautioned—

"Where is Wolf's Brother?

WHO, THEN, SPEAKS FOR WOLF?" **7**

BUT

150 *THE PEOPLE WERE DECIDED*

and their mind was firm

and the first people were sent

to choose a site for the first Long House

to clear a space for our Three Sisters

155 *to mold the land so that water*

would run away from our dwelling

so that all would be secure within

AND THEN WOLF'S BROTHER RETURNED

He asked about the New Place

160 *and said at once that we must choose another*

"You have chosen the Center Place

for a great community of Wolf" **8**

8 What is the
problem?

But we answered him

that many had already gone

165 *and that it could not wisely be changed*

and that surely Wolf could make way for us

as we sometimes make way for Wolf

But Wolf's Brother **counseled***—*

9 What caution
does Wolf's
Brother share
with his Native
American
people?

"I think that you will find

170 *that it is too small a place for both*

and that it will require more work then—

than change would presently require" **9**

BUT

   THE PEOPLE CLOSED THEIR EARS

175   and would not **reconsider**

   When the New Place was ready

      all the People rose up as one

         and took those things they found of value

         and looked at last upon their new home

> **reconsider**
> to think about whether a past action or decision should be changed

180 NOW CONSIDER HOW IT WAS FOR THEM

   This New Place

      had cool summers and winter protection

      and fast-moving streams

      and forests around us

185   filled with deer and squirrel

   there was room even for our Three Beloved Sisters

   AND THE PEOPLE SAW THAT THIS WAS GOOD

   AND DID NOT SEE

   WOLF WATCHING FROM THE SHADOWS! **10**

> **10** What problem has been caused because they didn't listen to Wolf's Brother?

apparent
easy to see or
understand

190 *BUT AS TIME PASSED*

  They began to see—

    for someone would bring deer or squirrel

      and hang him from a tree

      and go for something to contain the meat

195   *but would return*

        to find nothing hanging from the tree

          AND WOLF BEYOND

  AT FIRST

    This seemed to us an appropriate exchange—

200   *some food for a place to live*

  BUT

    *It soon became **apparent** that it was more than this—*

      for Wolf would sometimes walk between the dwellings

        that we had fashioned for ourselves

205   *and the women grew concerned*

          for the safety of the little ones

    Thinking of this

      they devised for a while an agreement with Wolf

        whereby the women would gather together

210   *at the edge of our village*

          and put out food for Wolf and his brothers

BUT IT WAS SOON APPARENT

    That this meant too much food

        and also Wolf grew bolder

215   coming in to look for food

            so that it was worse than before

WE HAD NO WISH TO TAME WOLF

AND SO

    Hearing the wailing of the women

220   the men **devised** a system

        whereby some ones among them

          were always alert to drive off Wolf

AND WOLF WAS SOON HIS OLD UNTAMED SELF

BUT

225   They soon discovered

        that this required so much energy

          that there was little left for winter preparations

        and the Long Cold began to look longer and colder

        with each passing day

230 THEN

    The men counseled together

    to choose a different **course** [11]

---

devise

to plan or invent something

course

the path or direction that someone or something moves along

---

[11] What changes happened with Wolf after the People moved into his territory?

THEY SAW

> *That neither providing Wolf with food*
>
> 235   *nor driving him off*
>
>   *gave the People a life that was pleasing*

THEY SAW

> *That Wolf and the People*
>
>   *could not live comfortably together*
>
> 240   *in such a small space*

THEY SAW

> *That it was possible*
>
>   *to hunt down this Wolf People*
>
>   *until they were no more*

245 *BUT THEY ALSO SAW*

> *That this would require much energy over many years*

THEY SAW, TOO,

> *That such a task would change the People:*
>
>   *they would become Wolf Killers*
>
> 250 *A People who took life only to sustain their own*
>
>   *would become a People who took life*
>
>   *rather than move a little*

> **12** How did the People want to change?

IT DID NOT SEEM TO THEM

THAT THEY WANTED TO BECOME SUCH A PEOPLE **12**

255 *AT LAST*

    One of the Eldest of the People

    spoke what was in every mind:

    "It would seem

       that Wolf's Brother's vision

260   *was sharper than our own*

    To live here indeed requires more work now

    than change would have made necessary

> **maintain**
> to continue having
> or doing something

Grandfather paused, making his knee a drum on which to **maintain** the rhythm of the chant, and then went on.

265 *NOW THIS WOULD BE A SIMPLE TELLING*

    OF A PEOPLE WHO DECIDED TO MOVE

       ONCE WINTER WAS PAST

EXCEPT

    THAT FROM THIS

270   *THE PEOPLE LEARNED A GREAT LESSON*

IT IS A LESSON

    WE HAVE NEVER FORGOTTEN

FOR

  At the end of their Council

275 *one of the Eldest rose again and said:*

   "Let us learn from this

    so that not again

     need the People build only to move

   Let us not again think we will gain energy

280   *only to lose more than we gain*

   We have learned to choose a place

    where winter storms are less

     rather than rebuild

   We have learned to choose a place

285   *where water does not stand*

     rather than sustain sickness

13 What is the lesson learned?

LET US NOW LEARN TO CONSIDER WOLF!" **13**

AND SO IT WAS

    That the People devised among themselves

290   *a way of asking each other questions*

        whenever a decision was to be made

        on a New Place or a New Way

    We sought to perceive the flow of energy

    through each new possibility

295   *and how much was enough*

      and how much was too much

UNTIL AT LAST

    Someone would rise

    and ask the old, old question

300   *to remind us of things*

      we do not yet see clearly enough to remember

"TELL ME NOW MY BROTHERS

TELL ME NOW MY SISTERS

WHO SPEAKS FOR WOLF?" **14**

> **14** What does the question really mean?

cherish
to treat with love or care; to hold dear

305 And so Grandfather's Song ended . . . and my father's voice grew still.

"Did the boy learn to sing with Wolf?" I asked.

"All may," my father answered.

"And did the People always remember to ask Wolf's
310 Question?"

My father smiled. "They remembered for a long time . . . a long time. And when the wooden ships came, bringing a new People, they looked at them and saw that what we accomplish by much thought
315 and considering the needs of all, they accomplish by building tools and changing the Earth, with much thought of winter and little of tomorrow. We could not teach them to ask Wolf's question. They did not understand he was their brother. We knew how long
320 it had taken us to listen to Wolf's voice. It seemed to us that These Ones could also learn. And so we **cherished** them . . . when we could . . . and held them off . . . when we must . . . and gave them time to learn." **15**

15 Who are the new People?

325 "Will they learn, do you think, my father? Will they learn?"

"Sometimes wisdom comes only after great foolishness. We still hope they will learn. I do not know even if our own People still ask their question.
330 I only know that at the last Great Council when we talked about the Small Ones in their wooden ships and decided that their way and our way might exist side by side—and decided, therefore, to let them live . . . I only know that someone rose to remind
335 them of the things we had not yet learned about these Pale Ones."

"He rose and he reminded us of what we had already learned, of how these New Ones believed that only one way was Right and all others Wrong.
340 He wondered out loud whether they would be as patient with us—once they were strong—as we were now with them. He wondered what else might be true for them that we did not yet see. He wondered how all these things—seen and unseen—might
345 affect our lives and the lives of our children's children's children. Then to remind us of the great difficulties that may arise from the simple **omission** of something we forgot to consider, he gazed slowly around the Council Circle and asked the ancient
350 question:

"TELL ME NOW MY BROTHERS

TELL ME NOW MY SISTERS

WHO SPEAKS FOR WOLF?" **16**

omission
the act of leaving something out or undone

16 Who is *Wolf* referring to now?

Being a descendant of an Iroquois healer and storyteller, Paula Underwood has brought the responsibility of teaching oral history to others onto herself. She was only 12 years old when she accepted the task of writing down her wisdom because she felt she had reached the age where others could benefit from her stories. One of these Learning Stories is *Who Speaks for Wolf*. "A learning story has no answers—only explorations." This story was passed down to Underwood from her father over many years. When she was 17, her father finally felt she had a grasp on all he could teach her from this learning story, and then it was her turn.

Critical Understandings

Read the prompts and respond using complete sentences. Refer to the chart on pages 14 and 15 to determine how to respond. Provide text evidence when requested.

1. Integrate information learned from the campfire discussion with content from Grandfather's Song to determine why Wolf felt comfortable with the People. Provide text evidence.

   _____

   _____

   _____

   _____

   _____

   _____

   Text Evidence from the campfire discussion: _____

   _____

   _____

   Text Evidence from the chant: _____

   _____

   _____

   _____

   _____

2. Trace the decision-making process that the People used before deciding where to move. Who and what was omitted from the decision-making process?

   _____

   _____

   _____

   _____

   _____

   _____

   _____

Critical Understandings (*cont.*)

3. Evaluate the People's move to the Center Place for a great community of Wolf from Wolf's Brother's perspective.

_____

_____

_____

_____

_____

4. Summarize the lesson learned when the People failed to consider Wolf.

_____

_____

_____

_____

_____

_____

_____

_____

_____

_____

Passage Comprehension

After listening to *Who Speaks for Wolf*, read the prompts and respond using complete sentences. Use the chart on pages 14 and 15 to determine how to respond. Provide text evidence when requested.

1. Trace the point of view in the story to determine the identity of Father.

_____
_____
_____
_____
_____
_____
_____
_____
_____

2. Integrate information from the text and the impact of the audio version to evaluate Grandfather's oratory skills.

_____
_____
_____
_____
_____
_____
_____
_____
_____
_____
_____

Passage Comprehension (*cont.*)

3. Trace and evaluate how the wolves' points of view changed regarding living with the People. Provide text evidence.

_____

_____

_____

_____

_____

_____

Text Evidence: _____

_____

_____

_____

_____

_____

_____

_____

4. Evaluate the impact of hearing Grandfather's Song the way it was intended.

_____

_____

_____

_____

_____

_____

_____

Passage Comprehension (*cont.*)

5. Summarize human interaction with the environment from the People's point of view.

_____

_____

_____

_____

_____

_____

_____

_____

6. Summarize human interaction with the environment from the new People's point of view.

_____

_____

_____

_____

_____

_____

_____

_____

_____

_____

_____

_____

Close Reading

Read the text.

Who Speaks for Wolf

Almost at the edge of the circle of light cast by Central Fire—Wolf was standing. His eyes reflected the fire's warmth with a colder light. Wolf stood there, staring at the fire.

A boy of eight winters was watching Wolf—as **immobile** as Wolf—as
5 fascinated. Finally, the boy turned to Grandfather, warming his old bones from winter's first chill.

"Why does Wolf stand there and only watch the fire?"

"Why do you?" Grandfather replied.

And then the boy remembered that he had sat there, ever since the fire
10 was lit, watching the flames—until Wolf came. Now, instead, he watched Wolf. He saw that it was because Wolf was so different from him, yet also watched the fire, and that there seemed no fear in Wolf. It was this the boy did not understand.

Beyond where Wolf was standing there was a hill—still so close to the
15 Central Fire that the boy was surprised to see the dim outline of another Wolf face. This one was looking at the moon.

Moon-Looking-Wolf began to sing her song. More and more joined her until at last even Wolf-Looks-at-Fire chortled in his throat the beginnings of a song. They sang for the Moon, and for each other, and for any who
20 might listen. They sang of how Earth was a good place to be, of how much beauty surrounds us, and of how all this is sometimes most easily seen in Moon and Fire.

The boy listened and—and wanted to do nothing else with his life but listen to Wolf singing.

Close Reading (*cont.*)

25 After a long and particularly beautiful song, Moon-Looking-Wolf quieted, and one by one her brothers joined her in silence, until even the most distant—crying "I am here! Don't forget me!"—made space for the night and watched—and waited. Wolf-Looks-at-Fire turned and left the clearing, joining his brothers near the hill.

30 "But I still don't understand," the boy continued. "Why does Wolf look at Fire? Why does he feel at home so close to our living space? Why does Wolf Woman begin her song on a hill so close to us who are not Wolf?"

"We have known each other for a long time," the old man answered. "We have learned to live with one another."

35 The boy still looked puzzled. Within himself he saw only the edges of understanding.

Grandfather was silent for a time—and then began at last the slow cadences of a chant. The boy knew with satisfaction that soon he would understand—would know Wolf better than before—would learn how it
40 had been between us.

Close Reading (*cont.*)

LONG AGO . . . LONG AGO . . . LONG AGO . . .

Grandfather chanted, the rhythm taking its place with Wolf's song as something appropriate for the forest.

LONG AGO

45 *Our People grew in number so that where we were*

> *was no longer enough*

Many young men

> *were sent out from among us*

>> *to seek a new place*

50 >>> *where the People might be who-they-were*

They searched

> *and they returned*

>> *each with a place selected*

>> *each determined his place was best*

55 *AND SO IT WAS*

> *That the People had a decision to make:*

>> *which of the many was most appropriate*

NOW, AT THAT TIME

> *There was one among the People*

60 >> *to whom Wolf was brother*

He was so much Wolf's brother

> *that he would sing their song to them*

>> *and they would answer him*

He was so much Wolf's brother

65 > *that their young*

>> *would sometimes follow him through the forest*

>> *and it seemed they meant to learn from him*

Close Reading (*cont.*)

SO IT WAS, AT THIS TIME

> *That the People gave That One a special name*

70 *They called him WOLF'S BROTHER*

> *and if any **sought** to learn about Wolf*

> *if any were curious*

> *or wanted to learn to sing Wolf's song*

> *they would sit beside him*

75 *and describe their curiosity*

> *hoping for a reply*

"Has it been since that time that we sing to Wolf?" the boy asked eagerly. "Was it he who taught us how?" He clapped his hands over his mouth to stop the tumble of words. He knew he had interrupted Grandfather's 80 Song.

The old man smiled, and the crinkles around his eyes spoke of other boys—and other times.

"Yes, even he!" he answered. "For since that time it has pleased many of our people to sing to Wolf and to learn to understand him."

85 Encouraged, the boy asked, "And ever since our hunters go to learn to sing to Wolf?"

"Many people go, not only hunters. Many people go, not only men," Grandfather chided. "For was it not Wolf Woman who began the song tonight? Would it then be appropriate if only the men among us replied?"

90 The boy looked crestfallen. He wanted so much to be a hunter—to learn Wolf's song, but he knew there was wisdom in Grandfather's words. Not only hunters learn from Wolf.

"But you have led me down a different path," the Old One was saying. "It would please me to finish my first song."

95 The boy settled back and waited to learn.

Close Reading (*cont.*)

AS I HAVE SAID

The people sought a new place in the forest

They listened closely to each of the young men

> *as they spoke of hills and trees*

100 *of clearings and running water*

> *of deer and squirrels and berries*

They listened to hear which place

> *might be drier in rain*

> *more protected in winter*

105 *and where our Three Sisters*

> *Corn, Beans, and Squash*

> *might find a place to their liking*

They listened

> *and they chose*

110 *Before they chose*

> *they listened to each young man*

Before they chose

> *they listened to each among them*

> *he who understood the flow of waters*

115 *she who understood Long House construction*

> *he who understood the storms of winter*

> *she who understood Three Sisters*

to each of these they listened

> *until they reached agreement*

120 *and the Eldest among them*

> *finally rose and said:*

> *"SO BE IT—*

> *FOR SO IT IS"*

Close Reading (*cont.*)

"BUT WAIT"

125   *Someone cautioned—*

"Where is Wolf's Brother?

WHO, THEN, SPEAKS FOR WOLF?"

BUT

THE PEOPLE WERE DECIDED

130   *and their mind was firm*

and the first people were sent

to choose a site for the first Long House

to clear a space for our Three Sisters

to mold the land so that water

135   *would run away from our dwelling*

so that all would be secure within

AND THEN WOLF'S BROTHER RETURNED

He asked about the New Place

and said at once that we must choose another

140   *"You have chosen the Center Place*

for a great community of Wolf"

But we answered him

that many had already gone

and that it could not wisely be changed

145   *and that surely Wolf could make way for us*

as we sometimes make way for Wolf

But Wolf's Brother **counseled**—

"I think that you will find

that it is too small a place for both

150   *and that it will require more work then—*

than change would presently require"

Close Reading (*cont.*)

BUT

  THE PEOPLE CLOSED THEIR EARS

   and would not **reconsider**

155 *When the New Place was ready*

  all the People rose up as one

   and took those things they found of value

   and looked at last upon their new home

 NOW CONSIDER HOW IT WAS FOR THEM

160 *This New Place*

  had cool summers and winter protection

  and fast-moving streams

  and forests around us

   filled with deer and squirrel

165 *there was room even for our Three Beloved Sisters*

 AND THE PEOPLE SAW THAT THIS WAS GOOD

  AND DID NOT SEE

   WOLF WATCHING FROM THE SHADOWS!

 BUT AS TIME PASSED

170 *They began to see—*

  for someone would bring deer or squirrel

   and hang him from a tree

   and go for something to contain the meat

   but would return

175 *to find nothing hanging from the tree*

   AND WOLF BEYOND

Close Reading (*cont.*)

AT FIRST

    This seemed to us an appropriate exchange—

        some food for a place to live

180 *BUT*

    It soon became **apparent** *that it was more than this—*

        for Wolf would sometimes walk between the dwellings

            that we had fashioned for ourselves

                and the women grew concerned

185   *for the safety of the little ones*

    Thinking of this

        they devised for a while an agreement with Wolf

            whereby the women would gather together

            at the edge of our village

190   *and put out food for Wolf and his brothers*

BUT IT WAS SOON APPARENT

    That this meant too much food

        and also Wolf grew bolder

        coming in to look for food

195   *so that it was worse than before*

WE HAD NO WISH TO TAME WOLF

AND SO

    Hearing the wailing of the women

        the men **devised** *a system*

200   *whereby some ones among them*

            were always alert to drive off Wolf

AND WOLF WAS SOON HIS OLD UNTAMED SELF

Close Reading (*cont.*)

BUT

    They soon discovered

205   that this required so much energy

           that there was little left for winter preparations

        and the Long Cold began to look longer and colder

           with each passing day

THEN

210 The men counseled together

        to choose a different **course**

THEY SAW

    That neither providing Wolf with food

        nor driving him off

215   gave the People a life that was pleasing

THEY SAW

    That Wolf and the People

        could not live comfortably together

           in such a small space

220 THEY SAW

    That it was possible

        to hunt down this Wolf People

        until they were no more

BUT THEY ALSO SAW

225 That this would require much energy over many years

Close Reading (*cont.*)

THEY SAW, TOO,

> *That such a task would change the People:*

> *they would become Wolf Killers*

> *A People who took life only to sustain their own*

230 > *would become a People who took life*

> *rather than move a little*

IT DID NOT SEEM TO THEM

> *THAT THEY WANTED TO BECOME SUCH A PEOPLE*

AT LAST

235 *One of the Eldest of the People*

> *spoke what was in every mind:*

> *"It would seem*

> > *that Wolf's Brother's vision*

> > *was sharper than our own*

240 *To live here indeed requires more work now*

> *than change would have made necessary*

Grandfather paused, making his knee a drum on which to **maintain** the rhythm of the chant, and then went on.

NOW THIS WOULD BE A SIMPLE TELLING

245 *OF A PEOPLE WHO DECIDED TO MOVE*

> *ONCE WINTER WAS PAST*

EXCEPT

> *THAT FROM THIS*

> > *THE PEOPLE LEARNED A GREAT LESSON*

Close Reading (*cont.*)

250 *IT IS A LESSON*

    WE HAVE NEVER FORGOTTEN

FOR

    At the end of their Council

      one of the Eldest rose again and said:

255   *"Let us learn from this*

          so that not again

            need the People build only to move

        Let us not again think we will gain energy

          only to lose more than we gain

260   *We have learned to choose a place*

          where winter storms are less

            rather than rebuild

        We have learned to choose a place

          where water does not stand

265   *rather than sustain sickness*

LET US NOW LEARN TO CONSIDER WOLF!"

Close Reading (*cont.*)

AND SO IT WAS

That the People devised among themselves

a way of asking each other questions

270   whenever a decision was to be made

on a New Place or a New Way

We sought to perceive the flow of energy

through each new possibility

and how much was enough

275   and how much was too much

UNTIL AT LAST

Someone would rise

and ask the old, old question

to remind us of things

280   we do not yet see clearly enough to remember

"TELL ME NOW MY BROTHERS

TELL ME NOW MY SISTERS

WHO SPEAKS FOR WOLF?"

Close Reading (*cont.*)

And so Grandfather's Song ended . . . and my father's voice grew still.

285 "Did the boy learn to sing with Wolf?" I asked.

"All may," my father answered.

"And did the People always remember to ask Wolf's Question?"

My father smiled. "They remembered for a long time . . . a long time. And when the wooden ships came, bringing a new People, they looked at 290 them and saw that what we accomplish by much thought and considering the needs of all, they accomplish by building tools and changing the Earth, with much thought of winter and little of tomorrow. We could not teach them to ask Wolf's question. They did not understand he was their brother. We knew how long it had taken us to listen to Wolf's voice. 295 It seemed to us that These Ones could also learn. And so we **cherished** them . . . when we could . . . and held them off . . . when we must . . . and gave them time to learn."

"Will they learn, do you think, my father? Will they learn?"

"Sometimes wisdom comes only after great foolishness. We still hope 300 they will learn. I do not know even if our own People still ask their question. I only know that at the last Great Council when we talked about the Small Ones in their wooden ships and decided that their way and our way might exist side by side—and decided, therefore, to let them live . . . I only know that someone rose to remind them of the things we had not 305 yet learned about these Pale Ones."

"He rose and he reminded us of what we had already learned, of how these New Ones believed that only one way was Right and all others Wrong. He wondered out loud whether they would be as patient with us—once they were strong—as we were now with them. He wondered 310 what else might be true for them that we did not yet see. He wondered how all these things—seen and unseen—might affect our lives and the lives of our children's children's children. Then to remind us of the great difficulties that may arise from the simple **omission** of something we forgot to consider, he gazed slowly around the Council Circle and asked 315 the ancient question:

> *"TELL ME NOW MY BROTHERS*
>
> *TELL ME NOW MY SISTERS*
>
> *WHO SPEAKS FOR WOLF?"*

Prepare to Write: Contrast Essay

Part A. Study the Prompt

Read the following prompt and determine the topic, directions, and purpose for writing:

Folklore from the German and Native American cultures casts the wolf in strikingly different roles. Write a multiparagraph essay contrasting three ways in which each text portrays the wolf. Use details from "The White Wolf of the Hartz Mountains" and *Who Speaks for Wolf* to support your interpretation of the cultural differences.

Topic: _____

Directions: _____

_____

_____

Purpose for Writing: _____

_____

_____

Part B. Write an Introduction

Set the stage for the sharply different views taken by these two cultures. Write a contrast thesis statement.

_____

_____

_____

_____

_____

_____

_____

_____

_____

_____

_____

_____

_____

Prepare to Write: Contrast Essay (*cont.*)

Part C. Map Your Argument

"The White Wolf of the Hartz Mountains"	
Characteristic	**Text Evidence**

Prepare to Write: Contrast Essay (*cont.*)

Who Speaks for Wolf	
Characteristic	**Text Evidence**

Part D. Write a Conclusion

Summarize your key points without being redundant.

_____

_____

_____

_____

_____

The Literary Analysis Writer's Checklist

Trait	Yes	No	Did the writer . . .?
Ideas and Content			clearly state the thesis of the essay
			analyze and evaluate the elements found in the literature
			focus each paragraph on the topic
			include effective support for the thesis by giving details, examples, explanations, and quotations from the texts
Organization			write an introductory paragraph that captures the reader's interest and cites the titles of the works and the names of the authors
			include in the introductory paragraph a clear viewpoint on the topic and a "map" for the essay that follows
			sequence body paragraphs logically and use transition sentences that make clear the relationship between the ideas
			write a conclusion that ties the analysis together and offers an evaluation of the particulars
Voice and Audience Awareness			think about the audience and purpose for writing
			write in a clear and engaging way that makes the audience want to read the work
Word Choice			find a unique way to say things; avoid sounding repetitive
			use words that are lively and specific to the content
Sentence Fluency			write complete sentences
			expand some sentences using the steps of Masterpiece Sentences
			use compound sentence elements and compound sentences
Conventions			capitalize words correctly:
			capitalize the first word of each sentence
			capitalize proper nouns, including people's names
			punctuate correctly:
			end sentences with a period, question mark, or exclamation mark
			use an apostrophe for possessive nouns and contractions
			use commas and/or semicolons correctly
			use grammar correctly:
			use the correct verb tense
			make sure the verb agrees with the subject in number
			use correct spelling

Let's Focus: "The Mysterious Human Brain"

Content Focus
mental health

Type of Text
_____

Author's Name _____

Author's Purpose _____

Big Ideas
Consider the following Big Ideas. Write your answer for each question.

Is it possible for a person to have multiple selves?

_____

_____

Should people be held responsible for their actions regardless of their mental health condition?

_____

_____

Informational Preview Checklist: "The Mysterious Human Brain" on pages 113–120.

☐ Title: What clue does it provide about the passage?

☐ Pictures and captions: What additional information is added here?

☐ Headings: How is the information organized?

☐ Illustrations: What information is in charts, graphs, or other illustrations?

Enduring Understandings
After reading the text . . .

_____

_____

_____

_____

_____

Key Passage Vocabulary: "The Mysterious Human Brain"

Read each word. Write the word in column 3. Then, circle a number to rate your knowledge of the word.

Vocabulary	Part of Speech	Write the Word	Rate the Word
inhibition	(n)		0 1 2 3
distinct	(adj)		0 1 2 3
controversial	(adj)		0 1 2 3
prone (to)	(adj)		0 1 2 3
media	(n)		0 1 2 3
standard	(n)		0 1 2 3
previously	(adv)		0 1 2 3
transport	(v)		0 1 2 3
image	(n)		0 1 2 3
implement	(v)		0 1 2 3

THE MYSTERIOUS HUMAN BRAIN

"Man is not truly one,
but truly two . . .
All human beings,
as we meet them,
are commingled out
of good and evil . . ."

Robert Louis Stevenson,
*The Strange Case of Dr. Jekyll
and Mr. Hyde*

"I have someone else that takes over when it's time for me to work and when I'm on stage, this alter ego that I've created that kind of protects me and who I really am."

—Beyoncé Knowles, on becoming Sasha Fierce

Alter Egos?

The comic book character Clark Kent, who sees a crime happening, rushes into a phone booth and
5 emerges as Superman. Bruce Banner loses control of his anger and transforms into a green version of himself: the Incredible Hulk. Dr.
10 Jekyll exits his laboratory void of **inhibitions** as the villainous Edward Hyde. All of these fictitious characters have another "self" that
15 they become when the need arises. We hear people talk about them, watch superheroes turn into them, and read about them in
20 literature. These alter egos entertain audiences in the world of fantasy. But are alter egos a part of our real world? **1**

25 The answer is yes. Many of us daydream that we are someone else—someone smarter, richer, or more famous. Some of us, like
30 Beyoncé, take on different personalities around different people and in different situations. Some of us love costume parties.
35 These are typical kinds of "alter egos." They express our imagination and help us explore who we are. But a person whose alter egos are
40 too "real" may have a mental illness called dissociative identity disorder. All-Pro running back Herschel Walker is one of these
45 people. He was diagnosed with this disorder shortly after he retired from the NFL. **2**

inhibition

a feeling of fear or embarrassment that keeps you from doing something

1 What is an alter ego?

2 How is Herschel Walker different from many of us?

"I would say that we wear different hats in different situations. You have a white hat for your home life. You have a red hat for work. You have a blue hat for hanging out with your friends. As an athlete, you've got a green hat for competition. But with DID, your hats get all mixed up, meaning that your hat for competition has now become your home hat, your home hat has become your work hat, your work hat has become some other hat, and so on. So now you're in trouble because your family can't relate to your competition hat, for example. Plus, you're feeling out of control and have no idea what's going on . . . your substitute comes in and takes over when you can't handle the situation."

—Herschel Walker, on having DID

Dissociative Identity Disorder

50 Dissociative identity disorder (DID) is a condition in which a single person has more than one **distinct** identity or self. People with DID switch their identities when under stress.
55 Some psychologists believe the condition to be most common among survivors of traumatic events. The condition seems to begin when a child copes with
60 trauma by convincing him- or herself that it is happening to someone else. The child tries to dissociate him- or herself from the experience. This
65 creates a trigger that causes the child to create alternate personalities called "alters" who take over. The alters can carry over into adulthood. A person
70 can lose control over when the personalities "switch" and may not remember what happens to them while they are switched. In fact, many people with the
75 disorder tell tales of memory loss and blackouts. **3**

Many people often mistakenly confuse DID with schizophrenia. Schizophrenia is a mental
80 disorder in which sufferers have difficulty telling the difference between what is real and what

distinct
separate; different

3 What does DID stand for?

controversial

stirring up disagreement or debate

is not real. (See the chart below for more information on
85 this disorder.) However, there are distinct characteristics of DID that distinguish it from schizophrenia. Sufferers of DID don't often see or hear things
90 that are not real, but instead have serious gaps in memory. In addition, their alters usually have recognizable personality types. They might be protectors,
95 frightened children, or even animals. The average number of alters in a person with DID is 10. Some victims claim to have many more. At one DID
100 conference, a woman by the name of Cassandra claimed to have more than 180 of them. **4**

4 What are the attributes of DID?

The Debate

Formerly known as multiple personality disorder, DID is
105 one of the most **controversial** mental disorders. Mental health professionals have studied this illness for years. They disagree on the causes
110 and its treatments. They even disagree on whether it exists.

Many believers consider the disorder a legitimate defense mechanism of children who
115 have been traumatized. Psychologists explain that traumatized children can create another "self" to endure the suffering in their place.
120 Young children have brains

Schizophrenia: Facts and Figures

What is it?	• a severe brain disorder	
	• should NOT be confused with dissociative identity disorder (DID)	
	• can be treated, but cannot be cured	
What are its causes?	• genetic factors	
	• developmental problems in the brain	
What are its symptoms?	Usually includes:	
	• delusions	• lack of emotion
	• hearing imaginary sounds	• brief, empty replies to questions
	• disordered thoughts	• lack of motivation
	Can also include:	
	• paranoia	
	• impaired memory, attention, problem-solving	
Who gets it?	• 1% of the population	
	• people from all cultures	
	• usually appears in early adulthood, between the ages of 15 and 25	

that are still growing and underdeveloped personalities. This makes them **prone** to "splitting" their personality
125 into "alters." Alters have their own memories and attitudes. These come into play when an alter controls the body and brain of the person with the
130 disorder. The person may not be aware of the disorder until much later in life. Instead, he or she might only feel a sense of forgetfulness or time lapse. **5**

135 Doubters of the disorder do not believe that multiple personalities can exist within a person. Their thinking goes like this. They agree that most
140 sufferers have probably been abused, which leads them to therapy. But, patients' mental instability makes them vulnerable to suggestions
145 by therapists. The therapists might suggest there are hidden memories. Patients feel as though their behavior is rationalized, or explained, and
150 they embrace the diagnosis. **6**

Other doubters argue that the definition of an alter personality is unclear. Some doctors refer to the symptoms as a form of
155 post-traumatic stress disorder (PTSD) instead of DID.

Most cases of DID have been reported in the United States and Canada. This has led
160 people to question the integrity of the disorder and the influence of **media**. Few reports of multiple personality disorder existed until the book and
165 movie *Sybil* were released in the 1970s. After this account of a woman with 16 alters, based on a true story, became known to the public, diagnoses of the
170 disorder significantly increased. Doubters say this is proof it is an imagined disorder. However, believers say it is proof that therapists were simply
175 misguided and undereducated about the disorder before the release. Having been educated, they knew what to look for and how to diagnose, which created
180 a natural increase in cases. **7**

In the Court of Law

Can someone with DID be held responsible for crimes committed by the alters? Each state in the United
185 States has its own **standard** for determining whether a person was legally insane, and therefore not responsible, at the time his or her crime
190 was committed. A defendant may be found not guilty by reason of insanity if "at the time of committing the act, he was laboring under such a
195 defect of reason from disease of the mind as not to know the nature and quality of the act he was doing, or if he did know it, that he did not know
200 what he was doing was wrong."

prone (to)
tending to do something or doing it naturally

media
TV, radio, newspapers, the Internet, and other forms of communication as a group

standard
something used to judge, measure, or define something else

5 How do believers defend DID?

6 How do doubters of DID defend their position?

7 How did the movie *Sybil* change things?

previously

earlier; before

transport

to move something from one place to another

8 Why is insanity a complicated concept for people diagnosed with DID?

9 Why was Grimsley found guilty?

10 Why was Denny-Shaffer found not guilty?

With DID, however, insanity is a complicated concept. If the alter knows what he or she is doing and knows that it
205 is wrong, is the person guilty or not guilty? Take a look at a couple of DID court cases. **8**

Robin Grimsley learned she might have cancer.
210 This psychological trauma, according to Grimsley, caused her alternate personality, Jennifer, to emerge. Grimsley described Jennifer as impulsive,
215 angry, fearful, and anxious, and as having a drinking problem. On one occasion, Grimsley drove after drinking and subsequently was charged
220 with driving under the influence of alcohol. In her defense, Grimsley said that when Jennifer, her alternate personality, is in control, Robin,
225 her primary personality, is not aware of what is going on and cannot control Jennifer's actions. Though Grimsley had **previously** been diagnosed
230 with DID, the court found her guilty of the crime. According to the court, an individual's criminal responsibility rests on the mental state of the alter in
235 control at the time of the crime. The court concluded that because the alter personality— Jennifer—was not unconscious at the time of the drunken

240 driving, Grimsley as a whole should be held criminally accountable. **9**

Bridget Denny-Shaffer disguised herself as a medical
245 student, entered a hospital nursery, took a newborn baby and **transported** the baby to another state, telling her ex-boyfriend that she had given
250 birth. Once captured, Denny-Shaffer was charged with kidnapping and transporting the infant across state lines. Her defense was that she was
255 unconscious and not aware of the kidnapping for all or part of those weeks. In fact, it was shown in court that at least two alter personalities, Rina
260 and Mother Superior, were in control. Denny-Shaffer was found not guilty. The court could not prove that the host personality was mentally aware
265 of the goings on, and thus she couldn't be held responsible for the actions of the alter egos. The host personality—rather than the alter in control—is
270 the person on trial. If the host personality isn't aware of what is happening, then by reason of insanity, the person is not responsible. **10**

275 Denny-Shaffer, like most criminals found not guilty by reason of insanity, was sentenced to time in a mental

institution. According to
280 the American Psychiatric
Association, persons found not
guilty by reason of insanity
are likely to spend the same
amount of time or more in a
285 psychiatric institution as they
would have in prison if found
guilty of the crime. However,
mentally ill people are often
found guilty and sent to prison
290 because treatments are offered
within prison walls. Are the
treatments equal? How are
people found to be mentally ill
treated in the United States? [11]

Sometimes it is not so
obvious. More than 65% of
those with a mental illness
will still lead a normal,
productive life.

Society's Treatment of the Mentally Ill

295 People who suffered from
mental illness during the 17th
and 18th centuries were treated
horribly. Those judged insane
were frequently admitted
300 to madhouses, workhouses,
poorhouses, and jails. Those
thought to be particularly
dangerous were put in restraints
and sentenced to confinement.
305 By the end of the 17th century,
the prevailing **image** of
the mentally ill was that of
uncontrollable, wild animals.

image
a picture in the
mind

[11] What is the
typical sentence
for many
mentally ill
criminals?

Top: *More like a jail than a mental hospital, this facility was built in 1784.*

Middle: *The Northern Michigan Asylum was established in 1885 and has been known as the "11th Street Academy." It looks more like a school.*

Bottom: *A modern psychiatric hospital in Helsingor, Denmark*

implement

to put something into action or put it to use

12 How has the treatment of people with mental illness changed over time?

Harsh treatment and restraint
310 with chains was thought to be needed therapy to suppress the animal instincts. Treatment in public asylums was similar to
315 prison life. The most notorious of these was Bedlam in England. It is said that at one time, spectators could pay to watch the patients there as a form of entertainment. Today,
320 the word *bedlam* is a common noun that means "a state of total confusion."

By the end of the 18th century, a moral treatment movement
325 developed. This movement **implemented** more humane and personalized approaches to treatment of the mentally ill. The following century saw
330 a growth in the number and size of insane asylums. Laws were introduced that allowed authorities to deal with those deemed insane. Unfortunately,
335 the institutions became overburdened with large numbers of people, leading to very few therapeutic activities.

13 Why is DID controversial?

The turn of the 20th century
340 saw even more changes. Advocates worked to improve the conditions in asylums, which were now known as hospitals. New treatments used
345 drugs to control symptoms. More and more patients were

released from institutions. Th public began to understand that a mental illness is a
350 disease, just like a physical illness. **12**

Remaining Questions

The debate over DID will like not be resolved anytime soon People will continue to debat
355 whether a person can have multiple personalities and whether DID is misdiagnosec Juries and judges will continu to argue whether all persons
360 should be held accountable for their actions, regardless of their mental state. Among the lingering questions, one fact remains. Since 1999, the
365 Department of Justice has found that more than half of the people in the nation's prisons are mentally ill—and far less than half of those
370 receive any mental health treatment.

Should people be imprisoned for crimes committed by alte egos? You decide. **13**

Out of the 10 leading causes of disability in the United States, four are mental disorders—bipolar disorder, schizophrenia, depression, and OCD.

Relative Clauses as Adjectives

Complete the following sentences by adding a relative pronoun from the chart.
Underline the relative clause serving as an adjective—the adjective clause.

Relative Pronoun	Function/Meaning	Example
who	subject or object pronoun for people	It was my mom *who* loved our trip to New York the most.
which	subject or object pronoun for animals and things; does not change the meaning of the sentence; set off with commas	Ellis Island, *which* is off the coast of New York, is a popular tourist attraction.
whose	possessive pronoun for people, animals, and things	We cheered for the Broadway performer, *whose* voice amazed us.
whom	object pronoun for people	It was the opera singer for *whom* I felt the most admiration.
that	subject or object pronoun for people, animals, and things; changes the meaning of the sentence	While in New York, many people visit the memorial *that* honors those who died in the 9/11 terrorist attacks.
where	subject or object pronoun for place nouns	During the summer, New York is a city *where* people can watch a Broadway show or a Yankees game.
when	subject or object pronoun for time nouns	The colder months, *when* baseball season is over, offer the opportunity to watch a football game or an opera.

Example:
The courtroom _____**where**_____ the trial was held was filled with reporters.

1. My alter ego, _____ I've created to protect myself, emerges when I am on stage.

2. Many fictitious characters have special powers _____ they use for good or evil purposes.

3. Someone _____ claims to have an alternative personality often suffers from losses of memory.

4. My alter ego Shelly, on _____ I blamed the crime, was sentenced to 5 years in prison.

5. The days _____ the alter personality emerges are filled with a sense of imminent danger.

Relative Clauses as Nouns

- Have a subject and a predicate but cannot stand alone
- Take the place of a noun: subject or object
- Answer the *who* or *what* question
- Begin with: *that, what, whatever, which, whichever, who, whoever, whom, whomever, whose*

Read each sentence and determine whether the underlined group of words is a noun clause. Place an X in the appropriate column.

	Noun Clause	Other
Ex: I would say <u>that we wear different hats in different situations</u>.	X	
1. Psychologists explain <u>that when children under the age of 6 are traumatized</u>, they create another "self" to endure the suffering in their place.		
2. He was diagnosed <u>with a mental illness</u> called dissociative identity disorder.		
3. They agree <u>that most sufferers have probably been abused</u>.		
4. All of these fictitious characters have another "self" <u>that they become when the need arises</u>.		
5. Laws were introduced <u>that allowed authorities to deal with those deemed insane</u>.		
6. The criminal forgot <u>which alter was in control</u> but knew it wasn't her.		
7. Multiple personalities <u>that conflict with each other</u> are often created during childhood.		
8. According to the jury, <u>whoever was in control at the time of the crime</u> is the guilty party.		

Adjective, Adverb, and Noun Clauses

Read each sentence and determine the function of the underlined clause. Sort them appropriately in the chart.

1. People <u>who suffered from mental illness during the 17th and 18th centuries</u> were treated horribly.

2. Since 1999, the Department of Justice has found <u>that more than half of the people in the nation's prisons are mentally ill</u>.

3. He was diagnosed with this disorder <u>shortly after he retired</u> from the NFL.

4. The comic book character Clark Kent, <u>who sees a crime happening</u>, rushes into a phone booth and emerges as Superman.

5. The condition seems to begin when a child copes with trauma by convincing him- or herself <u>that it is happening to someone else</u>.

6. This creates a trigger <u>that causes a child to create alternate personalities called "alters"</u> who take over.

7. This creates a trigger that causes a child to create alternate personalities called "alters" <u>who take over</u>.

8. A person can lose control over when the personalities "switch" and may not remember what happens to them <u>while they are switched</u>.

9. Having been educated, they knew <u>what to look for and how to diagnose</u>, which created a natural increase in cases.

10. The person may not be aware of the disorder until much later in life <u>because it usually only appears during trauma</u>.

Adjective Clause	Adverb Clause	Noun Clause

Active and Passive Voice

Rewrite each sentence to change the passive voice to active voice. Underline the verb in your new sentence and make sure the subject is doing the action.

> **Example:** Most cases <u>have been reported</u> in highly developed nations.
>
> Highly developed nations <u>have reported</u> most cases.

1. Robin Grimsley <u>was told</u> by the doctors about her cancer.

   _____

2. Jennifer <u>was described</u> by Grimsley as impulsive, angry, fearful, and anxious.

   _____

3. Grimsley <u>had been charged</u> by the police with driving under the influence of alcohol.

   _____

4. Grimsley <u>was found</u> guilty by the courts.

   _____

5. A baby from the hospital nursery <u>was taken</u> by Bridget Denny-Shaffer.

   _____

   _____

6. An alter <u>was created</u> by the abused child.

   _____

   _____

7. Criminals <u>are sent</u> to prison by juries.

   _____

   _____

8. The green hat <u>had been worn</u> by Walker while playing football.

   _____

   _____

Active Voice Optional Activity

Write 10 sentences about an event you recently attended. Use the active voice in your sentences.

1. _____

   _____

2. _____

   _____

3. _____

   _____

4. _____

   _____

5. _____

   _____

6. _____

   _____

7. _____

   _____

8. _____

   _____

9. _____

   _____

10. _____

    _____

Passage Comprehension

Reread "The Mysterious Human Brain." Respond to each prompt using complete sentences. Refer to the chart on pages 14 and 15 to determine how to respond to each prompt. Provide text evidence when requested.

1. Objectively summarize dissociative identity disorder.

_____

_____

_____

_____

_____

_____

_____

_____

_____

2. Integrate information from the primary text and text features (bulleted text box) to contrast schizophrenia and DID.

_____

_____

_____

_____

_____

_____

_____

_____

_____

_____

_____

_____

Passage Comprehension (*cont.*)

3. Trace the doubters' claims that DID is an "imagined disorder." Provide text evidence.

_____

_____

_____

_____

_____

_____

_____

Text Evidence: _____

_____

_____

4. Evaluate the merit of DID. Provide text evidence to support your evaluation.

_____

_____

_____

Text Evidence: _____

_____

_____

_____

_____

_____

_____

_____

_____

_____

Passage Comprehension (*cont.*)

5. Summarize and evaluate the outcomes of the DID court cases.

_____

_____

_____

_____

_____

_____

_____

_____

_____

_____

_____

6. Evaluate the author's point of view regarding society's treatment of the mentally ill.

_____

_____

_____

_____

_____

_____

_____

_____

_____

_____

_____

Close Reading

Read the text.

"The Mysterious Human Brain"

"Man is not truly one, but truly two . . . All human beings, as we meet them, are commingled out of good and evil . . ."

Robert Louis Stevenson, *The Strange Case of Dr. Jekyll and Mr. Hyde*

Alter Egos?

The comic book character Clark Kent, who sees a crime happening,
5 rushes into a phone booth and emerges as Superman. Bruce Banner loses control of his anger and transforms into a green version of himself: the Incredible Hulk. Dr. Jekyll exits his laboratory void of **inhibitions** as the villainous Edward Hyde. All of these fictitious characters have another "self" that they become when the need arises. We hear people
10 talk about them, watch superheroes turn into them, and read about them in literature. These alter egos entertain audiences in the world of fantasy. But are alter egos a part of our real world?

The answer is yes. Many of us daydream that we are someone else— someone smarter, richer, or more famous. Some of us, like Beyoncé,
15 take on different personalities around different people and in different situations. Some of us love costume parties. These are typical kinds of "alter egos." They express our imagination and help us explore who we are. But a person whose alter egos are too "real" may have a mental illness called dissociative identity disorder. All-Pro running back Herschel
20 Walker is one of these people. He was diagnosed with this disorder shortly after he retired from the NFL.

Close Reading (*cont.*)

Dissociative Identity Disorder

Dissociative identity disorder (DID) is a condition in which a single person has more than one **distinct** identity or self. People with DID switch their identities when under stress. Some psychologists believe the
25 condition to be most common among survivors of traumatic events. The condition seems to begin when a child copes with trauma by convincing him- or herself that it is happening to someone else. The child tries to dissociate him- or herself from the experience. This creates a trigger that causes the child to create alternate personalities called "alters" who
30 take over. The alters can carry over into adulthood. A person can lose control over when the personalities "switch" and may not remember what happens to them while they are switched. In fact, many people with the disorder tell tales of memory loss and blackouts.

Many people often mistakenly confuse DID with schizophrenia.
35 Schizophrenia is a mental disorder in which sufferers have difficulty telling the difference between what is real and what is not real. (See the chart on page 116 for more information on this disorder.) However, there are distinct characteristics of DID that distinguish it from schizophrenia. Sufferers of DID don't often see or hear things that are not real, but instead have
40 serious gaps in memory. In addition, their alters usually have recognizable personality types. They might be protectors, frightened children, or even animals. The average number of alters in a person with DID is 10. Some victims claim to have many more. At one DID conference, a woman by the name of Cassandra claimed to have more than 180 of them.

Close Reading (*cont.*)

The Debate

45 Formerly known as multiple personality disorder, DID is one of the most **controversial** mental disorders. Mental health professionals have studied this illness for years. They disagree on the causes and its treatments. They even disagree on whether it exists.

Many believers consider the disorder a legitimate defense mechanism
50 of children who have been traumatized. Psychologists explain that traumatized children can create another "self" to endure the suffering in their place. Young children have brains that are still growing and underdeveloped personalities. This makes them **prone** to "splitting" their personality into "alters." Alters have their own memories and attitudes.
55 These come into play when an alter controls the body and brain of the person with the disorder. The person may not be aware of the disorder until much later in life. Instead, he or she might only feel a sense of forgetfulness or time lapse.

Doubters of the disorder do not believe that multiple personalities can
60 exist within a person. Their thinking goes like this. They agree that most sufferers have probably been abused, which leads them to therapy. But, patients' mental instability makes them vulnerable to suggestions by therapists. The therapists might suggest there are hidden memories. Patients feel as though their behavior is rationalized, or explained, and
65 they embrace the diagnosis.

Other doubters argue that the definition of an alter personality is unclear. Some doctors refer to the symptoms as a form of post-traumatic stress disorder (PTSD) instead of DID.

Most cases of DID have been reported in the United States and Canada.
70 This has led people to question the integrity of the disorder and the influence of **media**. Few reports of multiple personality disorder existed until the book and movie *Sybil* were released in the 1970s. After this account of a woman with 16 alters, based on a true story, became known to the public, diagnoses of the disorder significantly increased. Doubters
75 say this is proof it is an imagined disorder. However, believers say it is proof that therapists were simply misguided and undereducated about the disorder before the release. Having been educated, they knew what to look for and how to diagnose, which created a natural increase in cases.

Close Reading (*cont.*)

In the Court of Law

80 Can someone with DID be held responsible for crimes committed by the alters? Each state in the United States has its own **standard** for determining whether a person was legally insane, and therefore not responsible, at the time his or her crime was committed. A defendant may be found not guilty by reason of insanity if "at the time of committing the act, he was laboring under such a defect of reason from disease of the mind 85 as not to know the nature and quality of the act he was doing, or if he did know it, that he did not know what he was doing was wrong." With DID, however, insanity is a complicated concept. If the alter knows what he or she is doing and knows that it is wrong, is the person guilty or not guilty? Take a look at a couple of DID court cases.

90 Robin Grimsley learned she might have cancer. This psychological trauma, according to Grimsley, caused her alternate personality, Jennifer, to emerge. Grimsley described Jennifer as impulsive, angry, fearful, and anxious, and as having a drinking problem. On one occasion, Grimsley drove after drinking and subsequently was charged with driving under 95 the influence of alcohol. In her defense, Grimsley said that when Jennifer, her alternate personality, is in control, Robin, her primary personality, is not aware of what is going on and cannot control Jennifer's actions. Though Grimsley had **previously** been diagnosed with DID, the court found her guilty of the crime. According to the court, an individual's 100 criminal responsibility rests on the mental state of the alter in control at the time of the crime. The court concluded that because the alter personality—Jennifer—was not unconscious at the time of the drunken driving, Grimsley as a whole should be held criminally accountable.

Close Reading (*cont.*)

Bridget Denny-Shaffer disguised herself as a medical student, entered
105 a hospital nursery, took a newborn baby, and **transported** the baby to
another state, telling her ex-boyfriend that she had given birth. Once
captured, Denny-Shaffer was charged with kidnapping and transporting
the infant across state lines. Her defense was that she was unconscious
and not aware of the kidnapping for all or part of those weeks. In fact, it
110 was shown in court that at least two alter personalities, Rina and Mother
Superior, were in control. Denny-Shaffer was found not guilty. The court
could not prove that the host personality was mentally aware of the
goings on, and thus she couldn't be held responsible for the actions of the
alter egos. The host personality—rather than the alter in control—is the
115 person on trial. If the host personality isn't aware of what is happening,
then by reason of insanity, the person is not responsible.

Denny-Shaffer, like most criminals found not guilty by reason of insanity,
was sentenced to time in a mental institution. According to the American
Psychiatric Association, persons found not guilty by reason of insanity
120 are likely to spend the same amount of time or more in a psychiatric
institution as they would have in prison if found guilty of the crime.
However, mentally ill people are often found guilty and sent to prison
because treatments are offered within prison walls. Are the treatments
equal? How are people found to be mentally ill treated in the United States?

Close Reading (*cont.*)

Society's Treatment of the Mentally Ill

125 People who suffered from mental illness during the 17th and 18th centuries were treated horribly. Those judged insane were frequently admitted to madhouses, workhouses, poorhouses, and jails. Those thought to be particularly dangerous were put in restraints and sentenced to confinement. By the end of the 17th century, the prevailing **image** of the
130 mentally ill was that of uncontrollable, wild animals. Harsh treatment and restraint with chains was thought to be needed therapy to suppress the animal instincts. Treatment in public asylums was similar to prison life. The most notorious of these was Bedlam in England. It is said that at one time, spectators could pay to watch the patients there as a form of
135 entertainment. Today, the word *bedlam* is a common noun that means "a state of total confusion."

By the end of the 18th century, a moral treatment movement developed. This movement **implemented** more humane and personalized approaches to treatment of the mentally ill. The following century saw a growth
140 in the number and size of insane asylums. Laws were introduced that allowed authorities to deal with those deemed insane. Unfortunately, the institutions became overburdened with large numbers of people, leading to very few therapeutic activities.

The turn of the 20th century saw even more changes. Advocates worked to
145 improve the conditions in asylums, which were now known as hospitals. New treatments used drugs to control symptoms. More and more patients were released from institutions. The public began to understand that a mental illness is a disease, just like a physical illness.

Close Reading (*cont.*)

Remaining Questions

The debate over DID will likely not be resolved anytime soon. People
150 will continue to debate whether a person can have multiple personalities
and whether DID is misdiagnosed. Juries and judges will continue to
argue whether all persons should be held accountable for their actions,
regardless of their mental state. Among the lingering questions, one fact
remains. Since 1999, the Department of Justice has found that more than
155 half of the people in the nation's prisons are mentally ill—and far less
than half of those receive any mental health treatment.

Should people be imprisoned for crimes committed by alter egos? You
decide.

Quick Write in Response to Reading

Juries evaluate the evidence and decide who is guilty or innocent. Closing arguments of the lawyers are often the last thing a jury hears and, thus, have the power to convince the jury of a person's guilt or innocence.

Imagine you are the defense attorney for a person with DID who is on trial for attacking a complete stranger. Your client claims that an "alter" identity took charge because he or she felt threatened. Write a closing argument in defense of your client, explaining why he or she should not be punished for this crime.

Note: Lawyers use facts, reason, and **emotions** to convince the jury.

_____

_____

_____

_____

_____

_____

_____

_____

_____

_____

_____

_____

_____

_____

_____

_____

_____

_____

_____

_____

Let's Focus: Graphic Novel of *The Strange Case of Dr. Jekyll and Mr. Hyde*

Content Focus   **Type of Text**
multiple personalities
good and evil   _____

Authors' Names _____

Authors' Purpose _____

Big Ideas

Consider the following Big Idea questions. Write your answer for each question.

Can people control their thoughts? Explain.

_____

_____

To what degree do our thoughts influence our actions? Explain.

_____

_____

Graphic Novel Preview Checklist: the graphic novel of *The Strange Case of Dr. Jekyll and Mr. Hyde* on pages 139–199.

☐ Title: What clue does it provide?

☐ Characters: What information is added here?

☐ Artwork: What do you notice at quick glance?

☐ Features: What other text features do you notice? Find the following:

- Narrative Box: page _____   • Thought Balloon: page _____

- Dialogue Balloon: page _____   • Panel: page _____

- Sound Effect: page _____

Point of View

Chapters 1–4: _____ Chapter 5: _____

Enduring Understandings

After reading the text . . .

_____

_____

Key Passage Vocabulary: Graphic Novel of *The Strange Case of Dr. Jekyll and Mr. Hyde*

Read each word. Write it in column 3. Then, circle a number to rate your knowledge of the word.

Vocabulary	Part of Speech	Write the Word	Rate the Word
attend	(v)		0 1 2 3
involved	(adj)		0 1 2 3
incident	(n)		0 1 2 3
conflict	(n)		0 1 2 3
challenge	(n)		0 1 2 3
formula	(n)		0 1 2 3
urge	(n)		0 1 2 3
reaction	(n)		0 1 2 3
research	(n)		0 1 2 3
obtain	(v)		0 1 2 3

STONE ARCH *Classic Fiction*

INTRODUCING . . .

POOLE,
THE BUTLER

GABRIEL UTTERSON

DR. HENRY JEKYLL

HASTIE LANYON

EDWARD HYDE

[1] Where does the story take place?

London, 1885. Gabriel Utterson walks with his cousin Richard Enfield... [1]

Say, Utterson, you see this property here?

Yes, we walk past it once a week, cousin.

Not long ago, a most remarkable event led me here. I'm surprised I've never told you.

Then tell me now.

CHAPTER 1

A STRANGE VILLAIN

"It happened some months ago, late at night in the Soho neighborhood."

"A young girl collided with a man coming out of a cross street." **2**

2 Why did the man beat the girl?

"Before the girl could even apologize, the man struck her down."

Horrible! You didn't let him get away with it?

Indeed not. While a doctor **attended** the girl, I chased the villain down!

attend
to take care of someone or something

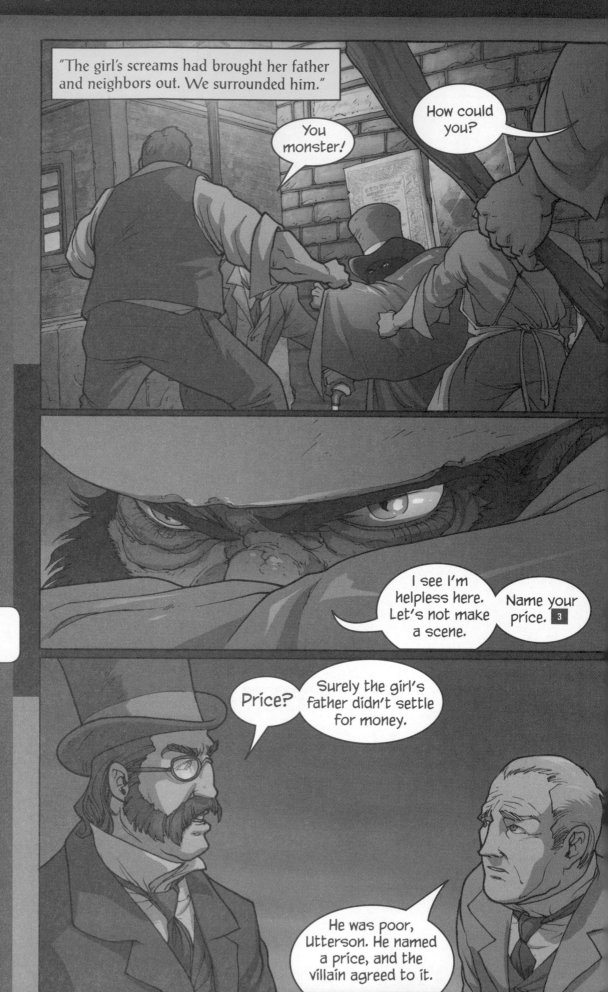

"The girl's screams had brought her father and neighbors out. We surrounded him."

You monster!

How could you?

3 Why did the crime go unreported?

I see I'm helpless here. Let's not make a scene.

Name your price. 3

Price?

Surely the girl's father didn't settle for money.

He was poor, Utterson. He named a price, and the villain agreed to it.

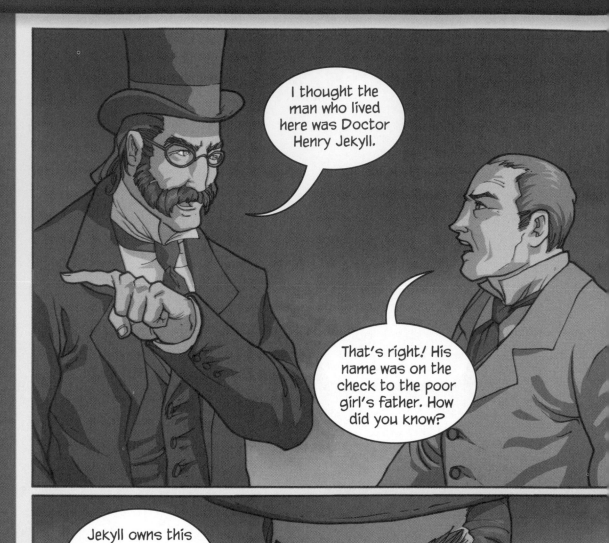

4 What is the connection between Dr. Henry Jekyll and Edward Hyde?

Hours later . . .

All this time and still no sign of—
[5]

Wait! Is that him?

[5] Where does Utterson wait for Edward Hyde?

Not so fast, Hyde!

What?! Let me go!

CHAPTER 2

MEETING MR. HYDE

6 Why does Utterson want to see Hyde's face?

involved
connected with; mixed up with

7 Where is Utterson going to go in the morning?

Early the next day . . .
Good morning, Mister Utterson.
Good morning, Poole. Is Dr. Jekyll in?
Yes sir. Please follow me.
Utterson! What a pleasant surprise. Come in, come in.
I'm glad to find you well. I've been worried.
CHAPTER 3
DR. HENRY JEKYLL

If that will be all, sir.

Yes, thank you, Poole.

Now, what causes you to worry, Utterson?

It's about that man in your will—Edward Hyde. I met him last night.

Is that so?

My cousin, Richard Enfield, has met him as well. He says Hyde came here for help after an **incident** in Soho.

Hyde has his own key to my laboratory in the back.

incident
an event or happening that is noticed or creates a stir

But why? Has he got some hold over you, Henry?

I fear that he means you harm. 8

8 Why was Utterson worried about Jekyll?

Unit 9   155

9 What hold do you think Jekyll has over Hyde?

10 What does "From both of me" mean?

Later, at the morgue . . .

Do you know this man?

His name is Hastie Lanyon, an old friend. What happened to him, Inspector?

He was attacked on the street. A young lady who lives nearby saw the whole thing.

We found this lying in the gutter.

May I see that?

My God, I've seen this before!
11

I believe I know where the murderer lives!

11 Where has Utterson seen the cane before?

Looks like he forgot to take his checkbook out of his pocket. You can't get far in this city without money.

If there's no money here, Hyde might try the bank.

Hyde won't try the bank, I'm sure of it.

There's someone else he can turn to for money.
12

12 Who will Hyde turn to for money?

A short time later . . .

Good morning, Poole. I must see Dr. Jekyll.

Right this way, sir.

The Doctor's in his laboratory out back. He's been there all night.

Henry! Are you ill?

No. I've had a terrible scare.

As have I, Henry. Our old friend Hastie Lanyon is dead.

He was murdered by Edward Hyde!

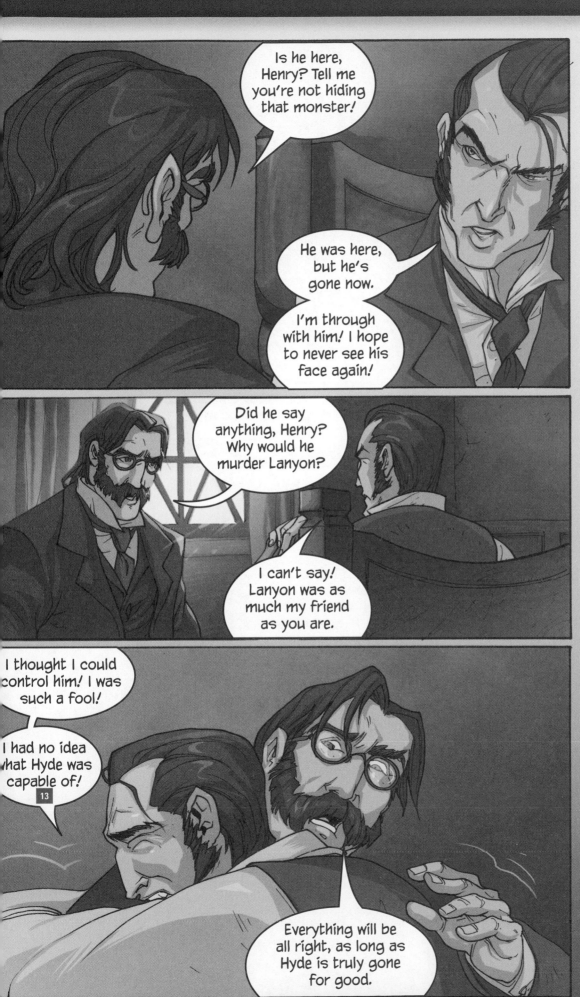

Is he here, Henry? Tell me you're not hiding that monster!

He was here, but he's gone now.

I'm through with him! I hope to never see his face again!

Did he say anything, Henry? Why would he murder Lanyon?

I can't say! Lanyon was as much my friend as you are.

I thought I could control him! I was such a fool!

I had no idea what Hyde was capable of!

Everything will be all right, as long as Hyde is truly gone for good.

13 Why is Jekyll so upset?

Weeks later, Dr. Jekyll's butler arrives at Utterson's house . . .

Poole! What brings you here? Is Henry ill?

Mister Utterson, there's something wrong. I've been afraid for about a week. I can bear it no more.

The Doctor has locked himself in his laboratory. I'm afraid for him, sir.

I think there's been foul play. Will you come with me and see for yourself?

Hyde has come back!! We must hurry!

At Dr. Jekyll's house . . .

God grant that there be nothing wrong.

Amen, Poole.

Why are all of Henry's servants still here? 14

They're all afraid, sir.

14 What are the servants afraid of?

15 Who is in the lab?

The next day . . .

Utterson, I'm glad you're still here. We're almost finished inside.

Any sign of Henry Jekyll, Inspector?

I'm afraid not. His body's not in there. We'll dig up the yard, but I doubt we'll find anything. **17**

17 Why does the inspector doubt they will find Henry Jekyll?

We might never know what happened to Doctor Jekyll.

We found this envelope addressed to you. Since you're Jekyll's attorney, we can't open it before you look at it.

Thank you, Inspector.

Back at Utterson's house . . .

What?

You don't confess unless you've done something wrong.

Henry Jekyll's Full Confession

Henry, what on earth could you have done?

"My name is Doctor Henry Jekyll. I was born in London to a wealthy family."

"My loving parents raised me in warmth and safety, wanting for nothing." 18

18 Who is writing the letter Utterson is reading?

"Growing up, I think I enjoyed school more than my friends did."

CHAPTER 5

JEKYLL'S CONFESSION

"I studied hard, got good grades, and didn't waste much time playing."

"My hard work earned me a place at the best college in England."

"There I met Hastie Lanyon, who introduced me to Gabriel Utterson."

"The three of us became great friends."

One mind, the high mind, seeks only beauty and goodness in life.

The other, the low mind, is vain and greedy, seeking only what's best for itself. **19**

19 What is the difference between the high mind and the low mind? Which mind did Jekyll listen to?

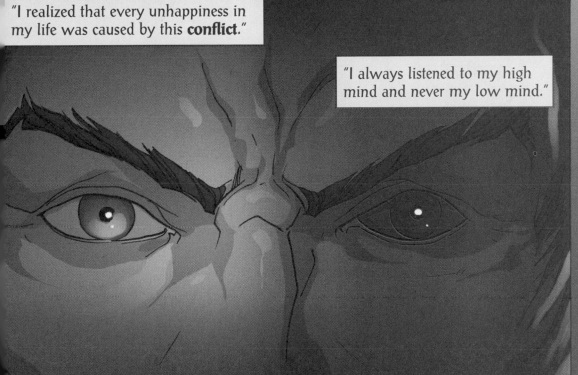

"I realized that every unhappiness in my life was caused by this **conflict**."

"I always listened to my high mind and never my low mind."

conflict

a clash or struggle between two sides or forces

"In time, I explained this discovery to my friend Lanyon. Like me, he was a man of science. I hoped he might understand."

A neat idea, but not worth anything.

It's not like you can give those minds their own separate bodies.

"He didn't take me seriously."

Goodnight, Henry! From both of me! Ha ha ha! 20

20 Which quote is a repeat of something said earlier in the story?

"Lanyon was only joking, but what if I could separate the high and low minds from each other?"

"I set out at once to work on this scientific **challenge**."

"The key was a certain rare salt I'd found from halfway around the world."

challenge

a problem or question that takes effort to solve

"I can't be more specific about the **formula** I created. I won't. I can promise you, however, that it worked."

formula

a mixture; a recipe

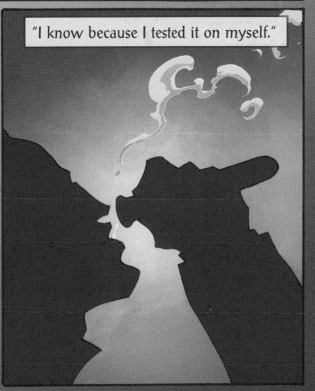

"I know because I tested it on myself."

AHHHHH!

"But instead, I changed." 21

No! It can't be!

Jekyll and Hyde were the same man?!

21 How did Jekyll change physically?

"The evil things it wanted to do! I'd denied such **urges** all my life!"

urge
a strong need or drive to do something

"My low mind could do every wicked thing I'd never let myself do before."

"But not yet. Not that night."

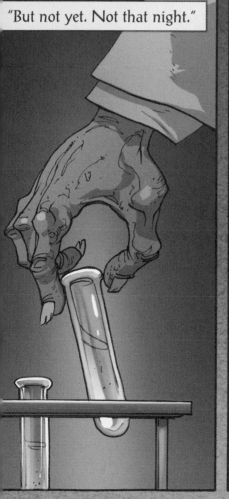

"I had to make sure the formula worked both ways."  22

22 Jekyll realized that he couldn't be both people at the same time. Why would that be scary?

"I simply became myself again."

"But that was good enough for me."

"Soon, I began using my formula every day. I even changed my name to Edward Hyde because I acted like a completely separate person." **23**

23 How often did Jekyll become Hyde?

"Something Hastie Lanyon would soon find out . . ."

"I expected Lanyon to be amazed. I hoped he'd be proud of me."

"Instead, all I saw in his eyes was horror!" **24**

24 Why was there horror in Lanyon's eyes?

Henry, what have you done?!

reaction

what someone feels, says, or does in response to something else

25 What does Jekyll see in the mirror now?

"Lanyon made me leave at once. I'd never seen him so upset."

"Lanyon's **reaction** made me question everything I'd done."

Had I gone too far? 25

"That night, I decided to set aside my formula."

"I woke the next day. To my relief, my low mind was blessedly quiet."

"But then . . ."

What on earth?

"My body burned and twisted inside. I became Edward Hyde!"

"Without my formula!"

"I rushed to my laboratory quickly, though I don't remember how."

"There, I mixed and drank my formula, half afraid it wouldn't work."

"How had it happened?"

I thought my low mind was at peace!

Now it almost seems to be fighting me for control!

"To my horror, this incident was just the first of many."

"Now, I changed for no reason, and I wasn't fully aware of my actions." 26

26 After Lanyon's rejection, what began happening to Jekyll?

Where am I? What have I done?!

"When I came to my senses, my clothes were stained with blood. My cane was broken."

What have I done!

"I wanted to get home and drink my formula, but I had to get rid of my bloodstained clothes first."

"Although I couldn't remember doing it, I must have killed my friend." 27

27 How does Jekyll know he killed Lanyon if he doesn't remember doing it?

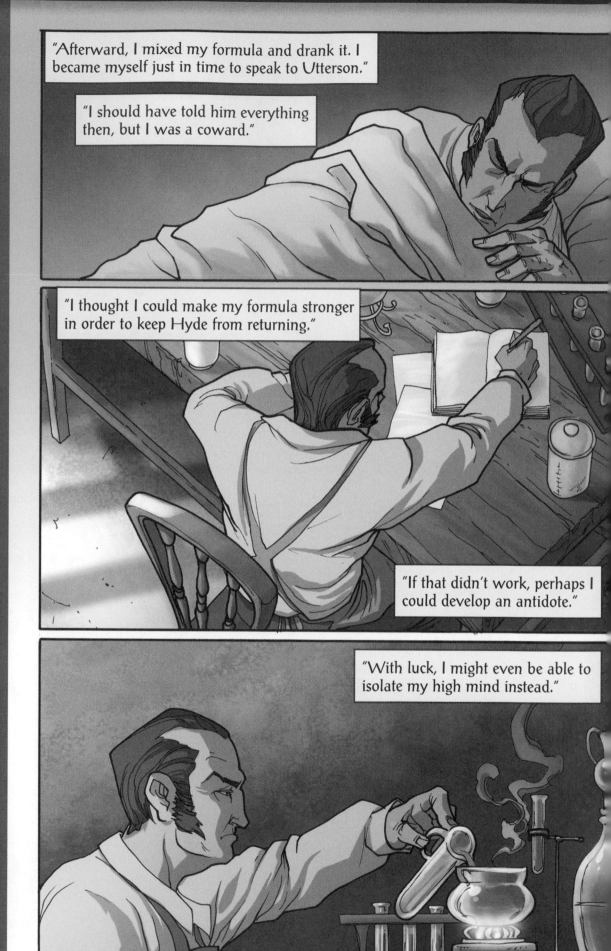

"But luck was not with me. Hyde found my new notes and destroyed them."

"He burned my original **research** notes too, so I couldn't use them." 28

research
the act of studying something or gathering information about it

28 Why did Hyde destroy the research notes?

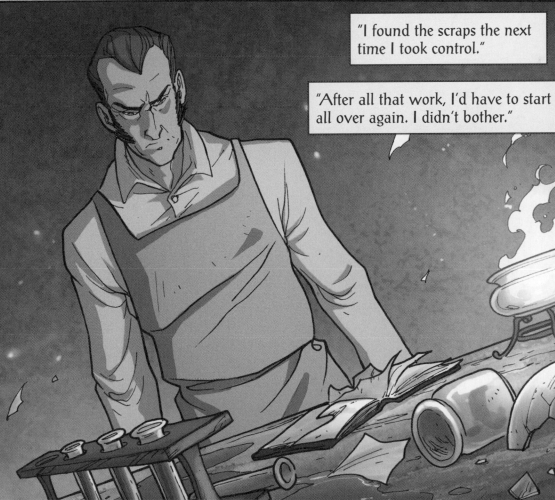

"I found the scraps the next time I took control."

"After all that work, I'd have to start all over again. I didn't bother."

"First, I did the hardest thing a human being has ever done."

"I disposed of the rare salt I **obtained** from halfway around the world."

obtain
to get; to gain

"Without it, my formula doesn't work."

"Second, I wrote a new will that doesn't include Hyde."

"Now, all that's left is to finish writing this confession."

"I understand now that I'm responsible for what Hyde has done."

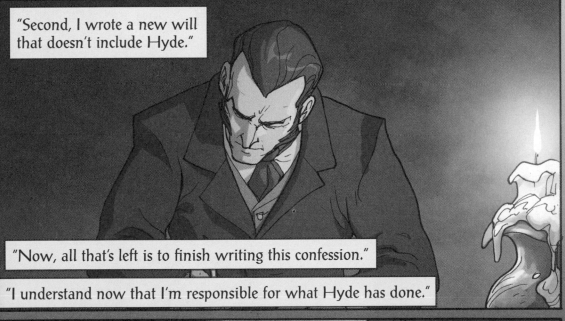

"But without my formula, he'll have to face justice for his crimes. This letter will make sure of that." 29

29 Why did Jekyll dispose of the formula?

Unit 9   **197**

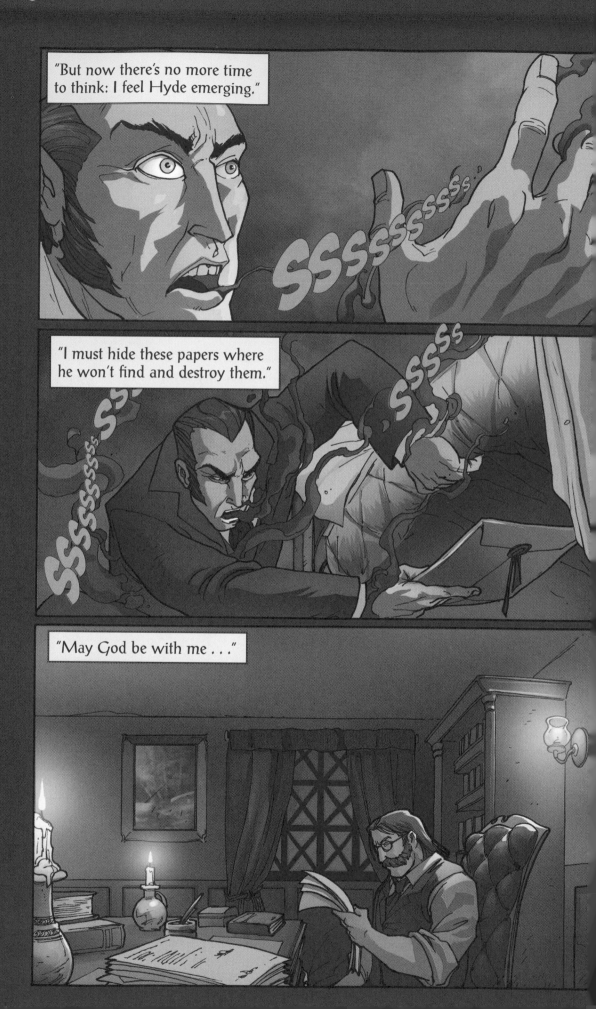

" . . . may God give me strength. Signed, Henry Jekyll."

Poor Henry.

No one else will ever learn the secret of the strange case of Dr. Jekyll and Mr. Hyde. 30

30 Why does Utterson vow to keep this a secret?

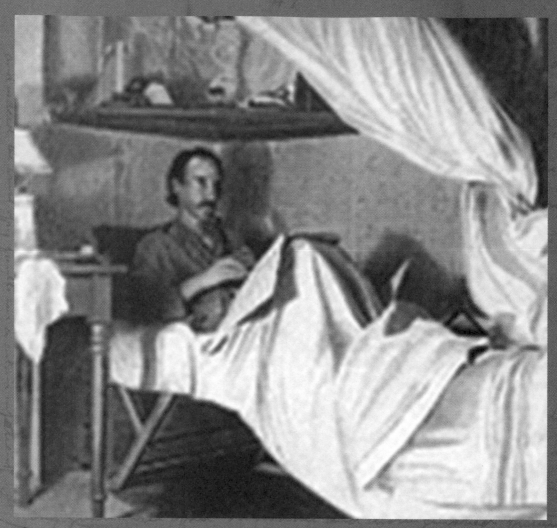

Robert Louis Stevenson

The effect of different personalities on the human condition, as well as the common theme of good vs. evil in literature, fascinated Robert Louis Stevenson. These types of stories are found in his earlier works. Stevenson's wife, Fanny, remembers when the infamous *Strange Case of Dr. Jekyll and Mr. Hyde* first started to form in his mind. "In the small hours of one morning . . . I was awakened by cries of horror from Louis. Thinking he had a nightmare, I awakened him. He said angrily: 'Why did you wake me? I was dreaming a fine boogey tale.' I had awakened him at the first transformation scene." Even though Stevenson was in bed and ill at the time, this didn't stop him from finishing the story that is one of the first literary works to begin exploring the origins and symptoms of split personalities, which later became known as dissociative identity disorder.

Dialogue

To rewrite dialogue, identify the speaker and include correct punctuation.

Example:

"Say, Utterson," asked Richard Enfield, "you see this property here?"

"Yes," responded Utterson, "we walk past it once a week, cousin."

Enfield continued, "Not long ago, a most remarkable event led me here. I'm surprised I've never told you."

"Then tell me now," implored Utterson.

Rewrite the following dialogue. Remember to identify the speaker, vary the verb, and include proper punctuation.

_____

_____

_____

_____

_____

_____

_____

_____

_____

_____

Critical Understandings

Refer to Chapters 1–3 of the graphic novel of *The Strange Case of Dr. Jekyll and Mr. Hyde*. Respond to each prompt using complete sentences. Refer to the chart on pages 14 and 15 to determine how to respond to each prompt.

1. Analyze the graphic treatment of the flashback on page 143.

_____

_____

_____

_____

_____

_____

_____

2. Relate the role Hastie Lanyon plays in the life of Edward Hyde to the role Judge Scott plays in the life of Jim Hall.

_____

_____

_____

_____

_____

_____

_____

_____

_____

_____

_____

_____

_____

_____

Critical Understandings (*cont.*)

3. Differentiate between Hyde's use of "I must have you for dinner some night" and Jekyll's use of the same statement.

_____

_____

_____

_____

_____

_____

_____

_____

_____

4. Assess the content in Dr. Jekyll's will.

_____

_____

_____

_____

_____

_____

_____

_____

_____

_____

_____

Passage Comprehension

Reread the graphic novel of *The Strange Case of Dr. Jekyll and Mr. Hyde*. Respond to each prompt using complete sentences. Refer to the chart on pages 14 and 15 to determine how to respond to each prompt.

1. Relate the visual image of Mr. Hyde to his character.

   _____

   _____

   _____

   _____

   _____

   _____

   _____

   _____

   _____

   _____

   _____

   _____

   _____

2. Differentiate between the low mind and the high mind.

   _____

   _____

   _____

   _____

   _____

   _____

   _____

   _____

   _____

Passage Comprehension (*cont.*)

3. Use the following excerpt from the text version of the story to assess the degree to which Bowen's graphic novel retelling stayed true to Stevenson's original novel.

"My provision of the salt, which had never been renewed since the date of the first experiment, began to run low. I sent out for a fresh supply, and mixed the draught; the ebullition followed, and the first change of colour, not the second; I drank it and it was without efficiency. You will learn from Poole how I have had London ransacked; it was in vain; and I am now persuaded that my first supply was impure, and that it was that unknown impurity which lent efficacy to the draught.

About a week has passed, and I am now finishing this statement under the influence of the last of the old powders. This, then, is the last time, short of a miracle, that Henry Jekyll can think his own thoughts or see his own face (now how sadly altered!) in the glass."

_____

_____

_____

_____

_____

_____

_____

_____

4. Utterson claims that Hyde has some hold over Jekyll. Assess the strength of Dr. Jekyll's counterclaim that he has a hold over Hyde. Is his reasoning sound with sufficient, relevant evidence to support his claim?

_____

_____

_____

_____

_____

_____

_____

Passage Comprehension (*cont.*)

5. Analyze the connection between Dr. Jekyll and Mr. Hyde and dissociative identity disorder.

_____

_____

_____

_____

_____

_____

_____

_____

_____

_____

_____

_____

6. Relate Dr. Jekyll to Robin Grimsley and the outcome of her trial.

_____

_____

_____

_____

_____

_____

_____

_____

_____

_____

Close Reading

Read the text.

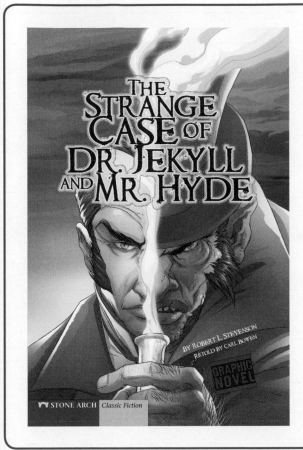

Close Reading (*cont.*)

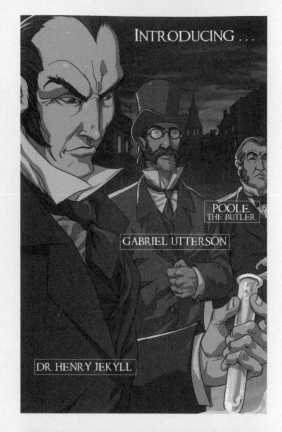

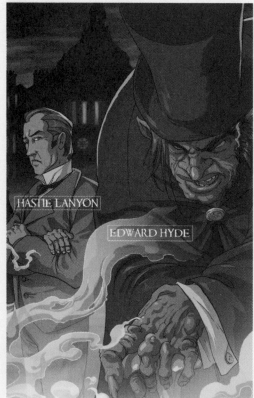

Close Reading (*cont.*)

Close Reading (*cont.*)

Close Reading (*cont.*)

Close Reading (*cont.*)

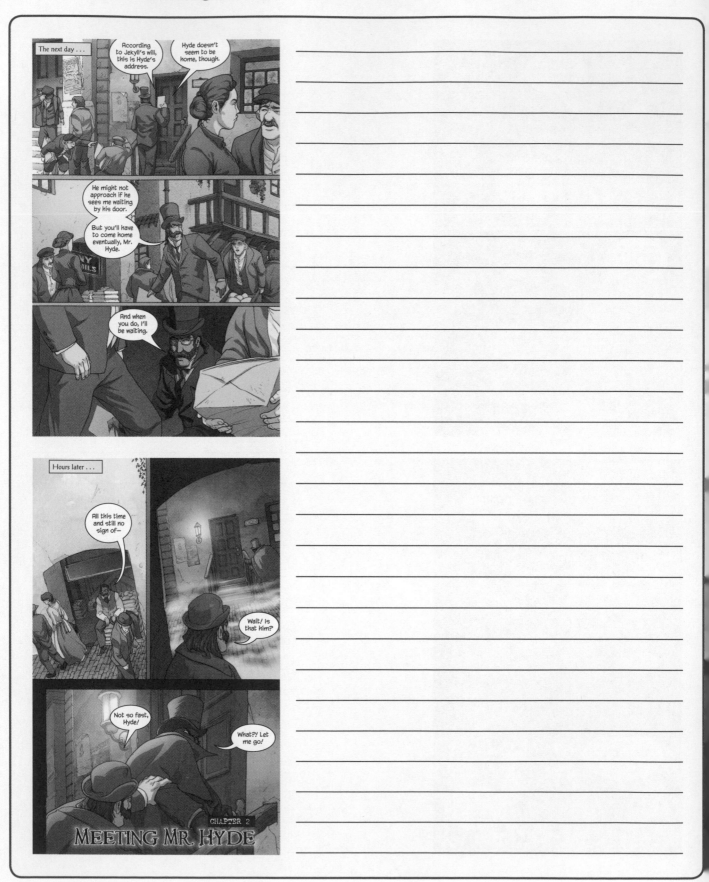

Close Reading (*cont.*)

Close Reading (*cont.*)

Close Reading (*cont.*)

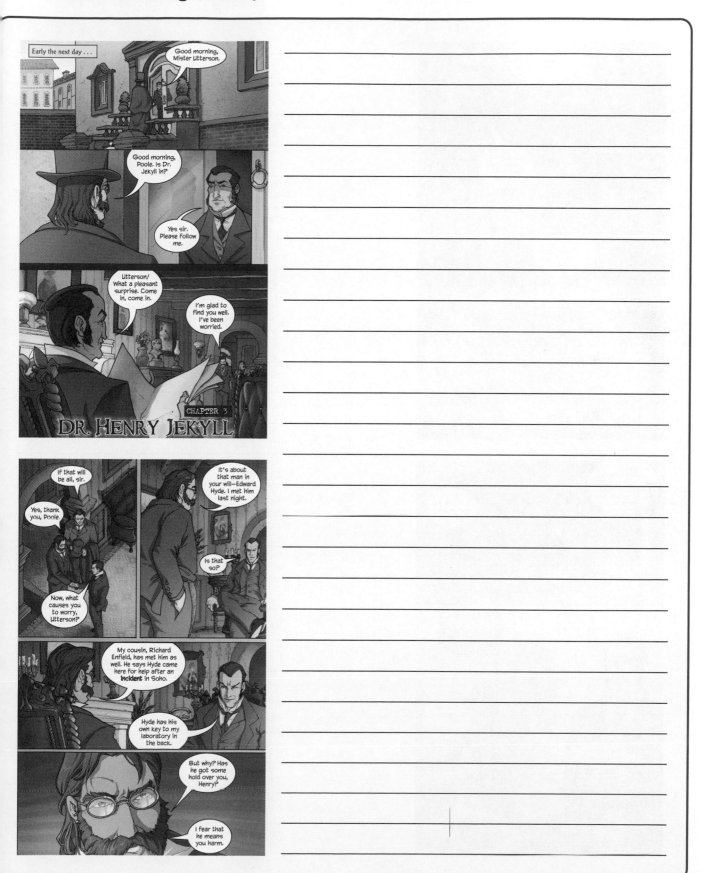

Close Reading (*cont.*)

Close Reading (*cont.*)

Close Reading (cont.)

Close Reading (*cont.*)

Close Reading (*cont.*)

Close Reading (*cont.*)

Close Reading (*cont.*)

Close Reading (*cont.*)

Close Reading (*cont.*)

Close Reading (*cont.*)

Close Reading (*cont.*)

Close Reading (*cont.*)

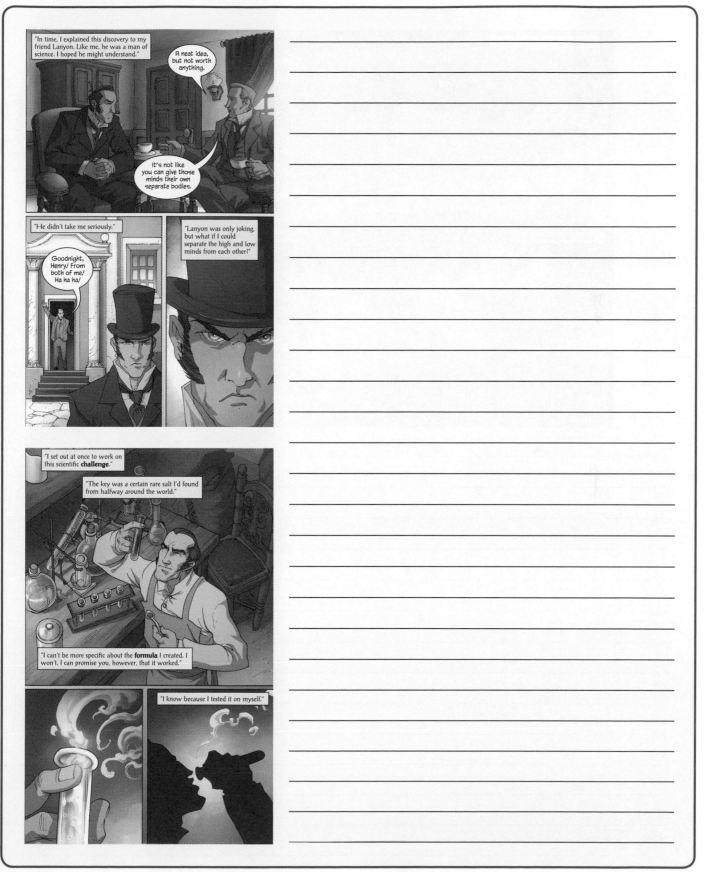

Close Reading (*cont.*)

Close Reading (*cont.*)

Close Reading (*cont.*)

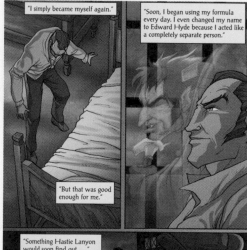

Close Reading (*cont.*)

Close Reading (*cont.*)

Close Reading (*cont.*)

Close Reading (*cont.*)

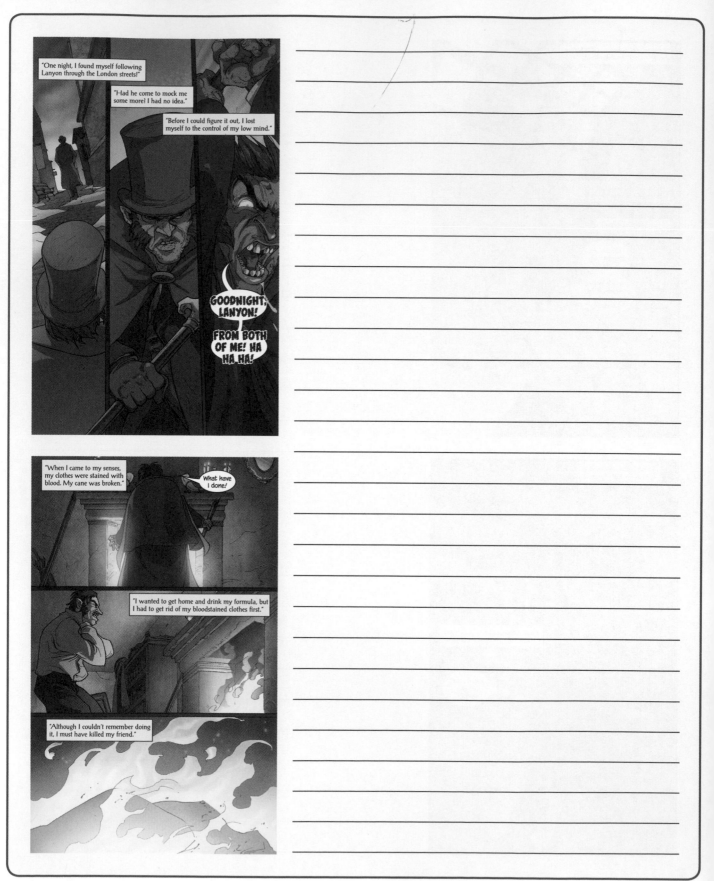

Close Reading (*cont.*)

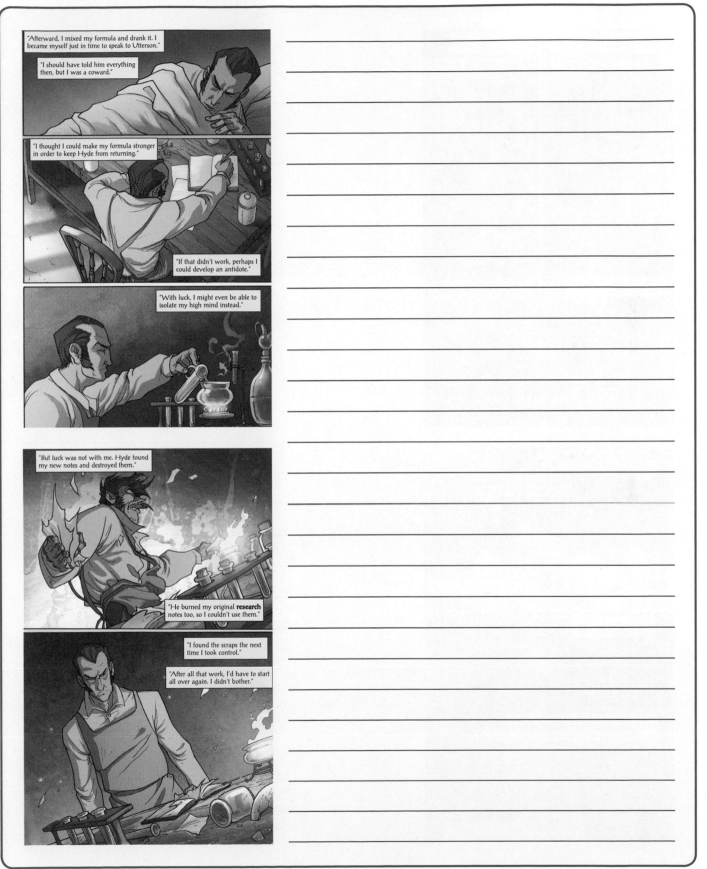

Close Reading (*cont.*)

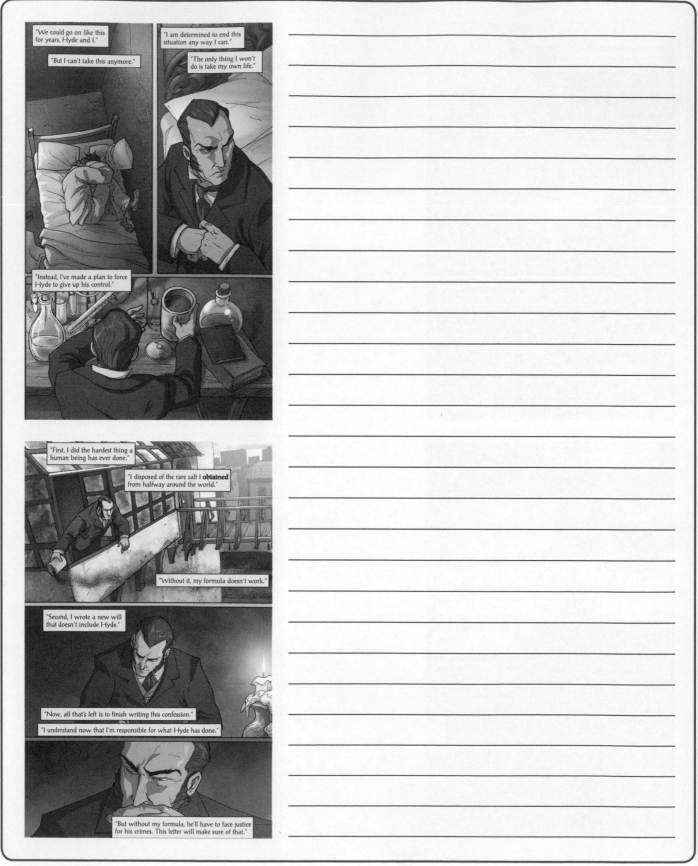

Close Reading (*cont.*)

Prepare to Write: Narrative

Part A. Study the Prompt

Read the prompt and identify the topic, directions, and purpose for writing.

Choose one page from the graphic novel of *The Strange Case of Dr. Jekyll and Mr. Hyde* and rewrite it in third-person narrative.

Include the dialogue from the scene and identify the speakers.
Use descriptive words to paint the scenes shown in pictures in the text.

Topic: _____

_____

Directions: _____

_____

_____

Purpose for writing: _____

_____

Part B. Introduce the Scene

After selecting a page, write an introduction that sets up the action in the scene and helps the reader understand how the scene is connected to what has previously happened in the story.

Setting: _____

_____

Characters: _____

_____

What led up to this? _____

Introduction: _____

_____

_____

_____

_____

_____

Prepare to Write: Narrative (*cont.*)

Part C. Map Your Scene

Explain the events on the page:

_____

_____

_____

_____

Describe what you see in each scene:

_____

_____

_____

Identify the characters' dialogue:

_____

_____

_____

_____

_____

_____

_____

Prepare to Write: Narrative (*cont.*)

Part D. Upgrade the Dialogue

Rewrite the dialogue from each panel. Identify the speaker and reference the chart below to find synonyms for *said* and *asked*.

Common Word	Upgrades
said	responded, replied, commented, stated, remarked
said (softly)	whispered, mumbled, muttered
said (loudly)	barked, bellowed, exclaimed, roared, shouted, shrieked, yelled
asked	begged, demanded, implored, inquired, insisted, pleaded

_____

_____

_____

_____

_____

_____

_____

_____

Part E. Conclude the Scene

Write a conclusion that connects the events in the scene to the action in the upcoming scenes.

_____

_____

_____

_____

_____

_____

_____

_____

_____

The Narrative Writer's Checklist

Trait	Yes	No	Did the writer . . .?
Ideas and Content			include characters, setting, plot
			create an opening that grabs the reader's attention
			include enough description so that the reader can picture the characters and setting
			include dialogue between characters
Organization			create an initiating event, conflict (or rising action), and climax
			include a resolution, as well as a conclusion that ties everything up
			create a clear sequence of events
Voice and Audience Awareness			think about the audience and purpose for writing
			write in a clear and engaging way that makes the audience want to read the work; select a point of view (1st or 3rd person) and maintain it consistently
Word Choice			find a unique way to say things
			use words that are lively and specific to the content
Sentence Fluency			write complete sentences
			expand some sentences using the steps of Masterpiece Sentences
			use compound sentence elements and compound sentences
Conventions			capitalize words correctly:
			capitalize the first word of each sentence
			capitalize proper nouns, including people's names
			punctuate correctly:
			end sentences with a period, question mark, or exclamation mark
			use an apostrophe for possessive nouns and contractions
			use commas and/or semicolons correctly
			use grammar correctly:
			use the correct verb tense
			make sure the verb agrees with the subject in number
			use correct spelling

Let's Focus: North High School letter

Content Focus
dress code

Type of Text
_____

Author's Name _____

Author's Purpose _____

Big Ideas

Consider the following Big Ideas. Write your answer for each question.

Is a person's success in life affected by the way he or she dresses? Explain.

_____

_____

Are people treated differently based on their appearance? Explain.

_____

_____

Informational Preview Checklist: North High School letter on pages 245–252.

☐ Title: What clue does it provide about the passage?

☐ Pictures and Captions: What additional information is added here?

☐ Headings: How is the information organized?

☐ Features: What other text features do you notice?

Enduring Understandings

After reading the text . . .

_____

_____

_____

_____

_____

Key Passage Vocabulary: North High School letter

Read each word. Write the word in column 3. Then, circle a number to rate your knowledge of the word.

Read the Word	Part of Speech	Write the Word	Rate the Word
priority	(n)		0　1　2　3
truancy	(n)		0　1　2　3
enforce	(v)		0　1　2　3
enhance	(v)		0　1　2　3
distracted	(adj)		0　1　2　3
principle	(n)		0　1　2　3
resist	(v)		0　1　2　3
appropriate	(adj)		0　1　2　3
restrictive	(adj)		0　1　2　3
consultation	(n)		0　1　2　3

NORTH HIGH SCHOOL

Tradition • Pride • Excellence

1776 North Main Street
Pleasantville, Ohio 43200
614-555-4320

Jan Dogan, Principal

Bennett Baker, Asst. Principal

Marzetta Martinez, Asst. Principal

Peony Kim, Asst. Principal

August 1, 2013

Dear Parents:

Here at North High School, our top **priority** is to provide a safe and disciplined learning environment. Young people who are safe and secure
5 are better students. In response to growing levels of violence in our schools, declining performance on tests, and increasing **truancy**, the school board feels it is necessary to address a major cause of all three—student dress. **1**

10 In 1994, Long Beach, California, became the first large school district to implement a uniform policy. Within one year of adopting the policy, Long Beach reported many successes. The overall crime rate fell by 91%, school suspensions dropped by 90%, sex
15 offenses were reduced by 96%, incidents of vandalism declined 69%, and assaults in the elementary and middle schools decreased by 85%. These results were proof that uniforms were the right fit. Their policy has been replicated throughout the country
20 by districts in New York City, Houston, Dallas, Washington, D.C., New Orleans, Detroit, Atlanta, Boston, Chicago, Miami, Seattle, and St. Louis to name a few. It has been more than 10 years since the proof was publicized, and districts across the country
25 saw the benefit—now it is our time.

Research studies show that school dress affects school success. There appears to be a fundamental relationship between a person's dress and his or her

priority
something that is more important than something else

truancy
being away from school without permission

1 Student dress is being blamed for what three problems?

enforce

to make sure a rule or law is obeyed

enhance

to improve something

distracted

not focused on what you should be focused on

2 What impact did uniforms have on Ohio high schools?

3 What option was considered prior to establishing a uniform policy?

behavior. Virginia Draa, an assistant professor at
30 Youngstown State University, reviewed attendance
rates, as well as graduation and proficiency pass rates,
at 64 public high schools in Ohio. Her study concluded
that those schools with uniform policies improved in
attendance, graduation, and suspension rates. **2**

35 Our dress is material. It affects our performance
and motivation. People who work out of their home
feel their workday is more productive when they
are dressed professionally. They feel better about
themselves, which makes them feel as though what
40 they are producing is of higher value.

We have had a dress code across the district for
many years. However, enforcing the dress code by
sending violators to the office has been a problem.
They call home and wait for clothes to be brought
45 to school. Sometimes, they get an in-school
suspension. All this has only accomplished one
thing—less time actively engaged in learning.

Rather than rewriting a dress code that is difficult
to **enforce**, the school board has adopted a uniform
50 policy for all grade levels across the district. Even
former President Bill Clinton said in a radio
address, "If it means teenagers will stop killing
each other over designer jackets, then our public
schools should be able to require their students
55 to wear school uniforms." The adoption of this
school uniform policy will promote school safety,
increase learning time, and **enhance** the learning
environment—putting North High School on the
path to academic excellence. **3**

60 The uniform policy will eliminate a lot of problems
we have had in the past with school dress. Students'
choice of dress has caused other students to feel
threatened, intimidated, and even **distracted**.

Baggy pants, clothing of certain colors, bandannas,
65 and an emphasis on one side of the body (e.g., one
pant leg pulled up) can be interpreted as gang
dress. Dressing as a gang member intimidates
other students and spreads fear. This makes an
environment focused on academic success nearly
70 impossible to achieve.

Pants with large pockets, coats, purses, and
backpacks can hold a weapon or drugs. Students are
unable to feel safe and at ease in their classrooms
when they are worried about the contents of
75 another student's pockets or bags.

Though most offenders disagree on the definition of
"seductive," seductive clothing *is* a great distraction.
Bare midriffs, shoulders, backs, and legs, as well as
overly tight garments, visible underwear, and clothes
80 that draw attention to the bosom or buttocks (i.e.,
V-neck shirts and pants with words on the backside)
cause students to lose their focus and think about
other things.

Clothing advertising cigarettes or alcohol may
85 persuade other students to try these controlled
substances. Television has restricted the advertisement
of cigarettes and alcohol when minors are typically
watching TV, so it doesn't make sense to allow
students to advertise these things in school—a
90 gathering place for minors. Clothing that depicts
violence or foul language may also persuade students
to act in the same manner.

Name-brand and designer labels cause problems
as well. Some students have missed school because
95 they didn't have fashionable clothes to wear or the
one pair of designer jeans was being laundered.
If students are not distracted by the distinction

principle

a belief about what is important or how you should act

resist

to say "no" to something you want but shouldn't have

4 In what ways are clothes a distraction during school?

between the "haves" and the "have nots," they will be able to zero in on what is truly important—
100 learning and growing. **4**

When a child feels safe and unthreatened in school, he or she makes better grades and is a much happier person. Students are excited to come to school when they are dressed well, and they will embrace better
105 moral **principles**. The potential benefits of school uniforms include:

- improving attendance;

- decreasing economic discrimination;

- decreasing violence and theft;

110 • decreasing gang violence;

- improving self-discipline;

- helping parents and students **resist** peer pressure;

- helping students concentrate on their
115 schoolwork; and

- helping staff recognize intruders who come to the school.

Thank you for taking the time to read this letter. I thank you in advance for your cooperation in
120 making our new uniform policy a success. Please read the uniform policy on the following pages, and prepare your child for the upcoming school year.

Sincerely,

5 How does a child need to feel while in school to make good grades and be happy?

Jon Dogan

Principal Dogan **5**

NORTH HIGH SCHOOL

1776 North Main Street
Pleasantville, Ohio 43200
614-555-4320

Jan Dogan, Principal

Bennett Baker, Asst. Principal

Marzetta Martinez, Asst. Principal

Peony Kim, Asst. Principal

Tradition • Pride • Excellence

Uniform Policy

125 **School Uniforms**

You are required to wear a school uniform at all times while attending school or any school-sponsored activity (unless special permission is given).

> **appropriate**
> fitting; right for a certain time and place

130 **A. Basic Uniforms**

<u>Girls:</u> The basic uniform for girls is a long- or short-sleeved gray polo shirt with plain solid-colored brown pants or skorts of cotton fabric. Dresses may be worn but must be solid brown
135 with short or long sleeves and follow the other requirements of this policy. If skorts or a dress is worn, legs must be covered in nude-colored full-length panty hose. Wear brown leather shoes that tie or buckle.

140 <u>Boys:</u> The basic uniform for boys is a long- or short-sleeved gray polo shirt with plain solid-colored brown pants of cotton fabric with a brown leather belt. Wear brown leather shoes that tie or buckle. **6**

> **6** What is the difference between acceptable dress for boys and acceptable dress for girls?

145 Clothing must be the **appropriate** size for you, not oversized or undersized. The waist of the garment shall be worn so that the waistband is at the waist and not below the waist. You may not wear baggy/saggy pants.

150 Shirts must cover the midriff, back, and sides at all times; should be fastened with no visible cleavage or undergarments; and may not have a visible manufacturer's logo.

restrictive

limiting; keeping someone from having full freedom

consultation

discussion; conversation

7 What body parts can be visible?

155 Skorts and dresses shall be worn no shorter than "mid-thigh." Mid-thigh is determined by placing your student ID at the top of the knee. The garment must touch the ID (using normal posture). **7**

B. Alternatives

160 In addition to the above basic uniform, the principal may designate:

1. school-sponsored T-shirts with a crew neck; and

165 2. more **restrictive** dress code requirements, if approved by the school's administration.

Each school will provide students/parents with a copy of the school's dress code.

C. Exceptions

170 If you enter the school district after the start of the school year, you will have a grace period of ten (10) school days before being required to wear the school uniform.

175 You may wear special clothing necessary for a school-sponsored activity, as permitted by the principal.

If you are enrolled in a career academy, you may wear the uniform of that program.

8 What are the exceptions to the rule?

180 The superintendent, in **consultation** with the principal, may waive the school uniform policy on a case-by-case basis for reasons such as, but not limited to, medical necessity or sincerely held religious belief. **8**

D. Outer Garments

185 You may wear coats, jackets, sweatshirts, sweaters, or other appropriate outer garments when necessary due to weather conditions or for other legitimate reasons. The outer garments must be of the appropriate size for you and shall not be overly baggy or violate any other 190 provisions of the dress code.

All backpacks and purses must be see-through. **9**

You may not wear:

1. clothing that is not properly fastened;

2. clothing that is torn or has holes, or pants 195 that are frayed;

3. visible undergarments, sleepwear, or outer garments traditionally designed as undergarments such as boxer shorts or bras;

4. outer garments or accessories (such as 200 backpacks, jewelry, and purses) that have slogans, signs, images, or symbols that:

   • promote drugs, alcohol, tobacco, gang identification, weapons, or inappropriate behavior, or

   205 • denigrate or promote discrimination for or against an individual or group.

5. hats, headgear, or other head coverings, except when approved by office staff;

6. body-piercing jewelry, except for earrings 210 on the ears; all other body-piercings must be removed or concealed;

7. jewelry or accessories that may be used as weapons, such as chains, spiked jewelry, or arm bands;

215 8. unnatural hair coloring; (colors other than blonde, brown, black, or auburn)

9. combs, curlers, or hair picks; or

10. sunglasses inside the school building. **10**

9 Why do bags need to be see-through? Could this ever be embarrassing?

10 What accessories CAN be worn?

E. Discipline

220 The principal or designee has the authority to decide whether your clothing complies with school board policy.

If the principal determines that your clothing does not comply with school board policy,
225 your parent/guardian may be asked to bring an appropriate change of clothes to school or you may be asked to leave an after-school activity. You may also receive a disciplinary consequence for violating the school's dress code policy.
230 Repeated violations may result in progressively more serious consequences. **11**

> **11** What are the consequences for failing to comply with the dress code?

Gerunds: Verbs as Nouns

A verb form that ends in -ing and functions as a noun is called a gerund.
A gerund answers the *who* or *what* question.

Function: swim + -ing	Examples
Verb	She is **swimming** laps in the pool.
Gerund	**Swimming** is good exercise.
Gerund phrase	**Swimming** *with goggles* protects your eyes from the chlorine.

Read each sentence and determine if the underlined word is functioning as
a verb or as a gerund. Place an X in the proper column to identify its function.

	Gerund	Verb
Examples: The dress code is <u>changing</u> soon.		X
<u>Changing</u> the dress code will improve student behavior.	X	
1. <u>Dressing</u> as a gang member intimidates other students and spreads fear.		
2. They are <u>waiting</u> in the office for more appropriate clothes.		
3. <u>Dressing</u> seductively is a great distraction to the opposite sex.		
4. However, <u>enforcing</u> the dress code by sending violators to the office has been a problem.		
5. <u>Rewriting</u> the dress code was a task for the school board.		
6. The school board is <u>adopting</u> a school uniform policy that promotes school safety.		
7. The uniform policy is <u>eliminating</u> a lot of the problems that we have had in the past with school dress.		
8. A safe environment promotes student <u>learning</u>.		
9. Her clothes are <u>distracting</u> others and keeping them form learning.		
10. <u>Advertising</u> for cigarettes is no longer allowed on television.		

Participles: Verbs as Adjectives

Present and past participles can be used to describe nouns. They answer the adjective questions *which one* or *what kind*.

Participles as Adjectives	Examples
Present participle	The dress code enhances the **learning** environment.
Past participle	Her **shredded** jeans violated the dress code.
Participial phrase • Set off by commas	His T-shirt, **covered with vulgar language**, was not appropriate for school.

Part A

Read each sentence and determine if the underlined word is functioning as a verb or as an adjective. Place an X in the proper column to identify its function.

	Adjective	Verb
Examples: Students are <u>fleeing</u> the school to avoid wearing uniforms.		X
The <u>fleeing</u> students will be arrested for truancy.	X	
1. Here at North High School, our top priority is to provide a safe and <u>disciplined</u> learning environment.		
2. In response to growing levels of violence in our schools, declining performance on tests, and <u>increasing</u> truancy, the school board feels it is necessary to address the problem.		
3. Her study <u>concluded</u> that those schools with uniform policies improved in attendance, graduation, and suspension rates.		
4. <u>Intimidated</u> students have a hard time concentrating on school tasks.		
5. They <u>called</u> home and waited for clothes to be brought to school.		
6. The blouse, <u>advertising</u> an alcoholic beverage, violated the dress code.		
7. The new dress code prohibits <u>sagging</u> pants.		
8. Attending school <u>excited</u> students once they felt safe.		
9. The benefits of school uniforms <u>included</u> better attendance and less economic discrimination.		
10. Because of the new school uniform policy, our classrooms are filled with neatly <u>dressed</u> students.		

Participles: Verbs as Adjectives (*cont.*)

Part B

Write sentences with the following words, using each word as an adjective and as a verb.

1. distracting

Adjective: _____

_____

_____

Verb: _____

_____

_____

2. enhanced

Adjective: _____

_____

_____

Verb: _____

_____

_____

3. challenging

Adjective: _____

_____

_____

Verb: _____

_____

_____

Transitive and Intransitive Verbs with Masterpiece Sentences

Transitive verbs need a direct object (the answer to the *to what* question) to complete the meaning of a sentence. **Intransitive verbs** cannot take a direct object.

Verbs	Who/What?	Did What?	To What?
Transitive	The vase	holds	flowers
Intransitive	The performers	walked	*cannot answer*

Use the following kernel sentences and questions to write expanded sentences. Identify the verb as transitive or intransitive by writing "T" or "I" in the right margin of the page.

how many	what kind	what	did what	to what	where
The	dress	code	prohibits		

how many	what kind	who	did what	to what	where
A	new	student	enrolled		

how many	what kind	who	did what	to what	when
		school board	adopted		

how many	what kind	who	did what	to what	where
	nervous		walked		

how many	what kind	who	did what	to what	where
			left		

Passage Comprehension

Reread the North High School letter. Respond to each prompt using complete sentences. Refer to the chart on pages 14 and 15 to determine how to respond to each prompt.

1. Relate dress to academic performance.

_____

_____

_____

_____

_____

_____

_____

_____

_____

_____

_____

_____

2. Analyze the effectiveness of the basic uniform in achieving safety and increased learning time.

_____

_____

_____

_____

_____

_____

_____

_____

_____

Passage Comprehension (*cont.*)

3. Analyze the decision to adopt a uniform policy at North High School rather than rewrite the current dress code policy.

_____

_____

_____

_____

_____

_____

_____

_____

_____

_____

4. Using your own experiences, assess the claim that "There appears to be a fundamental relationship between a person's dress and his or her behavior." Provide examples.

_____

_____

_____

_____

_____

_____

_____

_____

_____

_____

Passage Comprehension (*cont.*)

5. Use the information in the policy to differentiate between appropriate and inappropriate dress for boys.

_____

_____

_____

_____

_____

_____

_____

_____

_____

_____

6. Differentiate between North High School's uniform and the required clothing at your school.

_____

_____

_____

_____

_____

_____

_____

_____

_____

_____

_____

_____

Close Reading

Read the text.

North High School letter

Dear Parents:

Here at North High School, our top **priority** is to provide a safe and disciplined learning environment. Young people who are safe and secure are better students. In response to growing levels of violence in our
5   schools, declining performance on tests, and increasing **truancy**, the school board feels it is necessary to address a major cause of all three—student dress.

In 1994, Long Beach, California, became the first large school district to implement a uniform policy. Within one year of adopting the policy,
10   Long Beach reported many successes. The overall crime rate fell by 91%, school suspensions dropped by 90%, sex offenses were reduced by 96%, incidents of vandalism declined 69%, and assaults in the elementary and middle schools decreased by 85%. These results were proof that uniforms were the right fit. Their policy has been replicated throughout the country
15   by districts in New York City, Houston, Dallas, Washington, D.C., New Orleans, Detroit, Atlanta, Boston, Chicago, Miami, Seattle, and St. Louis to name a few. It has been more than 10 years since the proof was publicized, and districts across the country saw the benefit—now it is our time.

Research studies show that school dress affects school success. There
20   appears to be a fundamental relationship between a person's dress and his or her behavior. Virginia Draa, an assistant professor at Youngstown State University, reviewed attendance rates, as well as graduation and proficiency pass rates, at 64 public high schools in Ohio. Her study concluded that those schools with uniform policies improved in attendance, graduation, and
25   suspension rates.

Our dress is material. It affects our performance and motivation. People who work out of their home feel their workday is more productive when they are dressed professionally. They feel better about themselves, which makes them feel as though what they are producing is of higher value.

30   We have had a dress code across the district for many years. However, enforcing the dress code by sending violators to the office has been a problem. They call home and wait for clothes to be brought to school. Sometimes, they get an in-school suspension. All this has only accomplished one thing—less time actively engaged in learning.

Close Reading (*cont.*)

35 Rather than rewriting a dress code that is difficult to **enforce**, the school board has adopted a uniform policy for all grade levels across the district. Even former President Bill Clinton said in a radio address, "If it means teenagers will stop killing each other over designer jackets, then our public schools should be able to require their students to

40 wear school uniforms." The adoption of this school uniform policy will promote school safety, increase learning time, and **enhance** the learning environment—putting North High School on the path to academic excellence.

The uniform policy will eliminate a lot of problems we have had in the

45 past with school dress. Students' sloppy dress has caused other students to feel threatened, intimidated, and even **distracted**. Baggy pants, clothing of certain colors, bandannas, and an emphasis on one side of the body (e.g., one pant leg pulled up) can be interpreted as gang dress. Dressing as a gang member intimidates other students and spreads

50 fear. This makes an environment focused on academic success nearly impossible to achieve.

Pants with large pockets, coats, purses, and backpacks can hold a weapon or drugs. Students are unable to feel safe and at ease in their classrooms when they are worried about the contents of another student's pockets or bags.

55 Though most offenders disagree on the definition of "seductive," seductive clothing *is* a great distraction. Bare midriffs, shoulders, backs, and legs, as well as overly tight garments, visible underwear, and clothes that draw attention to the bosom or buttocks (i.e., V-neck shirts and pants with words on the backside) cause students to lose their focus and think about

60 other things.

Clothing advertising cigarettes or alcohol may persuade other students to try these controlled substances. Television has restricted the advertisement of cigarettes and alcohol when minors are typically watching TV, so it doesn't make sense to allow students to advertise these

65 things in school—a gathering place for minors. Clothing that depicts violence or foul language may also persuade students to act in the same manner.

Close Reading (*cont.*)

Name-brand and designer labels cause problems as well. Some students have missed school because they didn't have fashionable clothes to wear
70 or the one pair of designer jeans was being laundered. If students are not distracted by the distinction between the "haves" and the "have nots," they will be able to zero in on what is truly important—learning and growing.

When a child feels safe and unthreatened in school, he or she makes better grades and is a much happier person. Students are excited to come
75 to school when they are dressed well, and they will embrace better moral **principles**. The potential benefits of school uniforms include:

- improving attendance;

- decreasing economic discrimination;

- decreasing violence and theft;

80 • decreasing gang violence;

- improving self-discipline;

- helping parents and students **resist** peer pressure;

- helping students concentrate on their schoolwork; and

- helping staff recognize intruders who come to the school.

85 Thank you for taking the time to read this letter. I thank you in advance for your cooperation in making our new uniform policy a success. Please read the uniform policy on the following pages, and prepare your child for the upcoming school year.

Sincerely,

90 Principal Dogan

Close Reading (*cont.*)

Uniform Policy

School Uniforms

You are required to wear a school uniform at all times while attending school or any school-sponsored activity (unless special permission is given).

95 **A. Basic Uniforms**

<u>Girls:</u> The basic uniform for girls is a long- or short-sleeved gray polo shirt with plain solid-colored brown pants or skorts of cotton fabric. Dresses may be worn but must be solid brown with short or long sleeves and follow the other requirements of this policy. If skorts or a

100 dress is worn, legs must be covered in nude-colored full-length panty hose. Wear brown leather shoes that tie or buckle.

<u>Boys:</u> The basic uniform for boys is a long- or short-sleeved gray polo shirt with plain solid-colored brown pants of cotton fabric with a brown leather belt. Wear brown leather shoes that tie or buckle.

105 Clothing must be the **appropriate** size for you, not oversized or undersized. The waist of the garment shall be worn so that the waistband is at the waist and not below the waist. You may not wear baggy/saggy pants.

Shirts must cover the midriff, back, and sides at all times; should be

110 fastened with no visible cleavage or undergarments; and may not have a visible manufacturer's logo.

Skorts and dresses shall be worn no shorter than "mid-thigh." Mid-thigh is determined by placing your student ID at the top of the knee. The garment must touch the ID (using normal posture).

Close Reading (*cont.*)

115 **B. Alternatives**

In addition to the above basic uniform, the principal may designate:

1. school-sponsored T-shirts with a crew neck; and

2. more **restrictive** dress code requirements, if approved by the school's administration.

120 Each school will provide students/parents with a copy of the school's dress code.

C. Exceptions

If you enter the school district after the start of the school year, you will have a grace period of ten (10) school days before being required 125 to wear the school uniform.

You may wear special clothing necessary for a school-sponsored activity, as permitted by the principal.

If you are enrolled in a career academy, you may wear the uniform of that program.

130 The superintendent, in **consultation** with the principal, may waive the school uniform policy on a case-by-case basis for reasons such as, but not limited to, medical necessity or sincerely held religious belief.

D. Outer Garments

You may wear coats, jackets, sweatshirts, sweaters, or other 135 appropriate outer garments when necessary due to weather conditions or for other legitimate reasons. The outer garments must be of the appropriate size for you and shall not be overly baggy or violate any other provisions of the dress code.

All backpacks and purses must be see-through.

Close Reading (*cont.*)

140 You may not wear:

   1. clothing that is not properly fastened;

   2. clothing that is torn or has holes, or pants that are frayed;

   3. visible undergarments, sleepwear, or outer garments traditionally designed as undergarments such as boxer shorts or bras;

145

   4. outer garments or accessories (such as backpacks, jewelry, and purses) that have slogans, signs, images, or symbols that:

     • promote drugs, alcohol, tobacco, gang identification, weapons, or inappropriate behavior, or

150

     • denigrate or promote discrimination for or against an individual or group.

   5. hats, headgear, or other head coverings, except when approved by office staff;

   6. body-piercing jewelry, except for earrings on the ears; all other body-piercings must be removed or concealed;

155

   7. jewelry or accessories that may be used as weapons, such as chains, spiked jewelry, or arm bands;

   8. unnatural hair coloring; (colors other than blonde, brown, black, or auburn)

160   9. combs, curlers, or hair picks; or

   10. sunglasses inside the school building.

E. Discipline

The principal or designee has the authority to decide whether your clothing complies with school board policy.

165 If the principal determines that your clothing does not comply with school board policy, your parent/guardian may be asked to bring an appropriate change of clothes to school or you may be asked to leave an after-school activity. You may also receive a disciplinary consequence for violating the school's dress code policy. Repeated

170 violations may result in progressively more serious consequences.

Quick Write in Response to Reading

Write a letter in response to Ms. Dogan, principal of North High School. Express your support or criticism of the new dress code. Make sure your letter responds directly to specific arguments used to justify the adoption of a school uniform policy.

Arguments needing a response:

1. _____

2. _____

3. _____

Dear Ms. Dogan,

_____

_____

_____

_____

_____

_____

_____

_____

_____

_____

_____

_____

_____

_____

_____

_____

_____

_____

_____

Quick Write in Response to Reading (*cont.*)

_____

_____

_____

_____

_____

_____

_____

_____

_____

_____

_____

_____

_____

_____

_____

_____

_____

_____

_____

_____

Thank you,

A concerned North High student

Let's Focus: "Say Yes to Free Dress!"

Content Focus
self-expression

Type of Text
_____

Author's Name _____

Author's Purpose _____

Big Ideas
Consider the following Big Ideas. Write your answer for each question.

Does clothing reflect who you are on the inside?

_____

_____

How does society affect the definition of _appropriate dress_?

_____

_____

Informational Preview Checklist: "Say Yes to Free Dress!" on pages 270–273.

☐ Title: What clue does it provide?

☐ Pictures: What additional information is added here?

☐ Headings: What information do they provide?

☐ Margin Information: What vocabulary is important to understand this story?

☐ Features: What other text features do you notice?

Enduring Understandings
After reading the text . . .

_____

_____

_____

_____

_____

_____

Key Passage Vocabulary: "Say Yes to Free Dress!"

Read each word. Write the word in column 3. Then, circle a number to rate your knowledge of the word.

Read the Word	Part of Speech	Write the Word	Rate the Word
prefer	(v)		0 1 2 3
stifle	(v)		0 1 2 3
appalling	(adj)		0 1 2 3
survey	(n)		0 1 2 3
increase	(n)		0 1 2 3
contradict	(v)		0 1 2 3
individuality	(n)		0 1 2 3
ban	(v)		0 1 2 3
valid	(adj)		0 1 2 3
exaggeration	(n)		0 1 2 3

Say YES to Free Dress!

prefer

to like or choose one thing over another

stifle

to keep something from happening

appalling

so bad that it is shocking

survey

a set of questions asked of many different people in order to gather information on a topic

1 What features of our appearance tell a story?

2 Who limits your ability to dress how you please? Does the author agree or disagree with these limitations?

Notice what you are wearing right now. Does your T-shirt have words or pictures on it? Are your jeans, shorts, or shoes
5 in style? Does your jewelry have a special meaning to you?

We may not always be aware of it, but our clothes send strong messages to the people around
10 us. So do our accessories, our hairstyle, and all the "extras" that go with an outfit—devices, ear buds, backpacks, and bags. Your overall clothing message
15 might be "I'm an athlete," "I'm a rebel," or "I want to be a movie star." It might say that you love a particular sports team, that you love high fashion, or that you
20 **prefer** to be comfortable. **1**

Most of us take for granted our freedom to dress however we like. In some cases, however, people do not have this freedom.
25 Many schools have adopted uniforms or strict dress codes. Several nations have made it illegal to wear certain types of religious clothing in public.
30 Parents across the world forbid their children to wear clothes they consider "inappropriate."

These and other measures like them are a tragedy. They trample
35 on a basic human right—the freedom of expression, and in some cases the freedom of religion. They **stifle** growth and creativity. And, they should be
40 overturned. After taking a closer look at a few of these **appalling** bans on self-expression, you'll surely agree. **2**

Same Is Lame

In 2009–2010, about 19 percent
45 of public schools required their students to wear uniforms. Ten years earlier, only 12 percent did. In a **survey** by the U.S. Department of Education,
50 57 percent of schools reported that they had a "strict" dress code. This was a 10 percent **increase** from 10 years earlier.

What explains these frightening
55 increases? Supporters of school uniforms and strict dress codes say that when students are dressed "neatly," they behave better. They also claim that
60 students are less "distracted" by fashion and more focused on learning.

These arguments may sound good. In reality, though, they aren't credible. In fact, they **contradict** the very idea of education itself! School is supposed to be a place of learning, growth, and development. But strict dress codes send mixed messages to kids. On one hand, kids are being told to "learn and grow!" On the other, they are being told to "stay the same!" This sort of contradiction can only lead to confusion in the minds of dress-code kids—who are also the adults of tomorrow. **3**

The sobering truth is this: if young people are taught to conform, or be like everyone else, they will continue to conform in adulthood. How will more sameness solve the world's many problems? We are in desperate need of creative, original thinking. We need new energy and new ideas. We need young people who are taught to be bold and different.

"By instituting a uniform policy," says a leading child psychologist, "schools are taking away kids' **individuality**." In a democracy such as ours— one that values individuality so highly—this type of action should be considered a crime! I take my hat off to those who have tried to cure the problems in education with uniforms, but, it will never work. **4**

In truth, there is little proof to substantiate the benefits of school uniforms. According to the American Civil Liberties Union—an organization developed to defend and preserve the rights and liberties of individuals—there is no link between school uniforms and safety or good grades. Uniforms are simply an infringement on our rights as human beings. Add to that the fact that wearing a prescribed set of clothing every day alleviates free will, and you have a disastrous outcome. Administrators and teachers focus their attention on developing students' decision-making skills and ability to take responsibility for their actions. But both of these skills require real-world practice, something students would receive less of without the freedom to stand in front of their closets and choose what to present to their peers every day.

increase
a growth in size, number, or strength

contradict
to go against; to say the opposite of something

individuality
the state of being different from everyone else

3 What should happen at school?

4 Would the child psychologist agree with the heading, Same Is Lame?

FIRST AMENDMENT

Congress shall make no law respecting an establishment of religion, or prohibiting the free exercise thereof; or abridging the freedom of speech, or of the press; or the right of the people peaceably to assemble, and to petition the Government for a redress of grievances.

EXCERPT FROM THE FIRST AMENDMENT, 1791:

Congress shall make no law respecting an establishment of religion, or prohibiting the free exercise thereof; or abridging the freedom of speech, or of the press; or the right of the people peaceably to assemble, and to petition the Government for a redress of grievances.

ban

to forbid; to formally state that something must not be done, said, or used

valid

logical; based on good, clear thinking

exaggeration

a stretching of the truth; the act of making something seem bigger or more important than it really is

5 How is the United States connected to the laws in France?

6 What needs to be part of the very long journey of acceptance?

Belief Grief

In 2004, France **banned** certain religious clothing in schools and government buildings.
135 Several other nations have passed similar laws. These laws center mainly on religious head coverings worn by Muslim women. Supporters of the laws
140 say that wearing the veils or scarves encourages racism, especially after the events of September 11, 2001. (On that day, Muslim extremists attacked
145 buildings in New York City and Washington, D.C., killing thousands.) Others say that religious clothing in public places challenges the idea that
150 church and state should be separate. **5**

Some of these concerns are **valid**. Religious clothing can bring up negative feelings in
155 those who disagree with a religion's basic ideas. These negative feelings can sometimes lead to violence. And some people believe that religion
160 should have a greater role in government.

But these concerns do not justify laws that ban religious clothing. The laws are quick
165 fixes rather than real solutions. Instead of trying to prevent racism by getting rid of religious clothing, we should try to prevent racism through
170 education. People should take the time to learn about other religions and share their own beliefs in calm and non-threatening ways. Only this

175 will reduce racism and violence for good. And only this will convince people that every religion has a few extremists but is mainly made up of
180 regular folks who want to lead peaceful lives.

The bottom line is this: clothing doesn't create conflict, fear does. And we can't legislate fear
185 away. We have to do the hard work of accepting each other, getting to know each other, and learning from each other. We need to learn how to make our
190 differences a plus rather than a minus. Accepting all kinds of clothing is the necessary first step in this very long journey. **6**

Black Hole of Control

Most parents mean well. They
195 want their kids to grow up, be happy, do good work, and have healthy relationships. They want them to find their way in life and develop their gifts and talents.
200 But they also want their kids to be "normal." They want their kids to reflect positively on their own parenting. Parents think of their children as walking
205 billboards for their own success.

This may be a slight **exaggeration**. But it's true that most parents care what their kids look like on a day-to-day basis.
210 It's also true that many parents have very different standards for dress and overall appearance than their children do.

For example, a 2010 survey
215 showed that nearly 40 percent of young people between the

ages of 18 and 29 have tattoos. By contrast, only 15 percent of people their parents' age have
220 tattoos. These statistics reflect a trend that goes beyond tattoos. What was once considered taboo is quickly becoming the norm. This trend makes it hard
225 for parents to let go of their "kids"—even those aged 18 to 29! **7**

Naturally enough, this need for control expresses itself in
230 parental rules about how a child may or may not dress. Most six-year-olds don't care how they dress. But by the time a child reaches middle school, the mood
235 has shifted. Daily battles about clothes, makeup, and hairstyles become the norm. The louder the parent says "NO," the louder the child says "YES."

240 In fact, it's a natural reflex for a teen to say "yes" when a parent says "no." In early adolescence, kids begin to separate from their parents. They go on a mission
245 to find out who they are as individuals. The will to do this becomes even stronger as a teen matures. One very obvious and important way of asserting one's
250 identity is by wearing unique— and sometimes startling— clothes and accessories. **8**

Because it is a natural part of growing up, a teenager who
255 wants to wear blue hair, ripped jeans, or a nose ring should be permitted to do so. True, there are some limits to this idea. No child—or adult—should wear
260 clothes that are insulting or indecent. (We all know these

types of clothing when we see them.) But if the fashion choice is harmless, it should
265 be allowed. If a child wants to wear purple-striped jeans with an orange-and-black plaid top, his or her parents should say nothing but "Have a nice day!"
270 Then, they should congratulate themselves on raising such a creative, adventuresome kid. Creative self-expression must be in their jeans. **9**

275 And remember, parents: the best way a child can learn is through making a mistake. If an outfit is a terrible choice, your kids' friends will definitely let
280 them know! **10**

The Skinny

If you've noticed a theme in this argument, it might be "Your clothes reflect who you are." People have been expressing
285 themselves through clothing since the earliest humans realized they had a choice between buffalo skins and bear skins. Today, the choice
290 might be between skinny jeans and wide-legged pants. But the stakes are the same. Any attempt to limit our basic freedom to dress—in a school,
295 in a nation, or in a home—is an attempt to limit our very humanity.

So, go ahead and make a statement. Explore who you are.
300 Experiment with your style. Say "yes" to your own sense of dress. Self-expression is always in fashion. **11**

> **7** What do tattoos have to do with the way people dress?
>
> **8** How do you assert your identity?
>
> **9** Who determines whether dress is insulting or indecent?
>
> **10** What advice does the author give parents?
>
> **11** What is "The Skinny" on the author's point of view? Do you agree or disagree?

Critical Understandings

Reread the first section of "Say Yes to Free Dress!" Respond to each prompt using complete sentences. Refer to the chart on pages 14 and 15 to determine how to respond to each prompt.

1. Clarify the author's claim that most of us "take for granted" our freedom to dress how we like.

_____

_____

_____

_____

_____

2. Develop an argument against the author's claim that school uniforms stifle growth and creativity.

_____

_____

_____

_____

_____

3. Use your personal clothing choices to prove the author's claim that our clothing sends a message.

_____

_____

_____

_____

4. Write a four-line poem to support the author's claim that dress codes are bad.

_____

_____

_____

_____

_____

Prepare to Write: Short Story

Imagine living in Kalba, a land where everything is gray and brown. Lives are governed by strict laws, and every day is predictably the same as the previous day. It's the only world you know until an unexpected event provides the opportunity for something different. Use the template to plan your short story.

Setting:

When: _____   Where: _____

Characters and attributes:

1. _____

_____

2. _____

_____

3. _____

_____

Problem: _____

_____

_____

Solution: _____

_____

_____

Kick-off event (starts the story): _____

_____

_____

_____

_____

_____

_____

_____

_____

Passage Comprehension

Reread "Say Yes to Free Dress!" Respond to each prompt using complete sentences. Refer to the chart on pages 14 and 15 to determine how to respond to each prompt.

1. Use the First Amendment to prove the author's claim that the freedom of expression is a basic human right.

   _____

   _____

   _____

   _____

   _____

   _____

   _____

   _____

   _____

   _____

   _____

2. Use personal experience to support the author's claim that in early adolescence kids begin to separate from their parents.

   _____

   _____

   _____

   _____

   _____

   _____

3. Write a new title for the passage in support of the author's claim that your clothes reflect who you are and send a message. Take notice of the headings and current title before creating your title.

   _____

   _____

   _____

Passage Comprehension (*cont.*)

4. Use text evidence from the NHS letter and policy to develop an argument against the author's claim that laws and dress codes trample on a person's religious freedom.

_____

_____

_____

_____

_____

_____

_____

_____

_____

5. Clarify the author's quote "Clothing doesn't create conflict, fear does."

_____

_____

_____

_____

_____

_____

6. Prove the author's point that parents have a hard time "letting go of their kids."

_____

_____

_____

_____

_____

_____

Close Reading

Read the text.

"Say Yes to Free Dress!"

Notice what you are wearing right now. Does your T-shirt have words or pictures on it? Are your jeans, shorts, or shoes in style? Does your jewelry have a special meaning to you?

We may not always be aware of it, but our clothes send strong messages to
5 the people around us. So do our accessories, our hairstyle, and all the "extras" that go with an outfit—devices, ear buds, backpacks, and bags. Your overall clothing message might be "I'm an athlete," "I'm a rebel," or "I want to be a movie star." It might say that you love a particular sports team, that you love high fashion, or that you **prefer** to be comfortable.

10 Most of us take for granted our freedom to dress however we like. In some cases, however, people do not have this freedom. Many schools have adopted uniforms or strict dress codes. Several nations have made it illegal to wear certain types of religious clothing in public. Parents across the world forbid their children to wear clothes they consider
15 "inappropriate."

These and other measures like them are a tragedy. They trample on a basic human right—the freedom of expression, and in some cases the freedom of religion. They **stifle** growth and creativity. And, they should be overturned. After taking a closer look at a few of these **appalling** bans on
20 self-expression, you'll surely agree.

Close Reading (*cont.*)

Same Is Lame

In 2009–2010, about 19 percent of public schools required their students to wear uniforms. Ten years earlier, only 12 percent did. In a **survey** by the U.S. Department of Education, 57 percent of schools reported that they had a "strict" dress code. This was a 10 percent **increase** from 10 years earlier.

25 What explains these frightening increases? Supporters of school uniforms and strict dress codes say that when students are dressed "neatly," they behave better. They also claim that students are less "distracted" by fashion and more focused on learning.

These arguments may sound good. In reality, though, they aren't credible.
30 In fact, they **contradict** the very idea of education itself! School is supposed to be a place of learning, growth, and development. But strict dress codes send mixed messages to kids. On one hand, kids are being told to "learn and grow!" On the other, they are being told to "stay the same!" This sort of contradiction can only lead to confusion in the minds
35 of dress-code kids—who are also the adults of tomorrow.

The sobering truth is this: if young people are taught to conform, or be like everyone else, they will continue to conform in adulthood. How will more sameness solve the world's many problems? We are in desperate need of creative, original thinking. We need new energy and new ideas.
40 We need young people who are taught to be bold and different.

"By instituting a uniform policy," says a leading child psychologist, "schools are taking away kids' **individuality**." In a democracy such as ours—one that values individuality so highly—this type of action should be considered a crime! I take my hat off to those who have tried to cure
45 the problems in education with uniforms, but, it will never work.

In truth, there is little proof to substantiate the benefits of school uniforms. According to the American Civil Liberties Union—an organization developed to defend and preserve the rights and liberties of individuals— there is no link between school uniforms and safety or good grades.
50 Uniforms are simply an infringement on our rights as human beings. Add to that the fact that wearing a prescribed set of clothing every day alleviates free will, and you have a disastrous outcome. Administrators and teachers focus their attention on developing students' decision-making skills and ability to take responsibility for their actions. But both of these
55 skills require real-world practice, something students would receive less of without the freedom to stand in front of their closets and choose what to present to their peers every day.

Close Reading (*cont.*)

Belief Grief

In 2004, France **banned** certain religious clothing in schools and government buildings. Several other nations have passed similar laws.
60 These laws center mainly on religious head coverings worn by Muslim women. Supporters of the laws say that wearing the veils and scarves encourages racism, especially after the events of September 11, 2001. (On that day, Muslim extremists attacked buildings in New York City and Washington, D.C., killing thousands.) Others say that religious
65 clothing in public places challenges the idea that church and state should be separate.

Some of these concerns are **valid**. Religious clothing can bring up negative feelings in those who disagree with a religion's basic ideas. These negative feelings can sometimes lead to violence. And some people
70 believe that religion should have a greater role in government.

But these concerns do not justify laws that ban religious clothing. The laws are quick fixes rather than real solutions. Instead of trying to prevent racism by getting rid of religious clothing, we should try to prevent racism through education. People should take the time to
75 learn about other religions and to share their own beliefs in calm and non-threatening ways. Only this will reduce racism and violence for good. And only this will convince people that every religion has a few extremists but is mainly made up of regular folks who want to lead peaceful lives.

80 The bottom line is this: clothing doesn't create conflict, fear does. And we can't legislate fear away. We have to do the hard work of accepting each other, getting to know each other, and learning from each other. We need to learn how to make our differences a plus rather than a minus. Accepting all kinds of clothing is the necessary first step in this very
85 long journey.

Close Reading (*cont.*)

Black Hole of Control

Most parents mean well. They want their kids to grow up, be happy, do good work, and have healthy relationships. They want them to find their way in life and develop their gifts and talents. But they also want their kids to be "normal." They want their kids to reflect positively on their own
90 parenting. Parents think of their children as walking billboards for their own success.

This may be a slight **exaggeration**. But it's true that most parents care what their kids look like on a day-to-day basis. It's also true that many parents have very different standards for dress and overall appearance
95 than their children do.

For example, a 2010 survey showed that nearly 40 percent of young people between the ages of 18 and 29 have tattoos. By contrast, only 15 percent of people their parents' age have tattoos. These statistics reflect a trend that goes beyond tattoos. What was once considered taboo is
100 quickly becoming the norm. This trend makes it hard for parents to let go of their "kids"—even those aged 18 to 29!

Naturally enough, this need for control expresses itself in parental rules about how a child may or may not dress. Most six-year-olds don't care how they dress. But by the time a child reaches middle school, the mood has
105 shifted. Daily battles about clothes, makeup, and hairstyles become the norm. The louder the parent says "NO," the louder the child says "YES."

Close Reading (*cont.*)

In fact, it's a natural reflex for a teen to say "yes" when a parent says "no." In early adolescence, kids begin to separate from their parents. They go on a mission to find out who they are as individuals. The will to do
110 this becomes even stronger as a teen matures. One very obvious and important way of asserting one's identity is by wearing unique—and sometimes startling—clothes and accessories.

Because it is a natural part of growing up, a teenager who wants to wear blue hair, ripped jeans, or a nose ring should be permitted to do
115 so. True, there are some limits to this idea. No child—or adult—should wear clothes that are insulting or indecent. (We all know these types of clothing when we see them.) But if the fashion choice is harmless, it should be allowed. If a child wants to wear purple-striped jeans with an orange-and-black plaid top, his or her parents should say nothing but
120 "Have a nice day!" Then, they should congratulate themselves on raising such a creative, adventuresome kid. Creative self-expression must be in their jeans.

And remember, parents: the best way a child can learn is through making a mistake. If an outfit is a terrible choice, your kids' friends will definitely
125 let them know!

The Skinny

If you've noticed a theme in this argument, it might be "Your clothes reflect who you are." People have been expressing themselves through clothing since the earliest humans realized they had a choice between buffalo skins and bear skins. Today, the choice might be between skinny
130 jeans and wide-legged pants. But the stakes are the same. Any attempt to limit our basic freedom to dress—in a school, in a nation, or in a home— is an attempt to limit our very humanity.

So go ahead and make a statement. Explore who you are. Experiment with your style. Say "yes" to your own sense of dress. Self-expression is
135 always in fashion.

Summarize and Scrutinize

Part A

Write an objective summary of one text from this unit. Your partner should choose the other text.

Passage: _____

Summary: _____

_____

_____

_____

_____

_____

_____

Part B

Identify the claims made by the author and the evidence used to support the claims.

Claim	Evidence/Support

Developing a Short Story

Refer to your notes on the Prepare to Write template on page 275.

Part A. Formulate a Title

_____

_____

Part B. Begin the Story

Choose one of the following strategies for beginning your story. Circle your choice and write your opening line(s).

- Provide a where or when
- Provide an action
- Introduce a character
- Make a simple but interesting comment
- Start a dialogue

Opening line(s): _____

_____

_____

_____

_____

_____

_____

_____

_____

_____

_____

_____

_____

Developing a Short Story (*cont.*)

Part C. Introduce the Characters

Sketch out how you will introduce the main characters to your readers.

_____

_____

_____

_____

_____

_____

_____

_____

_____

_____

_____

_____

_____

_____

_____

_____

_____

_____

_____

_____

_____

_____

_____

_____

Developing a Short Story (*cont.*)

Part D. Describe the Problem

Provide examples and elaborations to develop the problem.

_____

_____

_____

_____

_____

Part E. Develop the Solution

List the events that contribute to the solution and make it possible.

_____

_____

_____

_____

_____

_____

Part F. End the Story

Choose a strategy for ending your story. Circle your choice and write the closing lines of your short story.

- • Make an emotional connection
- • Focus on an important character
- • Reiterate the story's message
- • Reflect on the story's message

Closing sentences: _____

_____

_____

_____

_____

The Narrative Writer's Checklist

Trait	Yes	No	Did the writer . . .?
Ideas and Content			include characters, setting, plot
			create an opening that grabs the reader's attention
			include enough description so that the reader can picture the characters and setting
			include dialogue between characters
			create a title for the story
Organization			create an initiating event, conflict (or rising action), and climax
			include a resolution, as well as a conclusion that ties everything up
			create a clear sequence of events
Voice and Audience Awareness			think about the audience and purpose for writing
			write in a clear and engaging way that makes the audience want to read the work; select a point of view (1st or 3rd person) and maintain it consistently
Word Choice			find a unique way to say things
			use words that are lively and specific to the content
Sentence Fluency			write complete sentences
			expand some sentences using the steps of Masterpiece Sentences
			use compound sentence elements and compound sentences
Conventions			capitalize words correctly:
			capitalize the first word of each sentence
			capitalize proper nouns, including people's names
			punctuate correctly:
			end sentences with a period, question mark, or exclamation mark
			use an apostrophe for possessive nouns and contractions
			use commas and/or semicolons correctly
			use grammar correctly:
			use the correct verb tense
			make sure the verb agrees with the subject in number
			use correct spelling

Let's Focus: Excerpt from *The Good Earth*

Content Focus
arranged marriage
Chinese culture

Type of Text

_____

Author's Name _____

Author's Purpose _____

Big Ideas
Consider the following Big Idea questions. Write your answer for each question.

What factors are involved when choosing a lifelong mate?

_____

_____

What is the purpose of marriage?

_____

_____

Narrative Preview Checklist: the excerpt from *The Good Earth* on pages 291–298.

☐ Title: What clue does it provide about the passage?

☐ Pictures: What additional information is added here?

☐ Margin Information: What vocabulary is important to understand this story?

Enduring Understandings
After reading the text . . .

_____

_____

_____

_____

_____

Key Passage Vocabulary: Excerpt from *The Good Earth*

Read each word. Write the word in column 3. Then, circle a number to rate your knowledge of the word.

Read the Word	Part of Speech	Write the Word	Rate the Word
fruition	(n)		0 1 2 3
fashion	(v)		0 1 2 3
delicately	(adv)		0 1 2 3
cease	(v)		0 1 2 3
precious	(adj)		0 1 2 3
recklessly	(adv)		0 1 2 3
warped	(adj)		0 1 2 3
divert	(v)		0 1 2 3
mutinous	(adj)		0 1 2 3
acknowledgment	(n)		0 1 2 3

from

The Good Earth

by Pearl S. Buck

It was Wang Lung's marriage day. At first, opening
his eyes in the blackness of the curtains about his
bed, he could not think why the dawn seemed
different from any other. The house was still except
5   for the faint, gasping cough of his old father, whose
room was opposite to his own across the middle
room. Every morning the old man's cough was the
first sound to be heard. Wang Lung usually lay
listening to it and moved only when he heard it
10   approaching nearer and when he heard the door of
his father's room squeak upon its wooden hinges. **1**

But this morning he did not wait. He sprang up
and pushed aside the curtains of his bed. It was a
dark, ruddy dawn, and through a small square hole
15   of a window, where the tattered paper fluttered, a
glimpse of bronze sky gleamed. He went to the hole
and tore the paper away.

"It is spring and I do not need this," he muttered.

He was ashamed to say aloud that he wished the
20   house to look neat on this day. The hole was barely
large enough to admit his hand and he thrust it
out to feel of the air. A small soft wind blew gently
from the east, a wind mild and murmurous and
full of rain. It was a good omen. The fields needed
25   rain for **fruition**. There would be no rain this day,
but within a few days, if this wind continued, there
would be water. It was good. Yesterday he had said
to his father that if this brazen, glittering sunshine
continued, the wheat could not fill in the ear. Now
30   it was as if Heaven had chosen this day to wish him
well. Earth would bear fruit. **2**

He hurried out into the middle room, drawing on
his blue outer trousers as he went, and knotting
about the fullness at his waist his girdle of blue
35   cotton cloth. He left his upper body bare until he
had heated water to bathe himself. He went into

fruition
completion; a good
outcome

1 Who does Wang
Lung live with?

2 What is the
weather like on
Wang Lung's
wedding day?
Why is that a
problem?

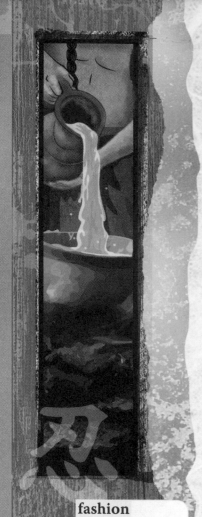

the shed which was the kitchen, leaning against the house, and out of its dusk an ox twisted its head from behind the corner next the door and lowed
40 at him deeply. The kitchen was made of earthen bricks as the house was, great squares of earth dug from their own fields, and thatched with straw from their own wheat. Out of their own earth had his grandfather in his youth **fashioned** also the oven,
45 baked and black with many years of meal preparing. On top of this earthen structure stood a deep, round, iron cauldron. **3**

This cauldron he filled partly full of water, dipping it with a half gourd from an earthen jar that stood
50 near, but he dipped cautiously, for water was precious. Then, after a hesitation, he suddenly lifted the jar and emptied all the water into the cauldron. This day he would bathe his whole body. Not since he was a child upon his mother's knee had anyone
55 looked upon his body. Today one would, and he would have it clean. **4**

He went around the oven to the rear, and selecting a handful of the dry grass and stalks standing in the corner of the kitchen, he arranged it **delicately** in the
60 mouth of the oven, making the most of every leaf. Then from an old flint and iron he caught a flame and thrust it into the straw and there was a blaze.

This was the last morning he would have to light the fire. He had lit it every morning since his mother
65 died six years before. He had lit the fire, boiled water, and poured the water into a bowl and taken it into the room where his father sat upon his bed, coughing and fumbling for his shoes upon the floor. Every morning for these six years the old man had
70 waited for his son to bring in hot water to ease him of his morning coughing. Now father and son could rest. There was a woman coming to the house. Never again would Wang Lung have to rise summer and winter at dawn to light the fire. He could lie in
75 his bed and wait, and he also would have a bowl of water brought to him, and if the earth were fruitful there would be tea leaves in the water. Once in some years it was so. **5**

fashion
to make; to shape

delicately
with a soft touch and great attention to detail

3 How has the earth been good to Wang Lung and his father?

4 What did Wang Lung treat himself to on his wedding day?

5 What is Wang Lung expecting of his new wife?

And if the woman wearied, there would be her
80 children to light the fire, the many children she
would bear to Wang Lung. Wang Lung stopped,
struck by the thought of children running in and
out of their three rooms. Three rooms had always
seemed much to them, a house half empty since his
85 mother died.

Now the grandsons were coming, grandsons upon
grandsons! They would have to put beds along the
walls and in the middle room. The house would be
full of beds. The blaze in the oven died down while
90 Wang Lung thought of all the beds there would
be in the half-empty house, and the water began
to chill in the cauldron. The shadowy figure of
the old man appeared in the doorway, holding his
unbuttoned garments about him. He was coughing
95 and spitting and he gasped, "How is it that there is
not water yet to heat my lungs?" **6**

Wang Lung stared and recalled himself and was
ashamed.

"This fuel is damp," he muttered from behind
100 the stove. "The damp wind—"

The old man continued to cough perseveringly
and would not **cease** until the water boiled. Wang
Lung dipped some into a bowl, and then, after a
moment, he opened a glazed jar that stood upon a
105 ledge of the stove and took from it a dozen or so of
the curled dried leaves and sprinkled them upon
the surface of the water. The old man's eyes opened
greedily and immediately he began to complain.

"Why are you wasteful? Tea is like eating silver." **7**

110 "It is the day," replied Wang Lung with a short
laugh. "Eat and be comforted."

The old man grasped the bowl in his shriveled,
knotty fingers, muttering, uttering little grunts.
He watched the leaves uncurl and spread upon the
115 surface of the water, unable to bear drinking the
precious stuff.

cease
to stop; to come to
an end

precious
very valuable; hard
to get and not to
be wasted

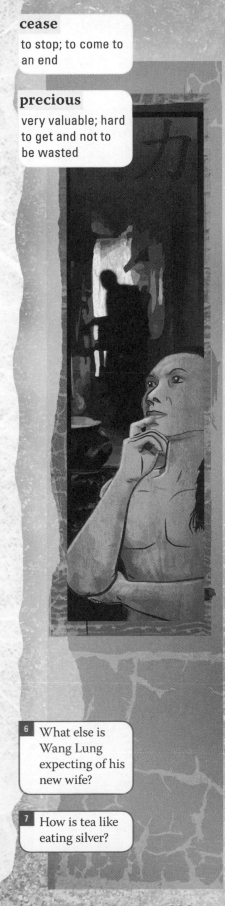

6 What else is
Wang Lung
expecting of his
new wife?

7 How is tea like
eating silver?

recklessly

carelessly; without concern for the harm that might be done

warped

bent out of shape

"It will be cold," said Wang Lung.

"True—true—" said the old man in alarm, and he began to take great gulps of the hot tea. He passed
120 into an animal satisfaction, like a child fixed upon its feeding. But he was not too forgetful to see Wang Lung dipping the water **recklessly** from the cauldron into a deep wooden tub. He lifted his head and stared at his son.

125 "Now there is water enough to bring a crop to fruit," he said suddenly.

Wang Lung continued to dip the water to the last drop. He did not answer.

"Now then!" cried his father loudly.

130 "I have not washed my body all at once since the New Year," said Wang Lung in a low voice. **8**

He was ashamed to say to his father that he wished his body to be clean for a woman to see. He hurried out, carrying the tub to his own room. The door
135 was hung loosely upon a **warped** wooden frame and it did not shut closely, and the old man tottered into the middle room and put his mouth to the opening and bawled, "It will be ill if we start the woman like this—tea in the morning water and all
140 this washing!"

"It is only one day," shouted Wang Lung. And then he added, "I will throw the water on the earth when I am finished and it is not all waste."

The old man was silent at this, and Wang Lung
145 unfastened his girdle and stepped out of his clothing. In the light that streamed in a square block from the hole he wrung a small towel from the steaming water and he scrubbed his dark slender body vigorously. Warm though he had
150 thought the air, when his flesh was wet he was cold, and he moved quickly, passing the towel in and out of the water until from his whole body there went up a delicate cloud of steam. Then he went to a box that had been his mother's and drew from it a
155 fresh suit of blue cotton cloth. He might be a little

8 How long has it been since Wang Lung washed his entire body?

cold this day without the wadding of the winter
garments, but he suddenly could not bear to put
them on against his clean flesh. The covering of
them was torn and filthy and the wadding stuck
160 out of the holes, grey and sodden. He did not want
this woman to see him for the first time with the
wadding sticking out of his clothes. Later she would
have to wash and mend, but not the first day. He
drew over the blue cotton coat and trousers a long
165 robe made of the same material—his one long
robe, which he wore on feast days only, ten days or
so in the year, all told. Then with swift fingers he
unplaited the long braid of hair that hung down his
back, and taking a wooden comb from the drawer
170 of the small, unsteady table, he began to comb out
his hair. **9**

His father drew near again and put his mouth to the
crack of the door.

"Am I to have nothing to eat this day?" he
175 complained. "At my age the bones are water in the
morning until food is given them."

"I am coming," said Wang Lung, braiding his hair
quickly and smoothly and weaving into the strands
a tasseled black silk cord.

180 Then after a moment he removed his long gown
and wound his braid about his head and went out,
carrying the tub of water. He had quite forgotten
the breakfast. He would stir a little water into
cornmeal and give it to his father. For himself he
185 could not eat. He staggered with the tub to the
threshold and poured the water upon the earth
nearest the door, and as he did so he remembered
he had used all the water in the cauldron for his
bathing and he would have to start the fire again.
190 A wave of anger passed over him at his father. **10**

"That old head thinks of nothing except his eating
and his drinking," he muttered into the mouth of
the oven; but aloud he said nothing. It was the last
morning he would have to prepare food for the old
195 man. He put a very little water into the cauldron,

9 What does
Wang Lung
wear on his
wedding day?

10 What did Wang
Lung forget to
do on his
wedding day?

divert
to cause someone or something to get off track or lose focus

drawing it in a bucket from the well near the door, and it boiled quickly and he stirred meal together and took it to the old man. **11**

Wang Lung went into his own room then, and drew
200 about him again the long blue robe and let down the braid of his hair. He passed his hand over his shaven brow and over his cheeks. Perhaps he had better be newly shaven? It was scarcely sunrise yet. He could pass through the Street of the Barbers
205 and be shaved before he went to the house where the woman waited for him. If he had the money he would do it.

He took from his girdle a small greasy pouch of grey cloth and counted the money in it. There were six
210 silver dollars and a double handful of copper coins. He had not yet told his father he had asked friends to sup that night. He had asked his male cousin, the young son of his uncle, and his uncle for his father's sake, and three neighboring farmers who lived in
215 the village with him. He had planned to bring back from the town that morning pork, a small pond fish, and a handful of chestnuts. He might even buy a few of the bamboo sprouts from the south and a little beef to stew with the cabbage he had raised
220 in his own garden. But this only if there were any money left after the bean oil and the soybean sauce had been bought. If he shaved his head he could not, perhaps, buy the beef. Well, he would shave his head, he decided suddenly. **12**

225 He left the old man without speech and went out into the early morning. In spite of the dark red dawn the sun was mounting the horizon clouds and sparkled upon the dew on the rising wheat and barley. The farmer in Wang Lung was **diverted** for
230 an instant and he stooped to examine the budding heads. They were empty as yet and waiting for the rain. He smelled the air and looked anxiously at the sky. Rain was there, dark in the clouds, heavy upon the wind. He would buy a stick of incense and place
235 it in the little temple to the Earth God. On a day like this he would do it.

11 What else does Wang Lung expect of his new wife?

12 How did Wang Lung treat himself on his wedding day?

mutinous
strongly wanting to rebel, or disobey someone in authority

240 He wound his way in among the fields upon the narrow path. In the near distance the grey city wall arose. Within that gate in the wall through which he would pass stood the great house where the woman had been a slave girl since her childhood, the House of Hwang. There were those who said, "It is better to live alone than to marry a woman who has been slave in a great house." But when he had

245 said to his father, "Am I never to have a woman?" his father replied, "With weddings costing as they do in these evil days and every woman wanting gold rings and silk clothes before she will take a man, there remain only slaves to be had for the poor." **13**

250 His father had stirred himself, then, and gone to the House of Hwang and asked if there were a slave to spare.

"Not a slave too young, and above all, not a pretty one," he had said.

255 Wang Lung had suffered that she must not be pretty. It would be something to have a pretty wife that other men would congratulate him upon having. His father, seeing his **mutinous** face, had cried out at him, "And what will we do with a pretty

260 woman? We must have a woman who will tend the house and bear children as she works in the fields, and will a pretty woman do these things? She will be forever thinking about clothes to go with her face! No, not a pretty woman in our house. We are

265 farmers. Moreover, who has heard of a pretty slave who was virgin in a wealthy house? All the young lords have had their fill of her. It is better to be first with an ugly woman than the hundredth with a beauty. Do you imagine a pretty woman will think

270 your farmer's hands as pleasing as the soft hands of a rich man's son, and your sun-black face as beautiful as the golden skin of the others who have had her for their pleasure?" **14**

Wang Lung knew his father spoke well.

275 Nevertheless, he had to struggle with his flesh before he could answer. And then he said violently, "At least, I will not have a woman who is pock-marked, or who has a split upper lip."

13 What is the background of Wang Lung's bride?

14 What criteria did Wang Lung's father require for his chosen wife?

acknowledgment
a sign or action that shows you know something is true

15 How much did Wang Lung's father pay for his wife?

"We will have to see what is to be had," his
280 father replied.

Well, the woman was not pock-marked nor had she a split upper lip. This much he knew, but nothing more. He and his father had bought two silver rings, washed with gold, and silver earrings, and
285 these his father had taken to the woman's owner in **acknowledgment** of betrothal. Beyond this, he knew nothing of the woman who was to be his, except that on this day he could go and get her. **15**

Pearl S. Buck

Pearl S. Buck, born Pearl Sydenstricker, was an American citizen who grew up with her family in China. Despite racial tensions in the early 1900s, Buck flourished in school, even when part of her family was forced to move to another city to escape a violent Chinese uprising. Buck held China close to her heart as she wrote, explaining, "My earliest knowledge of story, of how to tell and write stories, came to me in China . . . the novelist did not have the task of creating art but of speaking to the people." In 1917, Buck moved to a small town on the Huai River, a setting in her novel *The Good Earth*. A firm advocate for racial equality, Buck established Welcome House, Inc. due to the hatred toward Asian orphans, which became the first international interracial adoption agency. She went on to create safe places for Asian women and children affected by violence and poverty, and in 1938, Buck accepted the Nobel Prize in Literature "for her rich and truly epic descriptions of peasant life in China . . . ."

Participial Phrases

Participial Phrases	Examples

• Begin with participle
  – Present: -ing
  – Past: -ed and irregular
• Followed by objects and/or modifiers
	Using a flint and dry straw, Wang Lung lit the morning fire.
	Dressed in his wedding clothes, Wang Lung left the small cottage and headed to town.

Punctuation: • Set apart by commas if not essential for sentence meaning	The old man, ***exasperated with Wang Lung***, came to check on his morning tea.
Placement • As close as possible to the noun it describes	He found Wang Lung ***sitting in the kitchen***. NOT: ***Sitting in the kitchen***, he found Wang Lung.

Read each sentence and then underline the participial phrase.

Example:
At first, <u>opening his eyes in the blackness of the curtain about his bed</u>, he could not think why the dawn seemed different from any other.

1. The dawn, rising brightly above the horizon, seemed different from the others.

2. He sprang up and pushed aside the curtains hanging around his bed.

3. Tattered by the wind, a small square of paper covered the bedroom window.

4. Drawing on his blue outer trousers, he hurried out into the middle room.

5. The kitchen, made from earthen bricks, leaned against the house.

6. Pulled from the corner, dry grass and stalks fueled the fire beneath the cauldron.

7. Sitting on his bed, his father waited patiently for his cup of tea.

8. Dreaming of children, Wang Lung let his father's water get cold.

9. The shadowy figure, coughing in the doorway, glared at Wang Lung.

10. Tea leaves, sprinkled in the hot water, created a pleasing aroma.

Participial Phrase or Prepositional Phrase

Read each sentence and determine whether the underlined words form a participial phrase or a prepositional phrase. Sort the phrases into the chart below.

> **Examples:**
>
> Wang Lung dipped some water <u>into the bowl</u>.
>
> <u>Pushing aside the bed curtains</u>, Wang Lung quickly rose to greet the morning.

1. <u>On this morning</u>, he wanted the house to look neat and tidy.

2. A small soft wind blew gently <u>from the east</u>.

3. The wind, <u>blowing from the east</u>, was murmurous and full of rain.

4. The thatched straw roof was made <u>from their own wheat</u>.

5. <u>Filled with water</u>, the cauldron hung <u>above the earthen oven</u>.

6. <u>Walking behind the oven</u>, he selected a handful <u>of dry grass</u>.

7. <u>Striking an old flint and iron</u>, he caught a flame and thrust it <u>into the straw</u>.

8. <u>After this morning</u>, he would not have to light the morning fire.

9. <u>Coughing in the damp morning air</u>, the old man waited for his morning cup <u>of hot water</u>.

10. <u>Rising at dawn's first light</u>, Wang Lung had lit the oven and heated the water.

Participial Phrases	Prepositional Phrases
Pushing aside the bed curtains	into the bowl

Appositives

An **appositive**:

- Is a noun, pronoun, or noun phrase that serves to explain or identify another noun or pronoun
- Immediately precedes or follows the noun that it is identifying
- Is set off by commas unless it is essential to the meaning of a sentence

> **Examples:**
>
> The old man, a widower, lives with his son.
>
> Wang Lung, his only son, works hard to make a living on their farm.
>
> The young farmer Wang Lung is soon to be married.

Read each sentence. Underline the appositive in each sentence and draw an arrow to the noun it modifies.

> **Example:**
>
> He had asked his male cousin, the young son of his uncle, to sup that night.

1. The young woman, a slave in the House of Hwang, would soon be his wife.

2. Wang Lung, a poor farmer, worked tirelessly to tend to his fields.

3. Wang Lung's father, an old and sickly man, expected his son's wife to take care of him.

4. Wang Lung's mother, a hardworking farmer's wife, had been dead for six years.

5. Wang Lung, an anxious and excited bridegroom, walked to town to meet his new wife.

Appositives in Writing

Write one sentence that combines each pair of sentences by turning one sentence into an appositive. Remember to correctly punctuate each new sentence.

> **Example:**
>
> The stove is an earthen brick structure.
> His grandfather built the stove with clay from his farm.
>
> His grandfather built the stove, an earthen brick structure, with clay from his farm.

1. Wang Lung's father is a feeble old man.
    Wang Lung's father lives with him.

    _____

    _____

2. Wang Lung's new wife is a slave in the House of Hwang.
    Wang Lung's new wife lives in town.

    _____

    _____

3. Wang Lung is a dutiful son.
    Wang Lung takes good care of his father.

    _____

    _____

4. Arranged marriages are a common practice in rural China.
    Arranged marriages are frowned upon in the Western world.

    _____

    _____

5. Wang Lung's bride is a poor slave.
    The slave married Wang Lung for a chance for a better life.

    _____

    _____

Subject-Verb Agreement

- In a sentence, the subject noun and predicate verb must agree in number.
    - Singular subject + singular verb
    - Plural subject + plural verb
- Beware of the -s!
    - -s or -es makes a regular verb **singular: He *sits* quietly**.
    - -s or -es makes a regular noun **plural: The *boys* sit quietly**.
- Verb tense
    - Impacts present tense only for most verbs
    - Impacts present and past tense for the verb *be*

	Singular	Plural
Verb: *be*		
present tense	I am; you are; he is	you are; we are; they are
past tense	I was; you were; it was	you were; we were; they were
Verb: *have*		
present tense	I have; you have; he has	you have; we have; they have

Underline the kernel sentence. Then, determine if the kernel sentence is singular or plural and place an X in the appropriate column.

Sentence	Singular	Plural
Examples: <u>Wang Lung</u>, dreaming of a house full of children, <u>lights</u> the fire in the oven.	X	
<u>Wang Lung and his father</u> <u>sip</u> tea quietly in the dimly lit room.		X
1. The fire's flames burn brightly in the earthen stove.		
2. Farming is his life.		
3. The wind brings the promise of rain.		
4. Wang Lung and his new wife live in the simple farm cottage.		
5. Thoughts of a new life distract Wang Lung from his chores.		

Writing with Subject-Verb Agreement

Complete each sentence with the correct form of the subject or verb to maintain subject-verb agreement.

> **Examples:**
> Wang Lung _____is_____ thinking of his new life. (to be)
> The farmer's _____life_____ is a difficult and challenging one. (life)

1. Wang Lung and his father _____ about his new wife. (talk)

2. Children's _____ line the halls in Wang Lung's dreams. (bed)

3. In town, a young slave girl _____ for Wang Lung. (wait)

4. The residents of the House of Hwang _____ gifts for Wang Lung and his new wife. (have)

5. The wedding _____ are eager for the ceremony to begin. (guest)

6. The band _____ music as the couple enters. (play)

7. The family of the slave girl _____ she will be better off with Wang Lung. (hope)

8. Wang Lung's bath _____ longer than usual. (take)

9. Wang Lung and his bride _____ a new life together. (begin)

10. The festivities _____ for several hours. (last)

Passage Comprehension

Reread the excerpt from *The Good Earth*. Respond to each prompt using complete sentences. Refer to the chart on pages 14 and 15 to determine how to respond to each prompt.

1. Support Wang Lung's father's theory about pretty girls focusing more on clothes than work with a real-life example.

   _____

   _____

   _____

   _____

   _____

2. Develop an argument against the arranged marriage from the bride's point of view. Support your answer with text evidence.

   _____

   _____

   _____

   _____

   _____

3. Prove that though *The Good Earth* is written in third person, it is told from Wang Lung's point of view. Support your answer with text evidence.

   _____

   _____

   _____

   _____

   _____

   _____

   _____

   _____

Passage Comprehension (*cont.*)

4. Prove that the setting shaped the main character, Wang Lung.

_____

_____

_____

_____

_____

_____

5. Clarify how lines 250–280 fit into the overall plot.

_____

_____

_____

_____

_____

_____

_____

_____

6. Clarify the adage "You get what you pay for" as it relates to Wang Lung in *The Good Earth*.

_____

_____

_____

_____

_____

_____

_____

_____

Close Reading

Read the text.

from *The Good Earth*

It was Wang Lung's marriage day. At first, opening his eyes in the blackness of the curtains about his bed, he could not think why the dawn seemed different from any other. The house was still except for the faint, gasping cough of his old father, whose room was opposite to his own
5 across the middle room. Every morning the old man's cough was the first sound to be heard. Wang Lung usually lay listening to it and moved only when he heard it approaching nearer and when he heard the door of his father's room squeak upon its wooden hinges.

But this morning he did not wait. He sprang up and pushed aside the
10 curtains of his bed. It was a dark, ruddy dawn, and through a small square hole of a window, where the tattered paper fluttered, a glimpse of bronze sky gleamed. He went to the hole and tore the paper away.

"It is spring and I do not need this," he muttered.

He was ashamed to say aloud that he wished the house to look neat on
15 this day. The hole was barely large enough to admit his hand and he thrust it out to feel of the air. A small soft wind blew gently from the east, a wind mild and murmurous and full of rain. It was a good omen. The fields needed rain for **fruition**. There would be no rain this day, but within a few days, if this wind continued, there would be water. It was
20 good. Yesterday he had said to his father that if this brazen, glittering sunshine continued, the wheat could not fill in the ear. Now it was as if Heaven had chosen this day to wish him well. Earth would bear fruit.

Close Reading (*cont.*)

He hurried out into the middle room, drawing on his blue outer trousers
as he went, and knotting about the fullness at his waist his girdle of blue
25 cotton cloth. He left his upper body bare until he had heated water to
bathe himself. He went into the shed which was the kitchen, leaning
against the house, and out of its dusk an ox twisted its head from behind
the corner next the door and lowed at him deeply. The kitchen was made
of earthen bricks as the house was, great squares of earth dug from
30 their own fields, and thatched with straw from their own wheat. Out
of their own earth had his grandfather in his youth **fashioned** also the
oven, baked and black with many years of meal preparing. On top of this
earthen structure stood a deep, round, iron cauldron.

This cauldron he filled partly full of water, dipping it with a half gourd
35 from an earthen jar that stood near, but he dipped cautiously, for water
was precious. Then, after a hesitation, he suddenly lifted the jar and
emptied all the water into the cauldron. This day he would bathe his
whole body. Not since he was a child upon his mother's knee had anyone
looked upon his body. Today one would, and he would have it clean.

40 He went around the oven to the rear, and selecting a handful of the dry
grass and stalks standing in the corner of the kitchen, he arranged it
delicately in the mouth of the oven, making the most of every leaf. Then
from an old flint and iron he caught a flame and thrust it into the straw
and there was a blaze.

45 This was the last morning he would have to light the fire. He had lit it
every morning since his mother died six years before. He had lit the fire,
boiled water, and poured the water into a bowl and taken it into the room
where his father sat upon his bed, coughing and fumbling for his shoes
upon the floor. Every morning for these six years the old man had waited
50 for his son to bring in hot water to ease him of his morning coughing.
Now father and son could rest. There was a woman coming to the house.

Close Reading (*cont.*)

Never again would Wang Lung have to rise summer and winter at dawn to light the fire. He could lie in his bed and wait, and he also would have a bowl of water brought to him, and if the earth were fruitful there would
55 be tea leaves in the water. Once in some years it was so.

And if the woman wearied, there would be her children to light the fire, the many children she would bear to Wang Lung. Wang Lung stopped, struck by the thought of children running in and out of their three rooms. Three rooms had always seemed much to them, a house half
60 empty since his mother died.

Now the grandsons were coming, grandsons upon grandsons! They would have to put beds along the walls and in the middle room. The house would be full of beds. The blaze in the oven died down while Wang Lung thought of all the beds there would be in the half-empty house, and
65 the water began to chill in the cauldron. The shadowy figure of the old man appeared in the doorway, holding his unbuttoned garments about him. He was coughing and spitting and he gasped, "How is it that there is not water yet to heat my lungs?"

Wang Lung stared and recalled himself and was ashamed.

70 "This fuel is damp," he muttered from behind the stove. "The damp wind—"

The old man continued to cough perseveringly and would not **cease** until the water boiled. Wang Lung dipped some into a bowl, and then, after a moment, he opened a glazed jar that stood upon a ledge of the stove and
75 took from it a dozen or so of the curled dried leaves and sprinkled them upon the surface of the water. The old man's eyes opened greedily and immediately he began to complain.

"Why are you wasteful? Tea is like eating silver."

Close Reading (*cont.*)

"It is the day," replied Wang Lung with a short laugh. "Eat and be
80 comforted."

The old man grasped the bowl in his shriveled, knotty fingers, muttering, uttering little grunts. He watched the leaves uncurl and spread upon the surface of the water, unable to bear drinking the **precious** stuff.

"It will be cold," said Wang Lung.

85 "True—true—" said the old man in alarm, and he began to take great gulps of the hot tea. He passed into an animal satisfaction, like a child fixed upon its feeding. But he was not too forgetful to see Wang Lung dipping the water **recklessly** from the cauldron into a deep wooden tub. He lifted his head and stared at his son.

90 "Now there is water enough to bring a crop to fruit," he said suddenly.

Wang Lung continued to dip the water to the last drop. He did not answer.

"Now then!" cried his father loudly.

"I have not washed my body all at once since the New Year," said Wang
95 Lung in a low voice.

He was ashamed to say to his father that he wished his body to be clean for a woman to see. He hurried out, carrying the tub to his own room. The door was hung loosely upon a **warped** wooden frame and it did not shut closely, and the old man tottered into the middle room and put his
100 mouth to the opening and bawled, "It will be ill if we start the woman like this—tea in the morning water and all this washing!"

"It is only one day," shouted Wang Lung. And then he added, "I will throw the water on the earth when I am finished and it is not all waste."

Close Reading (*cont.*)

The old man was silent at this, and Wang Lung unfastened his girdle and
105 stepped out of his clothing. In the light that streamed in a square block
from the hole he wrung a small towel from the steaming water and he
scrubbed his dark slender body vigorously. Warm though he had thought
the air, when his flesh was wet he was cold, and he moved quickly, passing
the towel in and out of the water until from his whole body there went
110 up a delicate cloud of steam. Then he went to a box that had been his
mother's and drew from it a fresh suit of blue cotton cloth. He might be
a little cold this day without the wadding of the winter garments, but
he suddenly could not bear to put them on against his clean flesh. The
covering of them was torn and filthy and the wadding stuck out of the
115 holes, grey and sodden. He did not want this woman to see him for the
first time with the wadding sticking out of his clothes. Later she would
have to wash and mend, but not the first day. He drew over the blue
cotton coat and trousers a long robe made of the same material—his one
long robe, which he wore on feast days only, ten days or so in the year, all
120 told. Then with swift fingers he unplaited the long braid of hair that hung
down his back, and taking a wooden comb from the drawer of the small,
unsteady table, he began to comb out his hair.

His father drew near again and put his mouth to the crack of the door.

"Am I to have nothing to eat this day?" he complained. "At my age the
125 bones are water in the morning until food is given them."

"I am coming," said Wang Lung, braiding his hair quickly and smoothly
and weaving into the strands a tasseled black silk cord.

Close Reading (*cont.*)

Then after a moment he removed his long gown and wound his braid
about his head and went out, carrying the tub of water. He had quite
130 forgotten the breakfast. He would stir a little water into cornmeal and
give it to his father. For himself he could not eat. He staggered with the
tub to the threshold and poured the water upon the earth nearest the
door, and as he did so he remembered he had used all the water in the
cauldron for his bathing and he would have to start the fire again. A wave
135 of anger passed over him at his father.

"That old head thinks of nothing except his eating and his drinking," he
muttered into the mouth of the oven; but aloud he said nothing. It was
the last morning he would have to prepare food for the old man. He put
a very little water into the cauldron, drawing it in a bucket from the well
140 near the door, and it boiled quickly and he stirred meal together and took
it to the old man.

Wang Lung went into his own room then, and drew about him again
the long blue robe and let down the braid of his hair. He passed his hand
over his shaven brow and over his cheeks. Perhaps he had better be newly
145 shaven? It was scarcely sunrise yet. He could pass through the Street of
the Barbers and be shaved before he went to the house where the woman
waited for him. If he had the money he would do it.

Close Reading (*cont.*)

He took from his girdle a small greasy pouch of grey cloth and counted the money in it. There were six silver dollars and a double handful of
150 copper coins. He had not yet told his father he had asked friends to sup that night. He had asked his male cousin, the young son of his uncle, and his uncle for his father's sake, and three neighboring farmers who lived in the village with him. He had planned to bring back from the town that morning pork, a small pond fish, and a handful of chestnuts. He might
155 even buy a few of the bamboo sprouts from the south and a little beef to stew with the cabbage he had raised in his own garden. But this only if there were any money left after the bean oil and the soybean sauce had been bought. If he shaved his head he could not, perhaps, buy the beef. Well, he would shave his head, he decided suddenly.

160 He left the old man without speech and went out into the early morning. In spite of the dark red dawn the sun was mounting the horizon clouds and sparkled upon the dew on the rising wheat and barley. The farmer in Wang Lung was **diverted** for an instant and he stooped to examine the budding heads. They were empty as yet and waiting for the rain. He
165 smelled the air and looked anxiously at the sky. Rain was there, dark in the clouds, heavy upon the wind. He would buy a stick of incense and place it in the little temple to the Earth God. On a day like this he would do it.

He wound his way in among the fields upon the narrow path. In the near
170 distance the grey city wall arose. Within that gate in the wall through which he would pass stood the great house where the woman had been a slave girl since her childhood, the House of Hwang. There were those who said, "It is better to live alone than to marry a woman who has been slave in a great house." But when he had said to his father, "Am I never to have
175 a woman?" his father replied, "With weddings costing as they do in these evil days and every woman wanting gold rings and silk clothes before she will take a man, there remain only slaves to be had for the poor."

His father had stirred himself, then, and gone to the House of Hwang and asked if there were a slave to spare.

180 "Not a slave too young, and above all, not a pretty one," he had said.

Close Reading (*cont.*)

Wang Lung had suffered that she must not be pretty. It would be something to have a pretty wife that other men would congratulate him upon having. His father, seeing his **mutinous** face, had cried out at him, "And what will we do with a pretty woman? We must have a woman who
185 will tend the house and bear children as she works in the fields, and will a pretty woman do these things? She will be forever thinking about clothes to go with her face! No, not a pretty woman in our house. We are farmers. Moreover, who has heard of a pretty slave who was virgin in a wealthy house? All the young lords have had their fill of her. It is better to be first
190 with an ugly woman than the hundredth with a beauty. Do you imagine a pretty woman will think your farmer's hands as pleasing as the soft hands of a rich man's son, and your sun-black face as beautiful as the golden skin of the others who have had her for their pleasure?"

Wang Lung knew his father spoke well. Nevertheless, he had to struggle
195 with his flesh before he could answer. And then he said violently, "At least, I will not have a woman who is pock-marked, or who has a split upper lip."

"We will have to see what is to be had," his father replied.

Well, the woman was not pock-marked nor had she a split upper lip. This
200 much he knew, but nothing more. He and his father had bought two silver rings, washed with gold, and silver earrings, and these his father had taken to the woman's owner in **acknowledgment** of betrothal. Beyond this, he knew nothing of the woman who was to be his, except that on this day he could go and get her.

Quick Write in Response to Reading

Is an arranged marriage a good thing or a bad thing? Write an essay in which you attempt to persuade the reader to accept your position. Your opening paragraph should state your position, and you should elaborate each claim in a body paragraph. Remember, each body paragraph needs a topic sentence. Use the concluding paragraph to restate your position without sounding repetitive.

Quick Write in Response to Reading (*cont.*)

Let's Focus: Excerpt from *Nectar in a Sieve*

Content Focus
arranged marriage
Indian culture

Type of Text

_____

Author's Name _____

Author's Purpose _____

Big Ideas
Consider the following Big Idea questions. Write your answer for each question.

What role does economic status play in marriages today?

_____

_____

How have women's roles changed over time? Have those changes impacted men's roles in family and society?

_____

_____

Literary Preview Checklist: the excerpt from *Nectar in a Sieve* on pages 319–323.

☐ Title: What clue does it provide?

☐ Pictures: What additional information is added here?

☐ Margin Information: What vocabulary is important to understand this story?

Enduring Understandings
After reading the text . . .

_____

_____

_____

_____

_____

Key Passage Vocabulary: Excerpt from *Nectar in a Sieve*

Read each word. Write it in column 3. Then, circle a number to rate your knowledge of the word.

Read the Word	Part of Speech	Write the Word	Rate the Word
eligible	(adj)		0 1 2 3
justification	(n)		0 1 2 3
grudge	(n)		0 1 2 3
assess	(v)		0 1 2 3
regretfully	(adv)		0 1 2 3
preliminaries	(n)		0 1 2 3
retort	(n)		0 1 2 3
hoist	(v)		0 1 2 3
procession	(n)		0 1 2 3
decorous	(adj)		0 1 2 3

from

Nectar in a Sieve

by Kamala Markandaya

I kept Ira as long as I could but when she was past fourteen her marriage could be delayed no longer, for it is well known with what speed **eligible** young men are snapped up; as it was, most girls of her
5 age were already married or at least betrothed. The choice of go-between was not easy to make: Kali was the nearest to hand and the obvious one, but she was garrulous and self-opinionated: rejection of the young man she selected would involve a tedious
10 squabble. Besides, she had sons of her own and might well consider them suitable husbands, which I certainly could not, for they owned no land. Old Granny, on the other hand, would be the ideal go-between: she was old and experienced, knew very
15 well what to look for and never lacked patience; but for some years now I had not traded with her and she might with every **justification** refuse to act for me. But in the end it was to her I went. ▪

eligible
available and meets certain requirements

justification
a good reason or explanation

1 Use context to determine the meaning of *go-between*.

grudge

bad feelings toward someone because of something they did in the past

assess

to think something through in order to make a decision or judgment about it

regretfully

in a way that shows you wish something wasn't true or wasn't happening

preliminaries

activities that take place before an event

2 What merit is Ira's mom looking for in her future son-in-law?

3 How did Ira react to the news of her future husband?

"A dowry of one hundred rupees," I said. "A maiden
20 like a flower. Do your best for me and I shall be ever
in your debt. This I ask you," I said, looking straight
at her, "although Biswas takes my produce and for
you there has been nothing."

"I bear you no **grudge**, Rukmani," she replied.
25 "Times are hard and we must do what we can for
ourselves and our children. I will do my best."

Thereafter never a week went by but she brought
news of this boy or that, and she and I and Nathan
spent long hours trying to **assess** their relative
30 merits. At last we found one who seemed to fulfill
our requirements: he was young and well favoured,
the only son of his father from whom he would one
day inherit a good portion of land. **2**

"They will expect a large dowry," I said **regretfully**.
35 "One hundred rupees will not win such a husband,
we have no more."

"She is endowed with beauty," Old Granny said. "It
will make up for a small dowry—in this case."

She was right. Within a month the **preliminaries**
40 were completed, the day was fixed. Ira accepted our
choice with her usual docility; if she fretted at the
thought of leaving us and her brothers she showed
no sign. Only once she asked a little wistfully how
frequently I would be able to visit her, and, although
45 I knew such trips would have to be very rare since
her future home lay some ten villages away, I
assured her not a year would pass without my going
to see her two or three times. **3**

"Besides, you will not want me so often," I said. "This
50 home, your brothers, are all you have known so far,
but when you have your own home and your own
children you will not miss these . . . ."

She nodded slightly, making no comment, yet I
knew how bruised she must be by the imminent
55 parting. My spirit ached with pity for her, I longed
to be able to comfort her, to convince her that in

a few months' time her new home would be the most significant part of her life, the rest only a preparation . . . but before this joy must come the
60 stress of parting, the loneliness of beginning a new life among strangers, the strain of the early days of marriage; and because I knew this the words would not come **4**

Wedding day. Women from the village came to
65 assist. Janaki, Kali, many I hardly knew. We went with Ira to the river and, when she was freshly bathed, put on her the red sari I had worn at my own wedding. Its rich heavy folds made her look more slender than she was, made her look a
70 child . . . . I darkened her eyes with kohl and the years fell away more; she was so pitifully young I could hardly believe she was to be married, today.

The bridegroom arrived; his parents, his relatives, our friends, the priests. The drummer arrived and
75 squatted outside awaiting permission to begin; the fiddler joined him. There should have been other musicians—a flautist, a harmonium player, but we could not afford these. Nathan would have nothing we could not pay for. No debts, he insisted, no debts.
80 But I grudged Ira nothing: had I not saved from the day of her birth so that she should marry well? Now I brought out the stores I had put by month after month—rice and dhal and ghee, jars of oil, betel leaf, areca nuts, chewing tobacco and copra. **5**

85 "I didn't know you had so much," said Nathan in amazement.

"And if you had there would be little enough," I said with a wink at the women, "for men are like children and must grab what they see."

90 I did not wait for his **retort**, hearing only the laughter that greeted his sally, but went out to speak to the drummer. Arjun, my eldest son, was sitting next to the man, cautiously tapping the drum with three fingers as he had been shown.

retort
an angry or smart-aleck reply

4 How is Ira's mom feeling about Ira's impending wedding day?

5 How is Ira's wedding different from a wedding in your culture?

hoist

to lift or heave, usually something heavy

95 "There is plenty of food inside," I said to him. "Go and eat while there is still some left."

"I can eat no more," he replied. "I have been feasting all day."

Nevertheless he had made provision for the morrow:
100 I saw in his lap a bundle bulging with food; sugar syrup and butter had soaked through the cloth patchily. **6**

6 Why is Arjun's bundle bulging with food?

"Join your brothers," I said, **hoisting** him up. "The drummer is going to be busy."

105 He ran off, clinging tightly to his bundle. The wedding music began. Bride and groom were sitting uneasily side by side, Ira stiff in the heavy embroidered sari, white flowers in her hair, very pale. They did not look at each other. About them
110 were packed some fourteen or fifteen people—the hut could hold no more. The remainder sat outside on palm leaves the boys had collected.

"What a good match," everybody said. "Such a fine boy, such a beautiful girl, too good to be true." It
115 was indeed. Old Granny went about beaming: it was she who had brought the two parties together; her reputation as a matchmaker would be higher than ever. We none of us could look into the future. **7**

7 What phrase foreshadows bad news for this couple?

So they were married. As the light faded two
120 youths appeared bearing a palanquin for the newly married couple, lowered it at the entrance to the hut for them to step into. Now that it was time to go, Ira looked scared, she hesitated a little before entering: but already a dozen willing hands had
125 lifted her in. The crowd, full of good feeling, replete with food and drunk with the music, vicariously excited, pressed round, eagerly thrusting over their heads garland after garland of flowers; the earth was spattered with petals. In the midst of the crush
130 Nathan and I, Nathan holding out his hands to Ira in blessing, she with dark head bent low to receive it. Then the palanquin was lifted up, the torchbearers closed in, the musicians took their places. We

135 followed on foot behind, relatives, friends, well-wishers and hangers-on. Several children had added themselves to the company; they came after, jigging about in high glee, noisy and excited: a long, ragged tail-end to the **procession**. [8]

140 Past the fields, through the winding streets of the village we went, the bobbing palanquin ahead of us. Until we came at last to where, at a **decorous** distance, the bullock cart waited to take them away.

Then it was all over, the bustle, the laughter, the noise. The wedding guests departed. The throng
145 melted. After a while we walked back together to our hut. Our sons, tired out, were humped together asleep, the youngest clutching a sugary confection in one sticky fist. Bits of food lay everywhere. I swept the floor clean and strewed it with leaves. The
150 walls showed cracks, and clods of mud had fallen where people had bumped against them, but these I left for patching in the morning. The used plantain leaves I stacked in one heap—they would do for the bullocks. The stars were pale in the greying night
155 before I lay down beside my husband. Not to sleep but to think. For the first time since her birth, Ira no longer slept under our roof. [9]

procession
a group of people moving forward as part of a public event

decorous
polite, proper, and respectful

[8] What was the mood of the wedding? How was Ira feeling?

[9] How was Ira's mom feeling?

Kamala Purnaiya Taylor was born in rural India in 1924. In 1955, she published her first novel under the pen name **Kamala Markandaya**. She wrote about the struggles of rural and urban life in India. Taylor experienced similar struggles in her own life as she moved from the small village of her youth and was exposed to the radical differences between classes in Indian society. She was born to a privileged family but spent a good amount of time studying history and people from all walks of life in India. Because of her enlightening work, *Nectar in a Sieve* was named a notable book in 1955 by the American Library Association.

All Nature seems at work. Slugs leave their lair—
The bees are stirring—birds are on the wing—
And Winter, slumbering in the open air,
Wears on his smiling face a dream of Spring!
And I, the while, the sole unbusy thing,
Nor honey make, nor pair, nor build, nor sing.

Bloom, O ye amaranths! bloom for whom ye may,
For me ye bloom not! Glide, rich streams, away!
With lips unbrightened, wreathless brow, I stroll:
And would you learn the spells that drowse my soul?
Work without hope draws nectar in a sieve,
And hope without an object cannot live.

"Work Without Hope"
by Samuel Taylor Coleridge, 1825
The poem that inspired Kamala Markandaya's title

Critical Understandings

Reread lines 1–38 of the excerpt from *Nectar in a Sieve*. Respond to each prompt using complete sentences. Refer to the chart on pages 14 and 15 to determine how to respond to each prompt.

1. Compare Rukmani and Wang Lung's father in *The Good Earth*.

   _____

   _____

   _____

   _____

   _____

2. Contrast Kali and Old Granny.

   _____

   _____

   _____

   _____

   _____

   _____

   _____

3. Cite evidence that Old Granny was a good choice for go-between.

   _____

   _____

   _____

   _____

   _____

4. Demonstrate knowledge of arranged marriages in Eastern cultures by listing your qualities that a suitor's family would be interested in.

   _____

   _____

   _____

   _____

Compare-Contrast Essay Structure

Read the following essay. Follow the steps below.

- Highlight the thesis statement green.
- Highlight the topic sentence of each paragraph yellow.
- Label the body paragraphs.
- Label the concluding paragraph.
- Label the introductory paragraph.

_____
_____

Claire and Chad have been volunteers at the local community center for years. Both of them are reliable, energetic, and dedicated workers. Because of their unique strengths and weaknesses, they have very different roles at the center.

_____
_____

Claire possesses fabulous organizational skills. Implementing her ideas has saved the community center thousands of dollars and streamlined its operations. She created procedures for most of the activities that take place at the center, thus eliminating many of the problems that once plagued the facility. Because her abrupt attitude can rub people the wrong way, she enjoys working in the solitude of her office.

_____
_____

Chad, on the other hand, is very much a people person. While his organizational skills may be somewhat weak, he is very effective in dealing with the public. With his passion for the well-being of the community and his winning smile, he has worked tirelessly to get local businesses involved in the center. Through the submission of grant applications and securing business sponsorships, he has dramatically increased the center's budget. With these funds, the community center has been able to offer many different types of activities that appeal to a wide variety of citizens.

_____
_____

Facilities like the community center need volunteers with an array of skills and interests. Claire and Chad have been willing to donate their unique skill sets to the community center, and the community is definitely the better for it.

Passage Comprehension

Reread the excerpt from *Nectar in a Sieve*. Respond to each prompt using complete sentences. Refer to the chart on pages 14 and 15 to determine how to respond to each prompt.

1. Compare Ira's family values with Wang Lung's family values.

   _____

   _____

   _____

2. Contrast the goals of Rukmani with the goals of Wang Lung's father.

   _____

   _____

   _____

   _____

   _____

   _____

   _____

3. Use inferencing to compare and contrast the bride's point of view in both texts on arranged marriages.

   _____

   _____

   _____

   _____

   _____

   _____

   _____

   _____

   _____

   _____

Passage Comprehension (*cont.*)

4. Cite evidence to prove that Wang Lung's father and Ira's father had different roles in the family.

_____

_____

_____

_____

_____

_____

_____

_____

_____

_____

_____

_____

5. Demonstrate understanding of the life of Indian farmers by explaining the happenings of the wedding day.

_____

_____

_____

_____

_____

_____

_____

_____

_____

_____

_____

_____

Passage Comprehension (*cont.*)

6. Cite evidence to prove that Indian weddings are ceremonial.

_____

_____

_____

_____

_____

_____

_____

_____

_____

_____

_____

_____

_____

_____

_____

_____

_____

_____

_____

_____

_____

_____

_____

Close Reading

Read the text.

from *Nectar in a Sieve*

I kept Ira as long as I could but when she was past fourteen her marriage could be delayed no longer, for it is well known with what speed **eligible** young men are snapped up; as it was, most girls of her age were already married or at least betrothed. The choice of go-between was not easy
5 to make: Kali was the nearest to hand and the obvious one, but she was garrulous and self-opinionated: rejection of the young man she selected would involve a tedious squabble. Besides, she had sons of her own and might well consider them suitable husbands, which I certainly could not, for they owned no land. Old Granny, on the other hand, would be
10 the ideal go-between: she was old and experienced, knew very well what to look for and never lacked patience; but for some years now I had not traded with her and she might with every **justification** refuse to act for me. But in the end it was to her I went.

"A dowry of one hundred rupees," I said. "A maiden like a flower. Do your
15 best for me and I shall be ever in your debt. This I ask you," I said, looking straight at her, "although Biswas takes my produce and for you there has been nothing."

"I bear you no **grudge**, Rukmani," she replied. "Times are hard and we must do what we can for ourselves and our children. I will do my best."

20 Thereafter never a week went by but she brought news of this boy or that, and she and I and Nathan spent long hours trying to **assess** their relative merits. At last we found one who seemed to fulfill our requirements: he was young and well favoured, the only son of his father from whom he would one day inherit a good portion of land.

Close Reading (*cont.*)

25 "They will expect a large dowry," I said **regretfully**. "One hundred rupees will not win such a husband, we have no more."

"She is endowed with beauty," Old Granny said. "It will make up for a small dowry—in this case."

She was right. Within a month the **preliminaries** were completed, the
30 day was fixed. Ira accepted our choice with her usual docility; if she fretted at the thought of leaving us and her brothers she showed no sign. Only once she asked a little wistfully how frequently I would be able to visit her, and, although I knew such trips would have to be very rare since her future home lay some ten villages away, I assured her not a year would
35 pass without my going to see her two or three times.

"Besides, you will not want me so often," I said. "This home, your brothers, are all you have known so far, but when you have your own home and your own children you will not miss these . . . ."

She nodded slightly, making no comment, yet I knew how bruised she must
40 be by the imminent parting. My spirit ached with pity for her, I longed to be able to comfort her, to convince her that in a few months' time her new home would be the most significant part of her life, the rest only a preparation . . . but before this joy must come the stress of parting, the loneliness of beginning a new life among strangers, the strain of the early
45 days of marriage; and because I knew this the words would not come . . . .

Close Reading (*cont.*)

Wedding day. Women from the village came to assist. Janaki, Kali, many I hardly knew. We went with Ira to the river and, when she was freshly bathed, put on her the red sari I had worn at my own wedding. Its rich heavy folds made her look more slender than she was, made her look a
50 child . . . . I darkened her eyes with kohl and the years fell away more; she was so pitifully young I could hardly believe she was to be married, today.

The bridegroom arrived; his parents, his relatives, our friends, the priests. The drummer arrived and squatted outside awaiting permission to begin; the fiddler joined him. There should have been other musicians—a
55 flautist, a harmonium player, but we could not afford these. Nathan would have nothing we could not pay for. No debts, he insisted, no debts. But I grudged Ira nothing: had I not saved from the day of her birth so that she should marry well? Now I brought out the stores I had put by month after month—rice and dhal and ghee, jars of oil, betel leaf, areca nuts, chewing
60 tobacco and copra.

"I didn't know you had so much," said Nathan in amazement.

"And if you had there would be little enough," I said with a wink at the women, "for men are like children and must grab what they see."

I did not wait for his **retort**, hearing only the laughter that greeted his
65 sally, but went out to speak to the drummer. Arjun, my eldest son, was sitting next to the man, cautiously tapping the drum with three fingers as he had been shown.

"There is plenty of food inside," I said to him. "Go and eat while there is still some left."

70 "I can eat no more," he replied. "I have been feasting all day."

Nevertheless he had made provision for the morrow: I saw in his lap a bundle bulging with food; sugar syrup and butter had soaked through the cloth patchily.

Close Reading (*cont.*)

"Join your brothers," I said, **hoisting** him up. "The drummer is going to
75 be busy."

He ran off, clinging tightly to his bundle. The wedding music began.
Bride and groom were sitting uneasily side by side, Ira stiff in the heavy
embroidered sari, white flowers in her hair, very pale. They did not look
at each other. About them were packed some fourteen or fifteen people—
80 the hut could hold no more. The remainder sat outside on palm leaves the
boys had collected.

"What a good match," everybody said. "Such a fine boy, such a beautiful
girl, too good to be true." It was indeed. Old Granny went about beaming:
it was she who had brought the two parties together; her reputation as a
85 matchmaker would be higher than ever. We none of us could look into
the future.

So they were married. As the light faded two youths appeared bearing
a palanquin for the newly married couple, lowered it at the entrance
to the hut for them to step into. Now that it was time to go, Ira looked
90 scared, she hesitated a little before entering: but already a dozen willing
hands had lifted her in. The crowd, full of good feeling, replete with food
and drunk with the music, vicariously excited, pressed round, eagerly
thrusting over their heads garland after garland of flowers; the earth was
spattered with petals. In the midst of the crush Nathan and I, Nathan
95 holding out his hands to Ira in blessing, she with dark head bent low to
receive it. Then the palanquin was lifted up, the torchbearers closed in,
the musicians took their places. We followed on foot behind, relatives,
friends, well-wishers and hangers-on. Several children had added
themselves to the company; they came after, jigging about in high glee,
100 noisy and excited: a long, ragged tail-end to the **procession**.

Past the fields, through the winding streets of the village we went, the
bobbing palanquin ahead of us. Until we came at last to where, at a
decorous distance, the bullock cart waited to take them away.

Then it was all over, the bustle, the laughter, the noise. The wedding guests
105 departed. The throng melted. After a while we walked back together to
our hut. Our sons, tired out, were humped together asleep, the youngest
clutching a sugary confection in one sticky fist. Bits of food lay everywhere.
I swept the floor clean and strewed it with leaves. The walls showed cracks,
and clods of mud had fallen where people had bumped against them, but
110 these I left for patching in the morning. The used plantain leaves I stacked
in one heap—they would do for the bullocks. The stars were pale in the
greying night before I lay down beside my husband. Not to sleep but to
think. For the first time since her birth, Ira no longer slept under our roof.

Summarize and Scrutinize

Part A

Write an objective summary of one text from this unit. Your partner should choose the other text.

Passage: _____

_____

_____

_____

_____

_____

Part B

Use information from the story and the unit video to respond to the following prompts.

Describe the historical and cultural setting, i.e., what was life like in the culture at the time the book was set? _____

_____

_____

_____

_____

Describe the life of the main family in the story. Be sure to include their financial situation.

_____

_____

_____

_____

In what way did the setting of the story affect the thoughts and feelings of the characters and the message of the story? _____

_____

_____

_____

Prepare to Write: Compare-Contrast Essay

Part A. Study the Prompt

Read the following prompt and determine the topic, directions, and purpose for writing.

Use information provided in the two texts to write an essay that compares and contrasts the practice of arranged marriages in India and China.

Topic: _____

Directions: _____

_____

_____

Purpose for Writing: _____

_____

_____

Part B. Organize Information

Unique: *The Good Earth*   **Similar**   **Unique: *Nectar in a Sieve***

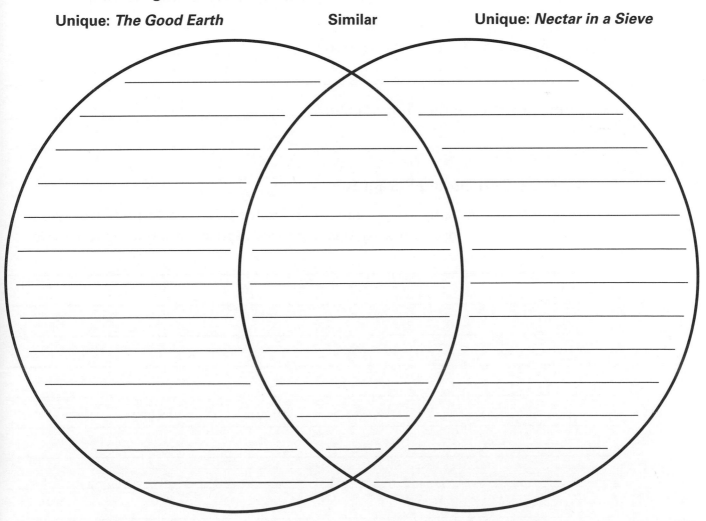

Prepare to Write: Compare-Contrast Essay (*cont.*)

Part C. Write Introductory Paragraph and Thesis Statement

The opening paragraph needs to contain an introduction to the topic. It should state the similarities between the two cultures and set the framework for examining the differences.

_____

_____

_____

_____

_____

_____

_____

Part D. Write Body Paragraph Topic Sentences

Write the topic sentences for the two paragraphs that will focus on the differences within each culture.

Examining practices in the Indian culture: _____

_____

Examining practices in the Chinese culture: _____

_____

Part E. Write Concluding Paragraph

Restate your thesis by using a different topic sentence pattern. Summarize differences and commonalities. Close with a personal perspective to avoid sounding repetitive.

_____

_____

_____

_____

_____

_____

_____

_____

The Literary Analysis Writer's Checklist

Trait	Yes	No	Did the writer . . .?
Ideas and Content			clearly state the thesis of the essay
			analyze and evaluate the elements found in the literature
			focus each paragraph on the topic
			include effective support for the thesis by giving details, examples, explanations, and quotations from the texts
Organization			write an introductory paragraph that captures the reader's interest and cites the titles of the works and the names of the authors
			include in the introductory paragraph a clear viewpoint on the topic and a "map" for the essay that follows
			sequence body paragraphs logically and use transition sentences that make clear the relationship between the ideas
			write a conclusion that ties the analysis together and offers an evaluation of the particulars
Voice and Audience Awareness			think about the audience and purpose for writing
			write in a clear and engaging way that makes the audience want to read the work
Word Choice			find a unique way to say things; avoid sounding repetitive
			use words that are lively and specific to the content
Sentence Fluency			write complete sentences
			expand some sentences using the steps of Masterpiece Sentences
			use compound sentence elements and compound sentences
Conventions			capitalize words correctly:
			capitalize the first word of each sentence
			capitalize proper nouns, including people's names
			punctuate correctly:
			end sentences with a period, question mark, or exclamation mark
			use an apostrophe for possessive nouns and contractions
			use commas and/or semicolons correctly
			use grammar correctly:
			use the correct verb tense
			make sure the verb agrees with the subject in number
			use correct spelling

Let's Focus: Part 1 of the Excerpt from *My Sister's Keeper*

Content Focus
savior sibling
family dynamics

Type of Text

_____

Author's Name _____

Author's Purpose _____

Big Ideas

Consider the following Big Idea questions. Write your answer for each question.

Should parents be able to make decisions for their minor children? Why or why not?

_____

_____

Is there a true "normal"? Or does the definition of *normal* change with circumstances? Explain.

_____

_____

Preview Checklist: Part 1 of the excerpt from *My Sister's Keeper* on pages 341–349.

☐ Title: What clue does it provide about the passage?

☐ Pictures: What additional information is added here?

☐ Margin Information: What vocabulary is important to understand this story?

Enduring Understandings

After reading the text . . .

_____

_____

_____

_____

Key Passage Vocabulary: from *My Sister's Keeper*, Part 1

Read each word. Write the word in column 3. Then, circle a number to rate your knowledge of the word.

Read the Word	Part of Speech	Write the Word	Rate the Word
acute	(adj)		0 1 2 3
donor	(n)		0 1 2 3
drastically	(adv)		0 1 2 3
collapse	(v)		0 1 2 3
assume	(v)		0 1 2 3
circumstance	(n)		0 1 2 3
wince	(v)		0 1 2 3
obstacle	(n)		0 1 2 3
inferno	(n)		0 1 2 3
friction	(n)		0 1 2 3

from

My Sister's Keeper
PART 1

by Jodi Picoult

If Mr. Webster had decided to put the word *freak* in his dictionary, *Anna Fitzgerald* would be the best definition he could give. It's more than just the way I look: refugee-skinny with absolutely no chest
5   to speak of, hair the color of dirt, connect-the-dot freckles on my cheeks that, let me tell you, do not fade with lemon juice or sunscreen or even, sadly, sandpaper. No, God was obviously in some kind of mood on my birthday, because he added to this
10 fabulous physical combination the bigger picture— the household into which I was born. **1**

My parents tried to make things normal, but that's a relative term. The truth is, I was never really a kid. To be honest, neither were Kate and Jesse. I
15 guess maybe my brother had his moment in the sun for the four years he was alive before Kate got diagnosed, but ever since then, we've been too busy looking over our shoulders to run headlong into growing up. You know how most little kids
20 think they're like cartoon characters—if an anvil drops on their heads they can peel themselves off the sidewalk and keep going? Well, I never once believed that. How could I, when we practically set a place for Death at the dinner table? **2**

1 Name two things that Anna is criticizing.

2 Why didn't Anna and her siblings live a "normal" childhood?

acute

serious; severe; sharp

donor

a person who gives something in order to help a person or group

drastically

quickly and to a great degree

3 Why does Anna end up in the hospital with Kate?

4 Why do you think Anna's mom spends her free time like this?

25 Kate has **acute** promyelocytic leukemia. Actually, that's not quite true—right now she doesn't have it, but it's hibernating under her skin like a bear, until it decides to roar again. She was diagnosed when she was two; she's sixteen now. *Molecular relapse*
30 and *granulocyte* and *portacath*—these words are part of my vocabulary, even though I'll never find them on any SAT. I'm an allogeneic **donor**—a perfect sibling match. When Kate needs leukocytes or stem cells or bone marrow to fool her body into
35 thinking it's healthy, I'm the one who provides them. Nearly every time Kate's hospitalized, I wind up there, too. **3**

None of which means anything, except that you shouldn't believe what you hear about me, least of
40 all that which I tell you myself.

As I am coming up the stairs, my mother comes out of her room wearing another ball gown. "Ah," she says, turning her back to me. "Just the girl I wanted to see."

45 I zip it up and watch her twirl. My mother could be beautiful, if she were parachuted into someone else's life. She has long dark hair and the fine collarbones of a princess, but the corners of her mouth turn down, like she's swallowed bitter news. She doesn't
50 have much free time, since a calendar is something that can change **drastically** if my sister develops a bruise or a nosebleed, but what she does have she spends at Bluefly.com, ordering ridiculously fancy evening dresses for places she is never going to go.
55 "What do you think?" she asks. **4**

The gown is all the colors of a sunset, and made out of material that swishes when she moves. It's strapless, what a star might wear sashaying down a red carpet—totally not the dress code for a
60 suburban house in Upper Darby, RI. My mother twists her hair into a knot and holds it in place. On her bed are three other dresses—one slinky and black, one bugle-beaded, one that seems impossibly small. "You look . . ."

65   *Tired.* The word bubbles right under my lips.

My mother goes perfectly still, and I wonder if I've said it without meaning to. She holds up a hand, shushing me, her ear cocked to the open doorway. "Did you hear that?"

70   "Hear what?"

"Kate."

"I didn't hear anything."

But she doesn't take my word for it, because when it comes to Kate she doesn't take anybody's word for

75   it. She marches upstairs and opens up our bedroom door to find my sister hysterical on her bed, and just like that the world **collapses** again. My father, a closet astronomer, has tried to explain black holes to me, how they are so heavy they absorb everything,

80   even light, right into their center. Moments like this are the same kind of vacuum; no matter what you cling to, you wind up being sucked in. **5**

"Kate!" My mother sinks down to the floor, that stupid skirt a cloud around her. "Kate, honey,

85   what hurts?"

Kate hugs a pillow to her stomach, and tears keep streaming down her face. Her pale hair is stuck to her face in damp streaks; her breathing's too tight. I stand frozen in the doorway of my own room,

90   waiting for instructions: *Call Daddy. Call 911. Call Dr. Chance.* My mother goes so far as to shake a better explanation out of Kate. "It's Preston," she sobs. "He's leaving Serena for good."

That's when we notice the TV. On the screen, a

95   blond hottie gives a longing look to a woman crying almost as hard as my sister, and then he slams the

collapse
to fall down or fall apart suddenly

5 Why is Anna's mom worried?

assume

to believe something is true without first making sure

circumstance

an event or situation; the state of things

6 What is wrong with Kate?

door. "But what hurts?" my mother asks, certain there has to be more to it than this.

"Oh my *God*," Kate says, sniffling. "Do you have
100 any idea how much Serena and Preston have been through? Do you?" **6**

That fist inside me relaxes, now that I know it's all right. Normal, in our house, is like a blanket too short for a bed—sometimes it covers you just fine,
105 and other times it leaves you cold and shaking; and worst of all, you never know which of the two it's going to be. I sit down on the end of Kate's bed. Although I'm only thirteen, I'm taller than her and every now and then people mistakenly **assume** I'm
110 the older sister. At different times this summer she has been crazy for Callahan, Wyatt, and Liam, the male leads on this soap. Now, I guess, it's all about Preston. "There was the kidnapping scare," I volunteer. I actually followed that story line; Kate
115 made me tape the show during her dialysis sessions.

"And the time she almost married his twin by mistake," Kate adds.

"Don't forget when he died in the boat accident. For two months, anyway." My mother joins the
120 conversation, and I remember that she used to watch this soap, too, sitting with Kate in the hospital.

For the first time, Kate seems to notice my mother's outfit. "What are you *wearing*?"

125 "Oh. Something I'm sending back." She stands up in front of me so that I can undo her zipper. This mail-order compulsion, for any other mother, would be a wake-up call for therapy; for my mom, it would probably be considered a healthy break. I wonder if
130 it's putting on someone else's skin for a while that she likes so much, or if it's the option of being able to send back a **circumstance** that just doesn't suit you. She looks at Kate, hard. "You're sure nothing hurts?" **7**

7 What circumstance is Anna referring to?

After my mother leaves, Kate sinks a little. That's
135 the only way to describe it—how fast color drains
from her face, how she disappears against the
pillows. As she gets sicker, she fades a little more,
until I am afraid one day I will wake up and not be
able to see her at all. "Move," Kate orders. "You're
140 blocking the picture."

So I go to sit on my own bed. "It's only the coming
attractions."

"Well, if I die tonight I want to know what I'm
missing." **8**

145 I fluff my pillows up under my head. Kate, as usual,
has swapped so that she has all the funchy ones that
don't feel like rocks under your neck. She's supposed
to deserve this, because she's three years older than
me or because she's sick or because the moon is in
150 Aquarius—there's *always* a reason. I squint at the
television, wishing I could flip through the stations,
knowing I don't have a prayer. "Preston looks like
he's made out of plastic."

"Then why did I hear you whispering his name last
155 night into your pillow?"

"Shut up," I say.

"*You* shut up." Then Kate smiles at me. "He probably
is gay, though. Quite a waste, considering the
Fitzgerald sisters are—" **Wincing**, she breaks off
160 mid-sentence, and I roll toward her.

"Kate?"

She rubs her lower back. "It's nothing."

It's her kidneys. "Want me to get Mom?"

wince
to make a face
in response to
something painful
or unpleasant

8 Why does Kate
want to see the
previews?

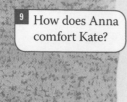

9 How does Anna comfort Kate?

"Not yet." She reaches between our beds, which are
165 just far apart enough for us to touch each other if
we both try. I hold out my hand, too. When we were
little we'd make this bridge and try to see how many
Barbies we could get to balance on it.

Lately, I have been having nightmares, where I'm cut
170 into so many pieces that there isn't enough of me to
be put back together.

❖

My father says that a fire will burn itself out, unless
you open a window and give it fuel. I suppose that's
what I'm doing, when you get right down to it;
175 but then again, my dad also says that when flames
are licking at your heels you've got to break a wall
or two if you want to escape. So when Kate falls
asleep from her meds I take the leather binder I
keep between my mattress and box spring and go
180 into the bathroom for privacy. I know Kate's been
snooping—I rigged up a red thread between the
zipper's teeth to let me know who was prying into
my stuff without my permission, but even though
the thread's been torn there's nothing missing
185 inside. I turn on the water in the bathtub so it
sounds like I'm in there for a reason, and sit down
on the floor to count.

If you add in the twenty dollars from the pawnshop,
I have $136.87. It's not going to be enough, but
190 there's got to be a way around that. Jesse didn't
have $2,900 when he bought his beat-up Jeep, and
the bank gave him some kind of loan. Of course,
my parents had to sign the papers, too, and I doubt
they're going to be willing to do that for me, given
195 the circumstances. I count the money a second
time, just in case the bills have miraculously
reproduced, but math is math and the total stays the
same. And then I read the newspaper clippings.

Campbell Alexander. It's a stupid name, in my
200 opinion. It sounds like a bar drink that costs too

much, or a brokerage firm. But you can't deny the man's track record. **10**

To reach my brother's room, you actually have to leave the house, which is exactly the way he likes it.
205 When Jesse turned sixteen he moved into the attic over the garage—a perfect arrangement, since he didn't want my parents to see what he was doing and my parents didn't really want to see. Blocking the stairs to his place are four snow tires, a small
210 wall of cartons, and an oak desk tipped onto its side. Sometimes I think Jesse sets up these **obstacles** himself, just to make getting to him more of a challenge.

I crawl over the mess and up the stairs, which
215 vibrate with the bass from Jesse's stereo. It takes nearly five whole minutes before he hears me knocking. "What?" he snaps, opening the door a crack.

"Can I come in?"

220 He thinks twice, then steps back to let me enter. The room is a sea of dirty clothes and magazines and leftover Chinese take-out cartons; it smells like the sweaty tongue of a hockey skate. The only neat spot is the shelf where Jesse keeps his special
225 collection—a Jaguar's silver mascot, a Mercedes symbol, a Mustang's horse—hood ornaments that he told me he just found lying around, although I'm not dumb enough to believe him.

Don't get me wrong—it isn't that my parents don't
230 care about Jesse or whatever trouble he's gotten himself mixed up in. It's just that they don't really have time to care about it, because it's a problem somewhere lower on the totem pole. **11**

obstacle
an object that is in someone's way

10 What do you think Anna is saving up for?

11 Why don't Anna's parents have time to care about what Jesse is doing?

inferno
a fire blazing out of control

Jesse ignores me, going back to whatever he was
235 doing on the far side of the mess. My attention is
caught by a Crock-Pot—one that disappeared out
of the kitchen a few months ago—which now sits
on top of Jesse's TV with a copper tube threaded
out of its lid and down through a plastic milk jug
240 filled with ice, emptying into a glass Mason jar.
Jesse may be a borderline delinquent, but he's
brilliant. Just as I'm about to touch the contraption,
Jesse turns around. "Hey!" He fairly flies over the
couch to knock my hand away. "You'll screw up the
245 condensing coil."

"Is this what I think it is?"

A nasty grin itches over his face. "Depends on what
you think it is." He jimmies out the Mason jar, so
that liquid drips onto the carpet. "Have a taste."

250 For a still made out of spit and glue, it produces
pretty potent moonshine whiskey. An **inferno** races
so fast through my belly and legs I fall back onto the
couch. "Disgusting," I gasp. **12**

12 What is Jesse
like?

Jesse laughs and takes a swig, too, although for
255 him it goes down easier. "So what do you want
from me?"

"How do you know I want something?"

"Because no one comes up here on a social call,"
he says, sitting on the arm of the couch. "And if it
260 was something about Kate, you would've already
told me."

"It *is* about Kate. Sort of." I press the newspaper
clippings into my brother's hand; they'll do a better
job explaining than I ever could. He scans them,
265 then looks me right in the eye. His are the palest
shade of silver, so surprising that sometimes when
he stares at you, you can completely forget what you
were planning to say.

270 "Don't mess with the system, Anna," he says bitterly. "We've all got our scripts down pat. Kate plays the Martyr. I'm the Lost Cause. And you, you're the Peacekeeper."

He thinks he knows me, but that goes both ways—and when it comes to **friction**, Jesse is an addict. I 275 look right at him. "Says who?" **13**

> **friction**
> disagreement or argument between people

> **13** Predict what Anna wants from Jesse.

As a successful fiction writer, Jodi Picoult makes it a mission to do extensive research for her novels to make sure her portrayal is as accurate as possible in a work of fiction. Research for her novel *Second Glance* led Picoult to the subject of stem cell research and its potential impact on society. "I personally am pro stem-cell research—there's too much good it can do to simply dismiss it. However, clearly, it's a slippery slope . . . I believe that we're all going to be forced to think about these issues within a few years . . . so why not first in fiction?" The book was published in 2003, but stem cell research continues to be a controversial issue. In all of her fiction, Picoult focuses on character development, as well as very detailed and accurate research, allowing the characters to present an issue from all points of view. She has captured the attention of many different genres, including fans of DC Comics as she wrote several issues for Wonder Woman. Her scope of creativity is not limited to one subject, and she touches on many sensitive topics such as autism in *House Rules*, our ability or inability to forgive evil in *The Storyteller*, and even musical theatre in *Over the Moon. My Sister's Keeper* was made into a feature film, and several of Picoult's other novels have been adapted into television movies.

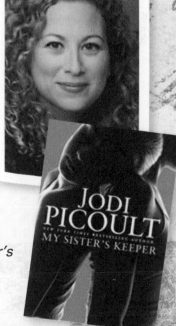

Phrasal Verbs

A **phrasal verb** is a verb phrase consisting of a verb followed by an adverb or a preposition. The adverb or preposition changes the meaning of the phrasal verb in idiomatic ways. Like an idiom, the meaning of the phrasal verb is different from the meanings of the individual words.

Phrasal Verb	Meaning	Phrasal Verb	Meaning
add up	add; total	**blow up**	cause to explode; destroy by explosives
break down	analyze; list the parts of separately	**bring up**	raise; care for from childhood
calm down	relax after being upset	**catch on**	learn; understand
catch up	get to the same point as someone else	**dream up**	invent; create
eat out	dine in a restaurant	**fill in**	complete (a printed form)
fill out	complete	**find out**	discover
get by	survive	**go on**	continue
hand in	submit	**hang up**	replace a telephone
leave out	omit	**look into**	investigate
look up	search for	**make up**	invent
pass down	teach or give something to the next generation	**play down**	minimize; lessen
point out	show; indicate	**put on**	put clothing or accessories on one's body
put out	extinguish	**run across**	find by accident
run down	slowly lose power so as to stop functioning	**run into**	meet unexpectedly
set up	arrange	**show up**	arrive; appear unexpectedly
shut up	stop talking	**take off**	leave the ground
throw away	discard	**turn on**	cause to function; start
turn down	reject; lower	**wake up**	awaken
wind up	finish; arrive at a place in the end; tighten the spring of a watch or machine	**work out**	solve; be successful

Phrasal Verbs (*cont.*)

Read each sentence and underline the phrasal verb. Circle the correct meaning for the phrasal verb.

> **Example:** "Shut up," Anna says.
> **a.** close the cabinet   **b.** stop talking   **c.** close the door

1. Sometimes I think Jesse sets up these obstacles himself, just to make getting to him more of a challenge.

   a. arranges   **b.** fixes   **c.** finds

2. I turn on the water in the bathtub so it sounds like I'm in there for a reason.

   a. swirl   **b.** splash   **c.** start

3. Anna's mom put on her newest ball gown and twirled around in it.

   a. wore   **b.** sewed   **c.** unwrapped

4. Mom calms down once she realizes Kate is just upset about characters on a show.

   a. cries   **b.** screams   **c.** relaxes

5. Anna finds out she is a perfect sibling match.

   a. searches   **b.** learns   **c.** examines

6. I purposely leave out the part about Kate wincing in pain.

   a. remember   **b.** omit   **c.** exit

7. I look at Jesse's face and know he is catching on.

   a. understanding   **b.** grabbing   **c.** leaving

8. I show up at Jesse's doorstep.

   a. display   **b.** rise   **c.** arrive

Phrasal Verb or Prepositional Phrase

Read each sentence and underline the phrasal verb or prepositional phrase. Write the underlined phrases in the correct column in the chart below.

> **Examples:**
> Anna <u>ran across</u> several interesting articles in the newspaper.
> Kate ran <u>across the street</u> to visit a friend.

1. Nearly every time Kate's hospitalized, I wind up there, too.

2. An abandoned path winds up the mountain and across a small creek.

3. Decorative lights were hung in the trees and around the patio.

4. Kate plays down her discomfort so as not to alarm her mom.

5. Anna hung up after making an appointment to meet Campbell Alexander.

6. When he finds out what Anna is planning, Jesse is stunned.

7. Anna doesn't want to give up the fight for her sister's life, but she is tired of being in the hospital.

8. Jesse runs down the stairs and leaves his garage apartment.

9. Anna shows up at Mr. Alexander's office and expects him to help her.

10. Mom looks into Kate's eyes to make sure she's telling the truth.

Phrasal Verbs	Prepositional Phrases
ran across	across the street

Verbs: *Be, Do, Have*

Be	Past		Present		Future	
Person	**Singular**	**Plural**	**Singular**	**Plural**	**Singular**	**Plural**
First	I *was*	we *were*	I *am*	we *are*	I *will be*	we *will be*
Second	you *were*	you *were*	you *are*	you *are*	you *will be*	you *will be*
Third	he *was*	they *were*	she *is*	they *are*	it *will be*	they *will be*

Main Verb: She *is* an excellent tennis player.
Helping Verb: She *is practicing* her serve.

Do	Past		Present		Future	
Person	**Singular**	**Plural**	**Singular**	**Plural**	**Singular**	**Plural**
First	I *did*	we *did*	I *do*	we *do*	I *will do*	we *will do*
Second	you *did*	you *did*	you *do*	you *do*	you *will do*	you *will do*
Third	he *did*	they *did*	she *does*	they *do*	it *will do*	they *will do*

Main Verb: He *does* his chores before school each morning.
Helping Verb: He *does get up* earlier than his sister.

Have	Past		Present		Future	
Person	**Singular**	**Plural**	**Singular**	**Plural**	**Singular**	**Plural**
First	I *had*	we *had*	I *have*	we *have*	I *will have*	we *will have*
Second	you *had*	you *had*	you *have*	you *have*	you *will have*	you *will have*
Third	he *had*	they *had*	she *has*	they *have*	it *will have*	they *will have*

Main Verb: I *have* his letter in my hand.
Helping Verb: I *have read* his letter several times.

Verbs: *Be, Do, Have (cont.)*

Read each sentence and underline the form of *be, do,* or *have* that is used in the sentence. Determine if it is used as a main verb or helping verb and place a check mark in the appropriate column.

Sentences with *be, do,* or *have*	Main Verb	Helping Verb
Examples: Jesse <u>is living</u> in the attic above the garage.		✓
Jesse's room <u>is</u> a mess.	✓	
1. Kate has acute promyelocytic leukemia.		
2. She was diagnosed as a toddler.		
3. My mother has long dark hair and the fine collarbones of a princess.		
4. The gown is all the colors of a sunset, and made out of material that swishes when she moves.		
5. My father, a closet astronomer, has tried to explain black holes to me.		
6. Her pale hair is stuck to her face in damp streaks.		
7. "Preston's leaving Serena for good," she sobs.		
8. Normal, in our house, is like a blanket too short for a bed.		
9. "Move," Kate orders. "You're blocking the picture."		
10. "So what do you want from me?" Jesse asks.		

Negative Statements

- The negative word *not* is added to the sentence after the helping verb and before the main verb:
  - Mother has tried on her new dress. (positive statement)
  - Mother has not tried on her new dress. (negative statement)
- If there is no helping verb, the proper form of *do* is added and followed by the word *not*:
  - Mother tried on her new dress. (positive statement)
  - Mother did not try on her new dress. (negative statement)
- *Not* is often written as a contraction:
  - I have not told Kate.
  - I haven't told Kate.
- Do not use two negative words to express a negative statement:
  - Incorrect: I have not done nothing.
  - Correct: I have not done anything.
    OR I have done nothing.

Negative/Positive Word Pairs	
Negative	**Positive**
none/no	any/some
no one	anyone/someone/everyone
nothing	anything/something
nobody	anybody/somebody
never	ever
neither/nor	either/or

Negative Statements (*cont.*)

Read each sentence and circle all of the words that express a negative.

> **Example:** The truth is, I was (never) really a kid.

1. To be honest, neither were Kate and Jesse.

2. Well, I never once believed that.

3. Actually, that's not quite true—right now she doesn't have it, but it's hibernating under her skin like a bear, until it decides to roar again.

4. None of which means anything, except that you shouldn't believe what you hear about me, least of all that which I tell you myself.

5. It's strapless, what a star might wear sashaying down a red carpet—totally not the dress code for a suburban house in Upper Darby, RI.

6. "Well, I didn't hear anything. "

7. But she doesn't take my word for it, because when it comes to Kate she doesn't take anybody's word for it.

8. "Don't forget when he died in the boat accident."

9. She looks at Kate, hard. "You're sure nothing hurts?"

10. I squint at the television, wishing I could flip through the stations, knowing I don't have a prayer.

11. She rubs her lower back. "It's nothing."

12. Lately, I have been having nightmares, where I'm cut into so many pieces that there isn't enough of me to be put back together.

13. Jesse didn't have $2,900 when he bought his beat-up Jeep, and the bank gave him some kind of loan.

14. But you can't deny the man's track record.

15. When Jesse turned sixteen he moved into the attic over the garage—a perfect arrangement, since he didn't want my parents to see what he was doing and my parents didn't really want to see.

Double Negatives

Rewrite each of the following sentences two ways to correct the double negative.

> **Example:** Mother hasn't gotten no new dresses today.
> <u>Mother hasn't gotten any new dresses today.</u>
> <u>Mother has gotten no new dresses today.</u>

1. I don't have nothing to say.

   _____

   _____

   _____

2. Jesse doesn't have no friends in his apartment.

   _____

   _____

   _____

3. Mother doesn't trust no one when it comes to Kate.

   _____

   _____

   _____

4. Anna doesn't expect nothing from her mom.

   _____

   _____

   _____

5. My parents don't have no time left to give Jesse or me.

   _____

   _____

   _____

   _____

Passage Comprehension

Reread Part 1 of the excerpt from *My Sister's Keeper*. Respond to each prompt using complete sentences. Refer to the chart on pages 14 and 15 to determine how to respond to each prompt.

1. Compare and contrast Anna and Kate.

_____

_____

_____

_____

_____

_____

_____

_____

2. Contrast Anna with Jesse.

_____

_____

_____

_____

_____

_____

_____

3. Cite evidence to prove that Kate's illness is life-threatening.

_____

_____

_____

_____

_____

_____

_____

Passage Comprehension (*cont.*)

4. Demonstrate understanding of the relationship between Anna and Kate through an illustration.

5. Cite evidence to prove that Anna is in conflict regarding her sister's illness.

6. Compare the section Black Hole of Control in Unit 10's "Say Yes to Free Dress!" to the Fitzgeralds' black hole.

Close Reading

Read the text.

> ### from *My Sister's Keeper*, PART 1
>
> If Mr. Webster had decided to put the word *freak* in his dictionary, *Anna Fitzgerald* would be the best definition he could give. It's more than just the way I look: refugee-skinny with absolutely no chest to speak of, hair the color of dirt, connect-the-dot freckles on my cheeks that, let me tell
> 5 you, do not fade with lemon juice or sunscreen or even, sadly, sandpaper. No, God was obviously in some kind of mood on my birthday, because he added to this fabulous physical combination the bigger picture—the household into which I was born.
>
> My parents tried to make things normal, but that's a relative term. The
> 10 truth is, I was never really a kid. To be honest, neither were Kate and Jesse. I guess maybe my brother had his moment in the sun for the four years he was alive before Kate got diagnosed, but ever since then, we've been too busy looking over our shoulders to run headlong into growing up. You know how most little kids think they're like cartoon characters—
> 15 if an anvil drops on their heads they can peel themselves off the sidewalk and keep going? Well, I never once believed that. How could I, when we practically set a place for Death at the dinner table?

Close Reading (*cont.*)

Kate has **acute** promyelocytic leukemia. Actually, that's not quite true—
right now she doesn't have it, but it's hibernating under her skin like a
20 bear, until it decides to roar again. She was diagnosed when she was two;
she's sixteen now. *Molecular relapse* and *granulocyte* and *portacath*—
these words are part of my vocabulary, even though I'll never find them
on any SAT. I'm an allogeneic **donor**—a perfect sibling match. When
Kate needs leukocytes or stem cells or bone marrow to fool her body into
25 thinking it's healthy, I'm the one who provides them. Nearly every time
Kate's hospitalized, I wind up there, too.

None of which means anything, except that you shouldn't believe what
you hear about me, least of all that which I tell you myself.

As I am coming up the stairs, my mother comes out of her room wearing
30 another ball gown. "Ah," she says, turning her back to me. "Just the girl I
wanted to see."

I zip it up and watch her twirl. My mother could be beautiful, if she were
parachuted into someone else's life. She has long dark hair and the fine
collarbones of a princess, but the corners of her mouth turn down, like
35 she's swallowed bitter news. She doesn't have much free time, since a
calendar is something that can change **drastically** if my sister develops a
bruise or a nosebleed, but what she does have she spends at Bluefly.com,
ordering ridiculously fancy evening dresses for places she is never going
to go. "What do you think?" she asks.

Close Reading (*cont.*)

40 The gown is all the colors of a sunset, and made out of material that swishes when she moves. It's strapless, what a star might wear sashaying down a red carpet—totally not the dress code for a suburban house in Upper Darby, RI. My mother twists her hair into a knot and holds it in place. On her bed are three other dresses—one slinky and black, one
45 bugle-beaded, one that seems impossibly small. "You look . . ."

Tired. The word bubbles right under my lips.

My mother goes perfectly still, and I wonder if I've said it without meaning to. She holds up a hand, shushing me, her ear cocked to the open doorway. "Did you hear that?"

50 "Hear what?"

"Kate."

"I didn't hear anything."

But she doesn't take my word for it, because when it comes to Kate she doesn't take anybody's word for it. She marches upstairs and opens up our
55 bedroom door to find my sister hysterical on her bed, and just like that the world **collapses** again. My father, a closet astronomer, has tried to explain black holes to me, how they are so heavy they absorb everything, even light, right into their center. Moments like this are the same kind of vacuum; no matter what you cling to, you wind up being sucked in.

60 "Kate!" My mother sinks down to the floor, that stupid skirt a cloud around her. "Kate, honey, what hurts?"

Kate hugs a pillow to her stomach, and tears keep streaming down her face. Her pale hair is stuck to her face in damp streaks; her breathing's too tight. I stand frozen in the doorway of my own room, waiting for
65 instructions: *Call Daddy. Call 911. Call Dr. Chance.* My mother goes so far as to shake a better explanation out of Kate. "It's Preston," she sobs. "He's leaving Serena for good."

That's when we notice the TV. On the screen, a blond hottie gives a longing look to a woman crying almost as hard as my sister, and then he
70 slams the door. "But what hurts?" my mother asks, certain there has to be more to it than this.

Close Reading (*cont.*)

"Oh my *God*," Kate says, sniffling. "Do you have any idea how much Serena and Preston have been through? Do you?"

75 That fist inside me relaxes, now that I know it's all right. Normal, in our house, is like a blanket too short for a bed—sometimes it covers you just fine, and other times it leaves you cold and shaking; and worst of all, you never know which of the two it's going to be. I sit down on the end of Kate's bed. Although I'm only thirteen, I'm taller than her and every now and then people mistakenly **assume** I'm the older sister. At different
80 times this summer she has been crazy for Callahan, Wyatt, and Liam, the male leads on this soap. Now, I guess, it's all about Preston. "There was the kidnapping scare," I volunteer. I actually followed that story line; Kate made me tape the show during her dialysis sessions.

"And the time she almost married his twin by mistake," Kate adds.

85 "Don't forget when he died in the boat accident. For two months, anyway." My mother joins the conversation, and I remember that she used to watch this soap, too, sitting with Kate in the hospital.

For the first time, Kate seems to notice my mother's outfit. "What are you *wearing*?"

90 "Oh. Something I'm sending back." She stands up in front of me so that I can undo her zipper. This mail-order compulsion, for any other mother, would be a wake-up call for therapy; for my mom, it would probably be considered a healthy break. I wonder if it's putting on someone else's skin for a while that she likes so much, or if it's the option of being able to send
95 back a **circumstance** that just doesn't suit you. She looks at Kate, hard. "You're sure nothing hurts?"

Close Reading (*cont.*)

After my mother leaves, Kate sinks a little. That's the only way to describe it—how fast color drains from her face, how she disappears against the pillows. As she gets sicker, she fades a little more, until I am afraid one
100 day I will wake up and not be able to see her at all. "Move," Kate orders. "You're blocking the picture."

So I go to sit on my own bed. "It's only the coming attractions."

"Well, if I die tonight I want to know what I'm missing."

I fluff my pillows up under my head. Kate, as usual, has swapped so that
105 she has all the funchy ones that don't feel like rocks under your neck. She's supposed to deserve this, because she's three years older than me or because she's sick or because the moon is in Aquarius—there's *always* a reason. I squint at the television, wishing I could flip through the stations, knowing I don't have a prayer. "Preston looks like he's made out
110 of plastic."

"Then why did I hear you whispering his name last night into your pillow?"

"Shut up," I say.

"*You* shut up." Then Kate smiles at me. "He probably is gay, though. Quite
115 a waste, considering the Fitzgerald sisters are—" **Wincing**, she breaks off mid-sentence, and I roll toward her.

"Kate?"

She rubs her lower back. "It's nothing."

It's her kidneys. "Want me to get Mom?"

120 "Not yet." She reaches between our beds, which are just far apart enough for us to touch each other if we both try. I hold out my hand, too. When we were little we'd make this bridge and try to see how many Barbies we could get to balance on it.

Close Reading (*cont.*)

Lately, I have been having nightmares, where I'm cut into so many pieces
125 that there isn't enough of me to be put back together.

My father says that a fire will burn itself out, unless you open a window
and give it fuel. I suppose that's what I'm doing, when you get right down
to it; but then again, my dad also says that when flames are licking at your
heels you've got to break a wall or two if you want to escape. So when
130 Kate falls asleep from her meds I take the leather binder I keep between
my mattress and box spring and go into the bathroom for privacy. I know
Kate's been snooping—I rigged up a red thread between the zipper's teeth
to let me know who was prying into my stuff without my permission, but
even though the thread's been torn there's nothing missing inside. I turn
135 on the water in the bathtub so it sounds like I'm in there for a reason, and
sit down on the floor to count.

If you add in the twenty dollars from the pawnshop, I have $136.87. It's
not going to be enough, but there's got to be a way around that. Jesse
didn't have $2,900 when he bought his beat-up Jeep, and the bank gave
140 him some kind of loan. Of course, my parents had to sign the papers,
too, and I doubt they're going to be willing to do that for me, given the
circumstances. I count the money a second time, just in case the bills
have miraculously reproduced, but math is math and the total stays the
same. And then I read the newspaper clippings.

145 Campbell Alexander. It's a stupid name, in my opinion. It sounds like a
bar drink that costs too much, or a brokerage firm. But you can't deny the
man's track record.

Close Reading (*cont.*)

150 To reach my brother's room, you actually have to leave the house, which is exactly the way he likes it. When Jesse turned sixteen he moved into the attic over the garage—a perfect arrangement, since he didn't want my parents to see what he was doing and my parents didn't really want to see. Blocking the stairs to his place are four snow tires, a small wall of cartons, and an oak desk tipped onto its side. Sometimes I think Jesse sets up these **obstacles** himself, just to make getting to him more of a 155 challenge.

I crawl over the mess and up the stairs, which vibrate with the bass from Jesse's stereo. It takes nearly five whole minutes before he hears me knocking. "What?" he snaps, opening the door a crack.

"Can I come in?"

160 He thinks twice, then steps back to let me enter. The room is a sea of dirty clothes and magazines and leftover Chinese take-out cartons; it smells like the sweaty tongue of a hockey skate. The only neat spot is the shelf where Jesse keeps his special collection—a Jaguar's silver mascot, a Mercedes symbol, a Mustang's horse—hood ornaments that he told me he just found 165 lying around, although I'm not dumb enough to believe him.

Don't get me wrong—it isn't that my parents don't care about Jesse or whatever trouble he's gotten himself mixed up in. It's just that they don't really have time to care about it, because it's a problem somewhere lower on the totem pole.

170 Jesse ignores me, going back to whatever he was doing on the far side of the mess. My attention is caught by a Crock-Pot—one that disappeared out of the kitchen a few months ago—which now sits on top of Jesse's TV with a copper tube threaded out of its lid and down through a plastic milk jug filled with ice, emptying into a glass Mason jar. Jesse may be a 175 borderline delinquent, but he's brilliant. Just as I'm about to touch the contraption, Jesse turns around. "Hey!" He fairly flies over the couch to knock my hand away. "You'll screw up the condensing coil."

Close Reading (*cont.*)

"Is this what I think it is?"

180 A nasty grin itches over his face. "Depends on what you think it is." He jimmies out the Mason jar, so that liquid drips onto the carpet. "Have a taste."

For a still made out of spit and glue, it produces pretty potent moonshine whiskey. An **inferno** races so fast through my belly and legs I fall back onto the couch. "Disgusting," I gasp.

185 Jesse laughs and takes a swig, too, although for him it goes down easier. "So what do you want from me?"

"How do you know I want something?"

"Because no one comes up here on a social call," he says, sitting on the arm of the couch. "And if it was something about Kate, you would've
190 already told me."

"It *is* about Kate. Sort of." I press the newspaper clippings into my brother's hand; they'll do a better job explaining than I ever could. He scans them, then looks me right in the eye. His are the palest shade of silver, so surprising that sometimes when he stares at you, you can
195 completely forget what you were planning to say.

"Don't mess with the system, Anna," he says bitterly. "We've all got our scripts down pat. Kate plays the Martyr. I'm the Lost Cause. And you, you're the Peacekeeper."

He thinks he knows me, but that goes both ways—and when it comes to
200 **friction**, Jesse is an addict. I look right at him. "Says who?"

Quick Write in Response to Reading

Kate's illness has had a dramatic impact on her relationship with her siblings. Describe the relationship between Anna and Kate. Consider what you know about their personalities and character traits and how these traits impact their relationship.

Let's Focus: Part 2 of the Excerpt from *My Sister's Keeper*

Content Focus
savior sibling
family dynamics

Type of Text
_____

Author's Name _____

Author's Purpose _____

Big Ideas
Consider the following Big Idea questions. Write your answer for each question.

Is it ethical to hurt one person to help another? Explain.

_____

_____

How do you decide whether to accept a given circumstance or fight it with everything you can?

_____

_____

Preview: Part 2 of the excerpt from *My Sister's Keeper* on pages 371–375.
Predict what will happen in this excerpt based on your knowledge of Part 1.

_____

_____

_____

_____

Enduring Understandings
After reading the text . . .

_____

_____

_____

_____

_____

Key Passage Vocabulary: from *My Sister's Keeper*, Part 2

Read each word. Write the word in column 3. Then, circle a number to rate your knowledge of the word.

Read the Word	Part of Speech	Write the Word	Rate the Word
lacking	(adj)		0 1 2 3
interrupt	(v)		0 1 2 3
verdict	(n)		0 1 2 3
consume	(v)		0 1 2 3
primitive	(adj)		0 1 2 3
tenacity	(n)		0 1 2 3
automatically	(adv)		0 1 2 3
exalted	(adj)		0 1 2 3
(on) behalf	(n)		0 1 2 3
experimental	(adj)		0 1 2 3

from

My Sister's Keeper
PART 2

by Jodi Picoult

Jesse agrees to wait for me in the parking lot. It's one of the few times I can recall him doing anything I tell him to do. I walk around to the front of the building, which has two gargoyles guarding 280 its entrance.

Campbell Alexander, Esquire's office is on the third floor. The walls are paneled with wood the color of a chestnut mare's coat, and when I step onto the thick Oriental rug on the floor, my sneakers sink an 285 inch. The secretary is wearing black pumps so shiny I can see my own face in them. I glance down at my cutoffs and the Keds that I tattooed last week with Magic Markers when I was bored. **1**

The secretary has perfect skin and perfect eyebrows 290 and honeybee lips, and she's using them to scream bloody murder at whoever's on the other end of the phone. "You cannot expect me to tell a judge that. Just because *you* don't want to hear Kleman rant and rave doesn't mean that *I* have to . . . no, 295 actually, that raise was for the exceptional job I do and the crap I put up with on a daily basis, and as

1 Where is Anna? Why is she feeling uncomfortable?

lacking

missing something; not having enough of something

interrupt

to say or do something that causes another person to stop doing something

verdict

a decision, a judgment, or a ruling

consume

to take in; to read or process information

2 What is the secretary basing her first impression on?

3 How does Anna get the secretary to change her mind?

a matter of fact, while we're on—" She holds the phone away from her ear; I can make out the buzz of disconnection. "Bastard," she mutters, and then
300 seems to realize I'm standing three feet away. "Can I help you?"

She looks me over from head to toe, rating me on a general scale of first impressions, and finding me severely **lacking**. I lift my chin and pretend
305 to be far more cool than I actually am. "I have an appointment with Mr. Alexander. At four o'clock." **2**

"Your voice," she says. "On the phone, you didn't sound quite so . . ."

Young?

310 She smiles uncomfortably. "We don't try juvenile cases, as a rule. If you'd like I can offer you the names of some practicing attorneys who—"

I take a deep breath. "Actually," I **interrupt**, "you're wrong. Smith v. Whately, Edmunds v. Womens
315 and Infants Hospital, and Jerome v. the Diocese of Providence all involved litigants under the age of eighteen. All three resulted in **verdicts** for Mr. Alexander's clients. And those were just in the past *year*."

320 The secretary blinks at me. Then a slow smile toasts her face, as if she's decided she just might like me after all. "Come to think of it, why don't you just wait in his office?" she suggests, and she stands up to show me the way. **3**

325 Even if I spend every minute of the rest of my life reading, I do not believe that I will ever manage to **consume** the sheer number of words routed high and low on the walls of Campbell Alexander, Esquire's office. I do the math—if there are 400
330 words or so on every page, and each of those legal

books are 400 pages, and there are twenty on a shelf and six shelves per bookcase—why, you're pushing nineteen million words, and that's only partway across the room.

335 I'm alone in the office long enough to note that his desk is so neat, you could play Chinese football on the blotter; that there is not a single photo of a wife or a kid or even himself; and that in spite of the fact that the room is spotless, there's a mug full of water
340 sitting on the floor.

I find myself making up explanations: it's a swimming pool for an army of ants. It's some kind of **primitive** humidifier. It's a mirage.

I've nearly convinced myself about that last one, and
345 am leaning over to touch it to see if it's real, when the door bursts open. I practically fall out of my chair and that puts me eye to eye with an incoming German shepherd, which spears me with a look and then marches over to the mug and starts to drink. **4**

350 Campbell Alexander comes in, too. He's got black hair and he's at least as tall as my dad—six feet— with a right-angle jaw and eyes that look frozen over. He shrugs out of a suit jacket and hangs it neatly on the back of the door, then yanks a file out
355 of a cabinet before moving to his desk. He never makes eye contact with me, but he starts talking all the same. "I don't want any Girl Scout cookies," Campbell Alexander says. "Although you do get Brownie points for **tenacity**. Ha." He smiles at his
360 own joke.

"I'm not selling anything."

He glances at me curiously, then pushes a button on his phone. "Kerri," he says when the secretary answers. "What is this doing in my office?"

primitive
simple and old-fashioned; an early model of something

tenacity
stubbornness; the quality of not giving up easily

4 What personality traits of Anna are evident in the office?

automatically
without thinking

exalted
of high value or status

(on) behalf
in someone's place or to help someone

experimental
using new methods or ideas that may or may not work

5 How does Alexander receive Anna's offer?

6 What connects Campbell Alexander to Kate?

365 "I'm here to retain you," I say.

The lawyer releases the intercom button. "I don't think so." **5**

"You don't even know if I have a case."

I take a step forward; so does the dog. For the first
370 time I realize it's wearing one of those vests with a red cross on it, like a St. Bernard that might carry rum up a snowy mountain. I **automatically** reach out to pet him. "Don't," Alexander says. "Judge is a service dog."

375 My hand goes back to my side. "But you aren't blind."

"Thank you for pointing that out to me."

"So what's the matter with you?"

The minute I say it, I want to take it back. Haven't I watched Kate field this question from hundreds of
380 rude people?

"I have an iron lung," Campbell Alexander says curtly, "and the dog keeps me from getting too close to magnets. Now, if you'd do me the **exalted** honor of leaving, my secretary can find you the name of
385 someone who—" **6**

But I can't go yet. "Did you really sue God?" I take out all the newspaper clippings, smooth them on the bare desk.

A muscle tics in his cheek, and then he picks
390 up the article lying on top. "I sued the Diocese of Providence, on **behalf** of a kid in one of their orphanages who needed an **experimental** treatment involving fetal tissue, which they felt violated Vatican II. However, it makes a much better
395 headline to say that a nine-year-old is suing God for being stuck with the short end of the straw in life." I just stare at him. "Dylan Jerome," the lawyer

admits, "wanted to sue God for not caring enough about him."

400 A rainbow might as well have cracked down the middle of that big mahogany desk. "Mr. Alexander," I say, "my sister has leukemia." **7**

"I'm sorry to hear that. But even if I were willing to litigate against God again, which I'm not, you can't
405 bring a lawsuit on someone else's behalf."

There is way too much to explain—my own blood seeping into my sister's veins; the nurses holding me down to stick me for white cells Kate might borrow; the doctor saying they didn't get enough the first
410 time around. The bruises and the deep bone ache after I gave up my marrow; the shots that sparked more stem cells in me, so that there'd be extra for my sister. The fact that I'm not sick, but I might as well be. The fact that the only reason I was born
415 was as a harvest crop for Kate. The fact that even now, a major decision about me is being made, and no one's bothered to ask the one person who most deserves it to speak her opinion.

There's way too much to explain, and so I do the
420 best I can. "It's not God. Just my parents," I say. "I want to sue them for the rights to my own body." **8**

> **7** What gives Anna hope?

> **8** What is Anna's life like?

Critical Understandings

Respond to each prompt using complete sentences. Refer to the chart on pages 14 and 15 to determine how to respond to each prompt.

1. Connect Principal Dogan's quote "How we dress does matter" with the secretary's first impression of Anna.

_____

_____

_____

_____

_____

_____

_____

_____

_____

_____

2. Illustrate Anna's maturity during her visit to the lawyer's office.

_____

_____

_____

_____

_____

_____

_____

_____

_____

_____

_____

Critical Understandings (*cont.*)

3. Synthesize the information in the last three paragraphs of the first excerpt with the first paragraph of the second excerpt to determine what Jesse values.

_____

_____

_____

_____

_____

_____

_____

_____

_____

_____

4. Assess Anna's statement ". . . I'm not sick, but I might as well be."

_____

_____

_____

_____

_____

_____

_____

_____

_____

_____

Passage Comprehension

Reread Part 2 of the excerpt from *My Sister's Keeper*. Respond to each prompt using complete sentences. Refer to the chart on pages 14 and 15 to determine how to respond to each prompt.

1. Illustrate the difference between the "normal" that Anna lives and the "normal" that she longs for.

_____

_____

_____

_____

_____

_____

_____

_____

2. Connect Anna's actions with the plot's suspense. Cite text evidence.

_____

_____

_____

_____

_____

_____

_____

_____

_____

_____

_____

Passage Comprehension (*cont.*)

3. Illustrate Anna's reason for suing her parents for the rights to her own body.

    _____

    _____

    _____

    _____

    _____

    _____

    _____

    _____

    _____

    _____

    _____

    _____

4. Synthesize Kate's point of view and Anna's parents' points of view to convince Anna to keep things as is.

    _____

    _____

    _____

    _____

    _____

    _____

    _____

    _____

    _____

    _____

    _____

Passage Comprehension (*cont.*)

5. Connect Kate to Campbell Alexander.

_____
_____
_____
_____
_____
_____
_____
_____
_____
_____
_____
_____

6. Use both excerpts to assess Anna's case for the rights to her own body.

_____
_____
_____
_____
_____
_____
_____
_____
_____
_____
_____
_____

Close Reading

Read the text.

---

from *My Sister's Keeper*, PART 2

Jesse agrees to wait for me in the parking lot. It's one of the few times I can recall him doing anything I tell him to do. I walk around to the front of the building, which has two gargoyles guarding its entrance.

5 Campbell Alexander, Esquire's office is on the third floor. The walls are paneled with wood the color of a chestnut mare's coat, and when I step onto the thick Oriental rug on the floor, my sneakers sink an inch. The secretary is wearing black pumps so shiny I can see my own face in them. I glance down at my cutoffs and the Keds that I tattooed last week with Magic Markers when I was bored.

10 The secretary has perfect skin and perfect eyebrows and honeybee lips, and she's using them to scream bloody murder at whoever's on the other end of the phone. "You cannot expect me to tell a judge that. Just because *you* don't want to hear Kleman rant and rave doesn't mean that *I* have to . . . no, actually, that raise was for the exceptional job I do and the 15 crap I put up with on a daily basis, and as a matter of fact, while we're on—" She holds the phone away from her ear; I can make out the buzz of disconnection. "Bastard," she mutters, and then seems to realize I'm standing three feet away. "Can I help you?"

Close Reading (*cont.*)

20 She looks me over from head to toe, rating me on a general scale of first impressions, and finding me severely **lacking**. I lift my chin and pretend to be far more cool than I actually am. "I have an appointment with Mr. Alexander. At four o'clock."

"Your voice," she says. "On the phone, you didn't sound quite so . . ."

Young?

25 She smiles uncomfortably. "We don't try juvenile cases, as a rule. If you'd like I can offer you the names of some practicing attorneys who—"

I take a deep breath. "Actually," I **interrupt**, "you're wrong. Smith v. Whately, Edmunds v. Womens and Infants Hospital, and Jerome v. the Diocese of Providence all involved litigants under the age of eighteen. All

30 three resulted in **verdicts** for Mr. Alexander's clients. And those were just in the past *year*."

The secretary blinks at me. Then a slow smile toasts her face, as if she's decided she just might like me after all. "Come to think of it, why don't you just wait in his office?" she suggests, and she stands up to show me

35 the way.

Even if I spend every minute of the rest of my life reading, I do not believe that I will ever manage to **consume** the sheer number of words routed high and low on the walls of Campbell Alexander, Esquire's office. I do the math—if there are 400 words or so on every page, and each of those

40 legal books are 400 pages, and there are twenty on a shelf and six shelves per bookcase—why, you're pushing nineteen million words, and that's only partway across the room.

Close Reading (*cont.*)

I'm alone in the office long enough to note that his desk is so neat, you could play Chinese football on the blotter; that there is not a single photo
45 of a wife or a kid or even himself; and that in spite of the fact that the room is spotless, there's a mug full of water sitting on the floor.

I find myself making up explanations: it's a swimming pool for an army of ants. It's some kind of **primitive** humidifier. It's a mirage.

I've nearly convinced myself about that last one, and am leaning over to
50 touch it to see if it's real, when the door bursts open. I practically fall out of my chair and that puts me eye to eye with an incoming German shepherd, which spears me with a look and then marches over to the mug and starts to drink.

Campbell Alexander comes in, too. He's got black hair and he's at least as
55 tall as my dad—six feet—with a right-angle jaw and eyes that look frozen over. He shrugs out of a suit jacket and hangs it neatly on the back of the door, then yanks a file out of a cabinet before moving to his desk. He never makes eye contact with me, but he starts talking all the same. "I don't want any Girl Scout cookies," Campbell Alexander says. "Although
60 you do get Brownie points for **tenacity**. Ha." He smiles at his own joke.

"I'm not selling anything."

He glances at me curiously, then pushes a button on his phone. "Kerri," he says when the secretary answers. "What is this doing in my office?"

"I'm here to retain you," I say.

65 The lawyer releases the intercom button. "I don't think so."

"You don't even know if I have a case."

Close Reading (*cont.*)

I take a step forward; so does the dog. For the first time I realize it's wearing one of those vests with a red cross on it, like a St. Bernard that might carry rum up a snowy mountain. I **automatically** reach out to
70 pet him. "Don't," Alexander says. "Judge is a service dog."

My hand goes back to my side. "But you aren't blind."

"Thank you for pointing that out to me."

"So what's the matter with you?"

The minute I say it, I want to take it back. Haven't I watched Kate field
75 this question from hundreds of rude people?

"I have an iron lung," Campbell Alexander says curtly, "and the dog keeps me from getting too close to magnets. Now, if you'd do me the **exalted** honor of leaving, my secretary can find you the name of someone who—"

But I can't go yet. "Did you really sue God?" I take out all the newspaper
80 clippings, smooth them on the bare desk.

A muscle tics in his cheek, and then he picks up the article lying on top. "I sued the Diocese of Providence, on **behalf** of a kid in one of their orphanages who needed an **experimental** treatment involving fetal tissue, which they felt violated Vatican II. However, it makes a much
85 better headline to say that a nine-year-old is suing God for being stuck with the short end of the straw in life." I just stare at him. "Dylan Jerome," the lawyer admits, "wanted to sue God for not caring enough about him."

A rainbow might as well have cracked down the middle of that big mahogany desk. "Mr. Alexander," I say, "my sister has leukemia."

90 "I'm sorry to hear that. But even if I were willing to litigate against God again, which I'm not, you can't bring a lawsuit on someone else's behalf."

Close Reading (*cont.*)

There is way too much to explain—my own blood seeping into my sister's veins; the nurses holding me down to stick me for white cells Kate might borrow; the doctor saying they didn't get enough the first time around.

95 The bruises and the deep bone ache after I gave up my marrow; the shots that sparked more stem cells in me, so that there'd be extra for my sister. The fact that I'm not sick, but I might as well be. The fact that the only reason I was born was as a harvest crop for Kate. The fact that even now, a major decision about me is being made, and no one's bothered to ask

100 the one person who most deserves it to speak her opinion.

There's way too much to explain, and so I do the best I can. "It's not God. Just my parents," I say. "I want to sue them for the rights to my own body."

Prepare to Write: Character Analysis Essay

Part A. Study the Prompt

Read the following prompt and determine the topic, directions, and purpose for writing.

Each character in the Fitzgerald family has developed unique ways to cope with Kate's illness. Write an essay that uses text evidence to describe Mom's, Jesse's, and Anna's coping mechanisms. If you were a member of the Fitzgerald family, which coping mechanism would you adopt?

Topic: _____

Directions: _____

_____

_____

Purpose for Writing: _____

_____

_____

Part B. Write an Introductory Paragraph and Thesis Statement

The opening paragraph needs to contain an introduction to the topic. It should state the similarities between the characters and their coping mechanisms and set the framework for examining and documenting the differences.

_____

_____

_____

_____

_____

_____

_____

_____

_____

_____

_____

_____

Prepare to Write: Character Analysis Essay (*cont.*)

Part C. Organize Information

Character	Coping Mechanism	Text Evidence
Mom		
Jesse		
Anna		

Prepare to Write: Character Analysis Essay (*cont.*)
Part D. Write Body Paragraph Topic Sentences

Write a topic sentence that introduces each character:

Mom: _____

_____

_____

Jesse: _____

_____

_____

Anna: _____

_____

_____

Prepare to Write: Character Analysis Essay (*cont.*)

Part E. Write a Conclusion

Restate your thesis by using a different topic sentence pattern. Summarize the characters' different strategies for coping. Close by adding your personal perspective on the character you would be like if you were a Fitzgerald.

_____

_____

_____

_____

_____

_____

_____

_____

_____

_____

_____

_____

_____

_____

_____

_____

_____

_____

_____

_____

_____

_____

The Literary Analysis Writer's Checklist

Trait	Yes	No	Did the writer . . .?
Ideas and Content			clearly state the thesis of the essay
			analyze and evaluate the elements found in the literature
			focus each paragraph on the topic
			include effective support for the thesis by giving details, examples, explanations, and quotations from the texts
Organization			write an introductory paragraph that captures the reader's interest and cites the titles of the works and the names of the authors
			include in the introductory paragraph a clear viewpoint on the topic and a "map" for the essay that follows
			sequence body paragraphs logically and use transition sentences that make clear the relationship between the ideas
			write a conclusion that ties the analysis together and offers an evaluation of the particulars
Voice and Audience Awareness			think about the audience and purpose for writing
			write in a clear and engaging way that makes the audience want to read the work
Word Choice			find a unique way to say things; avoid sounding repetitive
			use words that are lively and specific to the content
Sentence Fluency			write complete sentences
			expand some sentences using the steps of Masterpiece Sentences
			use compound sentence elements and compound sentences
Conventions			capitalize words correctly:
			capitalize the first word of each sentence
			capitalize proper nouns, including people's names
			punctuate correctly:
			end sentences with a period, question mark, or exclamation mark
			use an apostrophe for possessive nouns and contractions
			use commas and/or semicolons correctly
			use grammar correctly:
			use the correct verb tense
			make sure the verb agrees with the subject in number
			use correct spelling

from WHITE FANG

by Jack London

It was about this time that the newspapers were full of the daring escape of a convict from San Quentin prison. He was a ferocious man. He had been ill-made in the making. He had not been born right,
5   and he had not been helped any by the molding he had received at the hands of society. The hands of society are harsh, and this man was a striking sample of its handiwork. He was a beast—a human beast, it is true, but nevertheless so terrible a beast
10 that he can best be characterized as carnivorous. **1**

In San Quentin prison he had proved incorrigible. Punishment failed to break his spirit. He could die dumb-mad and fighting to the last, but he could not live and be beaten. The more fiercely he fought,
15 the more harshly society handled him, and the only effect of harshness was to make him fiercer. Straight-jackets to **restrain** him, starvation, and beatings and clubbings were the wrong treatment for Jim Hall; but it was the treatment he received. It
20 was the treatment he had received from the time he was a little pulpy, shapeable boy in a San Francisco slum—soft clay in the hands of society and ready to be formed into something. **2**

It was during Jim Hall's third term in prison that
25 he **encountered** a guard that was almost as great a beast as he. The guard treated him unfairly, lied about him to the warden, lost his credits, and persecuted him. The difference between them was that the guard carried a bunch of keys and a gun. Jim
30 Hall had only his naked hands and his teeth. But he sprang upon the guard one day and used his teeth on the other's throat just like any jungle animal.

restrain
to hold back

encounter
to meet; to come in contact with

1 What animal-like qualities does the prisoner have?

2 What kind of punishment did Jim Hall receive that did not lead to reform?

pursue

to chase; to go after

After this, Jim Hall went to live in the incorrigible cell. He lived there three years. The cell was of iron,
35 the floor, the walls, the roof. He never left this cell. He never saw the sky nor the sunshine. Day was a barely noticeable twilight and night was a black silence. He was in an iron tomb, buried alive. He saw no human face, spoke to no human thing. When his
40 food was shoved in to him, he growled like a wild animal. He hated all things. For days and nights he bellowed his rage loudly at the universe. Then, for weeks and months he never made a sound, in the black silence eating his very soul. He was a man
45 and a monstrosity, as fearful a thing of fear as ever imagined in the visions of a maddened brain. **3**

3 What was life like for Jim Hall before his attack on the prison guard and after his attack on the prison guard?

And then, one night, he escaped. The warders said it was impossible, but nevertheless the cell was empty, and half in half out of it lay the body of a
50 slain guard. Two other dead guards marked his trail through the prison to the outer walls, and he had killed with his hands to avoid noise.

He was armed with the weapons of the slain guards—a live arsenal that fled through the hills
55 **pursued** by the organized might of society. A heavy price of gold was upon his head. Greedy farmers hunted him with shotguns. His blood might pay off a loan or send a son to college. Public-spirited citizens took down their rifles and went out after
60 him. A pack of bloodhounds followed the way of his bleeding feet. And the sleuth-hounds of the law, the paid fighting animals of society, with telephone, and telegraph, and special train, clung to his trail night and day. **4**

4 Where did Jim Hall get his weapons?

65 Sometimes they came upon him, and men faced him like heroes, or stampeded through barbed-wire fences to the delight of the people reading the account at the breakfast table. It was after such encounters that the dead and wounded were carted
70 back to the towns, and their places filled by men eager for the manhunt.

And then Jim Hall disappeared. The bloodhounds **vainly** quested for him on the lost trail. Inoffensive, ordinary ranchers in remote valleys were held up by
75 armed men and **compelled** to identify themselves. While the remains of Jim Hall were discovered on a dozen mountainsides by greedy claimants for blood-money. **5**

In the meantime the newspapers were read at Sierra
80 Vista, not so much with interest as with anxiety, or worry. The women were afraid. Judge Scott pooh-poohed and laughed, but not with reason, for it was in his last days on the bench that Jim Hall had stood before him and received sentence. And in open
85 courtroom, before all men, Jim Hall had proclaimed that the day would come when he would wreak **vengeance** on the Judge that sentenced him.

For once, Jim Hall was right. He was innocent of the crime for which he was sentenced. It was a case, in
90 the language of thieves and police, of "railroading." Jim Hall was being "railroaded" to prison for a crime he had not committed. Because of the two prior convictions against him, Judge Scott imposed upon him a sentence of fifty years. **6**

95 Judge Scott did not know all things, and he did not know that he was party to a police conspiracy, that the evidence was hatched and falsified, that Jim Hall was guiltless of the crime charged. And Jim Hall, on the other hand, did not know that Judge Scott was
100 merely **ignorant**. Jim Hall believed that the judge knew all about it and was hand in glove with the police in the **promotion** of the monstrous injustice. So it was, when the doom of fifty years of living death was uttered by Judge Scott, that Jim Hall,
105 hating all things in the society that misused him, rose up and raged in the courtroom until dragged down by half a dozen of his blue-coated enemies. To him, Judge Scott was the keystone in the arch of injustice, and upon Judge Scott he emptied the
110 vials of his wrath and hurled the angry threats of his revenge yet to come. Then Jim Hall went to his living death . . . and escaped. **7**

vainly
without success; not achieving what one hoped to

compel
to make someone take a certain action

vengeance
the act of repaying one hurtful deed with another

ignorant
not knowing or having important information

promotion
an attempt to convince others that they should do, believe, or buy something

5 Why did so many men want to find Jim Hall?

6 What is Jim Hall's connection to Judge Scott?

7 In what ways are Jim Hall and Judge Scott both "falsely accused"?

from *White Fang*   **393**

advantage

something that puts you in a better position than others

ascent

an upward journey

8 Why do you think White Fang is introduced at this time?

9 Who is the strange god and the lovemaster?

Of all this White Fang knew nothing. But between him and Alice, the master's wife, there existed a
115 secret. Each night, after Sierra Vista had gone to bed, she rose and let in White Fang to sleep in the big hall. Now White Fang was not a house dog, nor was he permitted to sleep in the house; so each morning, early, she slipped down and let him out
120 before the family was awake. **8**

On one such night, while all the house slept, White Fang awoke and lay very quietly. And very quietly he smelled the air and read the message it bore of a strange god's presence. And to his ears came
125 sounds of the strange god's movements. White Fang burst into no furious outcry. It was not his way. The strange god walked softly, but more softly walked White Fang, for he had no clothes to rub against the flesh of his body. He followed silently. In the Wild
130 he had hunted live meat that was infinitely timid, and he knew the **advantage** of surprise.

The strange god paused at the foot of the great staircase and listened, and White Fang was as dead, so without movement was he as he watched and waited.
135 Up that staircase the way led to the lovemaster and to the lovemaster's dearest possessions. White Fang bristled, but waited. The strange god's foot lifted. He was beginning the **ascent**. **9**

Then it was that White Fang struck. He gave no
140 warning, with no snarl anticipated his own action.
Into the air he lifted his body in the spring that
landed him on the strange god's back. White Fang
clung with his forepaws to the man's shoulders, at
the same time burying his fangs into the back of the
145 man's neck. He clung on for a moment, long enough
to drag the god over backward. Together they
crashed to the floor. White Fang leaped clear, and,
as the man struggled to rise, was in again with the
slashing fangs. **10**

10 How did White
Fang complete
the mission
Alice had
given him?

*Wolf fang,
actual size*

Return of the Wolves

The wolf has taken on many images over time. It has been known as both the noblest animal and the vilest animal. Native Americans respect the wolf for its bravery, intelligence, **persistence**, hunting skills, and love of family. However, authors and storytellers have made the wolf the villain of many stories like *Little Red Riding Hood* and *The Three Pigs*. And of course Hollywood has put its spin on the wolf by creating horror films to scare us. But the true image of the wolf in North America today is one of **insecurity**. It is trying to fit back into the land over which it once reigned king. **1**

The wolf once ruled the West. Its spot at the top of the food chain was unchallenged for centuries. By the 1930s, however, this had changed. The wolf fell victim to overhunting and trapping. Laws did not protect it. By the early 1970s, the gray wolf had mostly vanished from the western United States. It was placed on the endangered species list. The federal government began a **relocation** project. Several dozen wolves were captured in Canada and released in Yellowstone National Park. This project was a great success. However, it created a division between people in the area. Some were for it. Others were against it. **2**

persistence
the ability to keep doing something even though it is difficult

insecurity
the state of not feeling safe or steady

relocation
the act of moving to a different place

1 What is your image of wolves?

2 How did the federal government protect wolves?

habitat
the natural home of a plant or animal

alter
to change

competition
the struggle between two or more people or groups who are trying to get the same thing

There have been many good things about the relocation of wolves to Yellowstone. For one, tourists love wolves. People who like seeing wildlife have come to the park to see the wolf in its **habitat** and to take pictures. Naturalists have seen the relocation of the wolf as a victory in returning the West to the way it used to be. In addition, the people who visit the park to see the wolves have boosted the economy greatly.

The reintroduction of wolves into Yellowstone has helped bring the elk population under control. Wolves are natural carnivores. Because elk and deer are their favorite meal, the populations of these animals have decreased. This is a positive change because the elk had overpopulated Yellowstone. **3**

Having too many elk had caused damage to aspen tree forests. This **altered** the beaver and bird populations. The flow of streams and rivers were changed as a result. The presence of wolves in the elk habitat creates what is called an "ecology of fear." Elk spend less time eating in one place. As a result, trees and shrubs grow back quicker. There's more variety in the plant life. In Yellowstone, researchers saw that open fields became more vegetated when they brought back wolves.

Because the wolf has returned, coyotes have been able to return to their natural habit of scavenging. Without wolves, coyotes had jumped up in the food chain. They could hunt animals without much **competition**. However, they struggled because they are not naturally good hunters. Having wolves in the area has provided more food for the coyotes. They feed on the remains of the wolves' kills. **4**

3 How has the reintroduction been good for the area?

4 How has the wolf's return affected elk, beavers, birds, coyotes, and aspen trees?

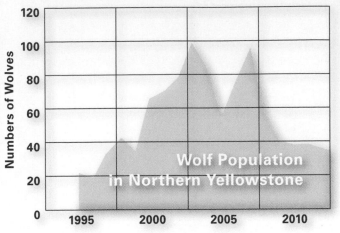

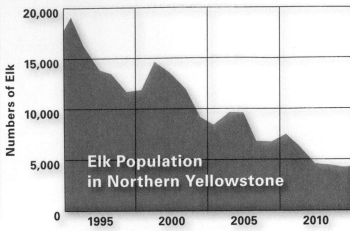

There have also been negative
100 **aspects** to reintroducing
wolves. Ranchers believe that
wolves pose a threat to the
sheep and cattle industries
of the areas surrounding
105 Yellowstone. Wolves hunt as
a pack. This makes herds of
sheep and cattle surrounding
the park vulnerable to their
attacks. Ranchers have
110 struggled to deal with the
wolves' presence. According to
ranchers, predatory livestock
deaths have increased as the
wolf population has increased.
115 Because wolves are now
protected by law, ranchers
feel defenseless. However, the
federal government pays the
ranchers for the loss of their
120 animals, and the actual losses
of livestock to wolves have been
relatively small.

Hunters, too, have been
affected by the hunting
125 skills of the wolf pack. The
declining numbers of large-
game animals such as elk and
deer in the areas surrounding
the park have made hunting

130 tougher. It is estimated that
in the surrounding areas, the
elk population has been cut in
half since the wolf's return to
Yellowstone. Elk have fallen
135 prey to the wolves, and they
have moved to higher ground
for safety. Hunters now have
fewer animals for their own
hunting activities. This in turn
140 affects the **economy** of the
surrounding areas because
fewer hunters buy hunting
permits. **5**

The battle of the wolf will
145 rage on. Naturalists, ranchers,
hunters, and people who
want to see the wolf return
to its historical home all
have valuable viewpoints.
150 The outcome must be a
compromise. But for now, deep
in the heart of Yellowstone
National Park, there are wolves.
Their lonesome howls can be
155 heard on the darkest nights.
Their shadowy images can be
seen gliding through the aspen
forests as they do what they do
best—survive. **6**

aspect
one part, element,
or angle of
something

decline
to grow smaller in
size or strength

economy
the flow of
money, goods,
and services in a
community

compromise
the settlement
reached when
each side in an
argument gives up
a part of what it
wants

5 How has the
reintroduction
of wolves been
bad?

6 What is your
viewpoint on the
reintroduction
of wolves?

The White Wolf of the Hartz Mountains

Adapted from a part of *The Phantom Ship*

By Captain Frederick Marryat

My oldest memories are of a simple, yet comfortable cottage in the Hartz Mountains. I lived with my father, brother, and sister. In summertime the landscape was beautiful; but during the severe
5 winter, it was desolate. In the winter we remained indoors, for the vicious wolves incessantly prowled about in the cold. **1**

1 How many people lived in the cottage?

In the winter, my father hunted; every day he left us and often locked the door to keep us inside. During
10 the short cold days of winter we would sit silent, longing for the happy hours when the snow would melt, and we should again be free.

One evening, the howl of a wolf, close under the window of the cottage, fell on our ears. My
15 father jumped up, seized his gun, and hastily left the cottage, locking the door after him. We anxiously waited.

We waited for some time, but the sound of the gun did not reach us. After several hours, my father
20 entered, with a young female and an old hunter. **2**

2 Who are the new arrivals in the cottage?

beckon

to signal to someone to come to you

reside

to live or stay in a place long-term

25

30

The female's features were very beautiful. Her hair was flaxen and bright as a mirror; her mouth, although somewhat large when it was open, showed the most brilliant teeth I have ever seen. But there was something about her eyes which made us children afraid; they were so restless, so sly; I could not at that time tell why, but I felt as if there was cruelty in her eyes; and when she **beckoned** us to come to her, we approached her with fear and trembling. Still she was beautiful, very beautiful. She spoke kindly to my brother and myself, patted our heads, and caressed us; but Marcella would not come near her; on the contrary, she slipped away and hid herself.

35

My father offered the young lady, whose name was Christina, his bed and he would remain at the fire, sitting up with her father. This arrangement was agreed to, and I and my brother crept into the other bed with Marcella, for we always slept together.

40

45

But we could not sleep; there was something so unusual, not only in seeing strange people, but in having those people sleep at the cottage, that we were bewildered. As for poor little Marcella, she was quiet, but trembled and sobbed the whole night. My father and the hunter remained drinking and talking before the fire. Our curious ears were ready to catch the slightest whisper.

50

They filled their mugs to the brim and drank to one another in the German fashion. The conversation was then carried on in a low tone; all that we could collect from it was that our new guest and his daughter were to **reside** in our cottage, at least for the present. After an hour, they both fell back in their chairs and slept.

55

When we awoke the next morning, we found that the hunter's daughter had risen before us. She came up to little Marcella and caressed her; the child burst into tears and sobbed as if her heart would break. **3**

3 Why didn't Marcella like Christina?

60 The hunter and his daughter stayed in the cottage.
My father and he went out hunting daily, leaving
Christina with us. She performed all the household
duties; was very kind to us children; and, gradually,
we grew to like her—even Marcella. But a great
65 change took place in my father; he was most
attentive to Christina. Often, after her father and we
were in bed, he would sit up with her, **conversing** in
a low tone by the fire. After three weeks of this, my
father asked for Christina's hand in marriage. Soon
70 after, the wedding took place.

My father repeated his vows after the hunter. "I
swear by all the spirits of the Hartz Mountains,
by all their power for good or for evil, that I take
Christina for my wedded wife; that I will protect
75 her, cherish her, and love her; that my hand shall
never be raised against her to harm her."

"And if I fail in this my vow, may all the vengeance
of the spirits fall upon me and upon my children;
may they **perish** by the vulture, by the wolf, or
80 by other beasts of the forest; may their flesh be
torn from their limbs, and their bones fade in the
wilderness; all this I swear."

My father hesitated, as he repeated the last words;
little Marcella could not restrain herself and burst
85 into tears. **4**

The next morning, the hunter mounted his horse
and rode away.

Things went on much as before the marriage, except
that our new stepmother did not show any kindness
90 towards us; indeed, during my father's absence, she
would often beat us, particularly little Marcella, and
her eyes would flash fire as she looked eagerly upon
the fair and lovely child.

converse
to talk with one or
more people

perish
to die

4 Why did Father
hesitate?

resolve

to make a firm decision to do something

seldom

rarely; not often

One night, my sister awoke me and my brother.

95 "What is the matter?" said Caesar.

"She has gone out," whispered Marcella.

"Gone out!"

"Yes, gone out the door, in her night-dress," replied the child. "I saw her."

100 What could bring her to leave the cottage, in such bitter wintry weather, was incomprehensible; we lay awake, and in about an hour we heard the growl of a wolf, close under the window.

"There is a wolf," said Caesar; "she will be torn 105 to pieces."

A few minutes afterwards, our stepmother appeared; she was in her night-dress, as Marcella had stated. She let down the latch of the door, so as to make no noise, went to a pail of water, and 110 washed her face and hands, and then slipped into the bed where my father lay.

We all three trembled, we hardly knew why, but we **resolved** to watch the next night. We did so—and many other nights as well, and always at about the 115 same hour, would our stepmother rise from her bed, and leave the cottage—and after she was gone, we invariably heard the growl of a wolf under our window, and always saw her, on her return, wash herself before she retired to bed. We observed, also, 120 that she **seldom** sat down to meals, and that when she did, she appeared to eat with dislike; but when the meat was being prepared, she would often put a raw piece into her mouth. **5**

5 What do you know about Christina so far?

My brother Caesar did not want to tell my father
125 until he knew more. He resolved to follow her out
and ascertain what she did. Marcella and I tried to
dissuade him; but he would not be deterred, and the
very next night he lay down in his clothes, and as
soon as our stepmother left the cottage, he jumped
130 up, took down my father's gun, and followed her.

Marcella and I waited in suspense. After a few
minutes, we heard the sound of a gun. It did not
awaken my father, and we lay trembling with
anxiety. In a minute afterwards, we saw our
135 stepmother enter the cottage—her dress was bloody.
I put my hand to Marcella's mouth to prevent her
crying out, although I was myself in great alarm.
Our stepmother looked to see if our father was
asleep, and then started a fire. **6**

6 Who was
shot?

140 "Who is there?" said my father, waking up.

"Lie still, dearest," replied my stepmother, "it is only
me; I have lighted the fire to warm some water; I am
not quite well."

My father turned round and was soon asleep, but
145 we watched our stepmother. She changed her
clothes and threw the garments she had worn into
the fire; and we then perceived that her right leg
was bleeding, as if from a gun-shot wound. She
bandaged it up and dressed herself.

150 Poor little Marcella, her heart beat quick as she
pressed me to her side—so indeed did mine. Where
was our brother, Caesar? How did my stepmother
receive the wound unless from his gun? At last
my father rose, and then, for the first time I spoke,
155 saying, "Father, where is my brother, Caesar?"

"Your brother!" exclaimed he, "why, where can
he be?"

rashness

a tendency to act without thinking something through

7 What does Christina want her husband to believe?

"Merciful Heaven! I thought as I lay very restless last night," observed our stepmother, "that I heard
160 somebody open the latch of the door; and dear husband, what has become of your gun?" **7**

My father cast his eyes up above the chimney, and perceived that his gun was missing. For a moment he looked perplexed, then seizing an axe, he went
165 out of the cottage without saying another word.

He did not remain away from us long. In a few minutes he returned, bearing in his arms the mangled body of my poor brother; he laid it down and covered up his face.

170 My stepmother rose up and looked at the body, while Marcella and I threw ourselves by its side, wailing and sobbing bitterly.

"Go to bed again, children," said she sharply. "Husband, your boy must have taken the gun
175 down to shoot a wolf, and the animal has been too powerful for him. Poor boy! He has paid dearly for his **rashness**."

8 Why didn't Marcella want him to tell what he knew?

My father made no reply; I wished to tell all, but Marcella, who saw my intention, held my arm and
180 looked at me so imploringly that I stopped. **8**

My father, therefore, was deceived; but Marcella and I, although we could not comprehend it, knew that our stepmother was in some way connected with my brother's death.

185 That day, my father went out and dug a grave, and when he laid the body in the earth, he piled up stones over it, so that the villainous wolves should not be able to dig it up. The shock of this tragedy was severe for my father; for several days he did
190 not hunt but uttered bitter vengeance against the wolves.

During this time of mourning, my stepmother's nocturnal wanderings continued with the same regularity as before. **9**

195 At last, my father took down his gun, and went hunting; but he soon returned and appeared bothered.

"Would you believe it, Christina, that the wolves— most evil of all animals—have actually dug up the 200 body of my poor boy, and now there is nothing left of him but his bones?"

Marcella looked at me, and I saw in her intelligent eyes all she would have uttered.

"A wolf growls under our window every night, 205 father," said I.

"Really?—why did you not tell me, boy?—wake me the next time you hear it."

I saw my stepmother turn away; her eyes flashed fire, and she gnashed her teeth. **10**

210 The spring finally came. The snow disappeared, and we were permitted to leave the cottage; but never would I leave, for one moment, my dear little sister, to whom, since the death of my brother, I was more attached than ever. I was afraid to leave her 215 alone with my stepmother, who appeared to have a particular pleasure in ill-treating the child. My father was now working his little farm, and I was able to assist him.

Marcella used to sit by us while we were at work, 220 leaving my stepmother alone in the cottage. As spring advanced, my stepmother decreased her nocturnal rambles, and we never heard the growl of the wolf under the window after I had spoken of it to my father.

9 What did Christina do on her nighttime wanderings?

10 Why is Christina upset?

225 One day, when my father and I were in the field, Marcella being with us, my stepmother came out, saying that she was going into the forest to collect some herbs my father wanted, and that Marcella must go to the cottage and watch the dinner.

230 Marcella went, and my stepmother disappeared in the forest. **11**

11 Predict what will happen next.

About an hour afterwards, we were startled by shrieks from the cottage. "Marcella has burnt herself, father," said I, throwing down my spade. My

235 father threw down his, and we both hastened to the cottage. Before we arrived, out darted a large white wolf. We rushed into the cottage and there saw poor little Marcella. Her body was extremely mangled, and the blood pouring from it had formed a large

240 pool on the cottage floor. My father's first intention had been to seize his gun and pursue, but he was checked by this horrid spectacle; he knelt down by his dying child and burst into tears. Marcella looked kindly at us for a few seconds and then closed her

245 eyes in death.

My father and I were still hovering over my sister's body when my stepmother came in. At the dreadful sight, she expressed much concern, but she did not appear to recoil from the sight of blood, as most

250 women do.

12 Where was Christina?

"Poor child!" said she, "it must have been that great white wolf which passed me just now and frightened me so." **12**

My father cried in agony.

255 I thought my father would never recover from the effects of this second tragedy. He mourned over the body of his sweet daughter and for several days would not bury her. At last he dug a grave for her close by that of my poor brother and took

260 every precaution that the wolves should not violate her remains.

I was now really miserable, as I lay alone in the bed which I had formerly shared with my brother and sister. I could not help thinking that my stepmother
265 was **implicated** in both their deaths, although I could not explain it. I no longer felt afraid of her; my heart was full of hatred and revenge.

The night after my sister was buried, as I lay awake, I saw my stepmother get up and go out of the
270 cottage. I waited some time, then dressed myself, and looked out through the door. The moon shone bright, and I could see the spot where my brother and sister had been buried; and to my horror, I perceived my stepmother busily removing the
275 stones from Marcella's grave. **13**

She was in her white night-dress, and the moon shone full upon her. She was digging with her hands and throwing away the stones behind her with all the ferocity of a wild beast. At last, she raised the
280 body to the side of the grave. I could bear it no longer; I ran to my father and awoke him.

"Father! Father! Dress yourself, and get your gun."

"What!" cried my father, "Is it the wolves?" **14**

He jumped out of bed, threw on his clothes, and in
285 his anxiety did not notice the absence of his wife. I opened the door, he went out, and I followed him.

Imagine his horror, when (unprepared as he was for such a sight) he beheld, as he advanced towards the grave, not a wolf, but his wife, in her night-dress, on
290 her hands and knees, crouching by the body of my sister, and tearing off large pieces of the flesh and devouring them with the viciousness of a wolf. She was too busy to be aware of our approach. My father dropped his gun; he breathed heavily, and then his
295 breath for a time stopped. I picked up the gun and put it into his hand. Suddenly he appeared as if rage had **restored** him to vigor; he leveled his piece, fired, and with a loud shriek, down fell the wretch whom he had married. **15**

implicated
thought to be involved in or guilty of something

restore
to bring back; to return something to its usual state

13 What is Christina going to do?

14 What does the narrator want to happen as indicated by the advice he has given his father?

15 Why did Father drop his gun? Why did his son put the gun back in his hand?

penalty

the price you pay for breaking a rule or doing something wrong

300 To our astonishment and horror, we found that instead of the dead body of my stepmother, we found the body of a large, white wolf.

For some time, my father remained in silence and deep thought. He then carefully lifted up the body
305 of my sister, replaced it in the grave, and covered it over as before. Raving like a madman, he then struck the head of the wolf with the heel of his boot. He walked back to the cottage, shut the door, and threw himself on the bed; I did the same.

310 Shortly after, we left the cottage forever and headed for Holland. We had not been many days in Amsterdam before my father was seized with a fever and died raving mad.

16 What is the narrator afraid of? Are his fears valid?

Now the question remains whether I am to pay the
315 **penalty** of the vow my father made on his wedding day? I am convinced that, in some way or another, I shall. **16**

WHO SPEAKS FOR WOLF

A Native American Learning Story

by Paula Underwood

immobile
completely still

Almost at the edge of the circle of light cast by Central Fire—Wolf was standing. His eyes reflected the fire's warmth with a colder light. Wolf stood there, staring at the fire.

5 A boy of eight winters was watching Wolf—as **immobile** as Wolf—as fascinated. Finally, the boy turned to Grandfather, warming his old bones from winter's first chill.

"Why does Wolf stand there and only watch
10 the fire?"

"Why do you?" Grandfather replied.

And then the boy remembered that he had sat there, ever since the fire was lit, watching the flames— until Wolf came. Now, instead, he watched Wolf.
15 He saw that it was because Wolf was so different from him, yet also watched the fire, and that there seemed no fear in Wolf. It was this the boy did not understand.

Beyond where Wolf was standing there was a hill—
20 still so close to the Central Fire that the boy was surprised to see the dim outline of another Wolf face. This one was looking at the moon.

Moon-Looking-Wolf began to sing her song. More and more joined her until at last even Wolf-Looks-
25 at-Fire chortled in his throat the beginnings of a song. They sang for the Moon, and for each other, and for any who might listen. They sang of how Earth was a good place to be, of how much beauty surrounds us, and of how all this is sometimes most
30 easily seen in Moon and Fire. **1**

1 Why do the wolves sing?

The boy listened and—and wanted to do nothing else with his life but listen to Wolf singing.

After a long and particularly beautiful song, Moon-Looking-Wolf quieted, and one by one her brothers
35 joined her in silence, until even the most distant—crying "I am here! Don't forget me!"—made space for the night and watched—and waited. Wolf-Looks-at-Fire turned and left the clearing, joining his brothers near the hill.

40 "But I still don't understand," the boy continued. "Why does Wolf look at Fire? Why does he feel at home so close to our living space? Why does Wolf Woman begin her song on a hill so close to us who are not Wolf?"

45 "We have known each other for a long time," the old man answered. "We have learned to live with one another."

The boy still looked puzzled. Within himself he saw only the edges of understanding.

50 Grandfather was silent for a time—and then began at last the slow cadences of a chant. The boy knew with satisfaction that soon he would understand—would know Wolf better than before—would learn how it had been between us. **2**

55 *LONG AGO . . . LONG AGO . . . LONG AGO . . .*

Grandfather chanted, the rhythm taking its place with Wolf's song as something appropriate for the forest.

2 What is the boy hoping that his grandfather will teach him? How will the grandfather teach him?

LONG AGO

60 *Our People grew in number so that where we were*

was no longer enough

Many young men

were sent out from among us

to seek a new place

65 *where the People might be who-they-were*

They searched

and they returned

each with a place selected

each determined his place was best **3**

3 Why did the
People need to
move?

70 *AND SO IT WAS*

That the People had a decision to make:

which of the many was most appropriate

NOW, AT THAT TIME

    There was one among the People

75   to whom Wolf was brother

    He was so much Wolf's brother

        that he would sing their song to them

        and they would answer him

    He was so much Wolf's brother

80   that their young

        would sometimes follow him through the forest

        and it seemed they meant to learn from him

SO IT WAS, AT THIS TIME

    That the People gave That One a special name

85   They called him WOLF'S BROTHER

    and if any **sought** to learn about Wolf

    if any were curious

        or wanted to learn to sing Wolf's song

        they would sit beside him

90   and describe their curiosity

        hoping for a reply **4**

> **sought**
> tried to do, find, or get something

> **4** Why was Wolf's Brother important?

"Has it been since that time that we sing to Wolf?" the boy asked eagerly. "Was it he who taught us how?" He clapped his hands over his mouth to stop

95 the tumble of words. He knew he had interrupted Grandfather's Song.

The old man smiled, and the crinkles around his eyes spoke of other boys—and other times.

"Yes, even he!" he answered. "For since that time it

100 has pleased many of our people to sing to Wolf and to learn to understand him."

Encouraged, the boy asked, "And ever since our hunters go to learn to sing to Wolf?"

"Many people go, not only hunters. Many people go,

105 not only men," Grandfather chided. "For was it not Wolf Woman who began the song tonight? Would it then be appropriate if only the men among us replied?"

The boy looked crestfallen. He wanted so much

110 to be a hunter—to learn Wolf's song, but he knew there was wisdom in Grandfather's words. Not only hunters learn from Wolf.

5 Why was the boy disappointed? What gave the boy hope?

"But you have led me down a different path," the Old One was saying. "It would please me to finish

115 my first song."

The boy settled back and waited to learn. 5

AS I HAVE SAID

The people sought a new place in the forest

They listened closely to each of the young men

120   *as they spoke of hills and trees*

            of clearings and running water

            of deer and squirrels and berries

They listened to hear which place

            might be drier in rain

125   *more protected in winter*

and where our Three Sisters

            Corn, Beans, and Squash

                might find a place to their liking **6**

They listened

130   *and they chose*

Before they chose

        they listened to each young man

Before they chose

        they listened to each among them

135   *he who understood the flow of waters*

            she who understood Long House construction

            he who understood the storms of winter

            she who understood Three Sisters

to each of these they listened

140   *until they reached agreement*

        and the Eldest among them

            finally rose and said:

                "SO BE IT—

                FOR SO IT IS"

6 Who are the Three Sisters? Why are crops referred to in familial terms?

counsel
to give advice or support to someone

7 Explain the attributes of the land they were seeking.

145 *"BUT WAIT"*

Someone cautioned—

"Where is Wolf's Brother?

WHO, THEN, SPEAKS FOR WOLF?" **7**

BUT

150 *THE PEOPLE WERE DECIDED*

and their mind was firm

and the first people were sent

to choose a site for the first Long House

to clear a space for our Three Sisters

155 *to mold the land so that water*

would run away from our dwelling

so that all would be secure within

AND THEN WOLF'S BROTHER RETURNED

He asked about the New Place

160 *and said at once that we must choose another*

"You have chosen the Center Place

for a great community of Wolf" **8**

8 What is the problem?

But we answered him

that many had already gone

165 *and that it could not wisely be changed*

and that surely Wolf could make way for us

as we sometimes make way for Wolf

But Wolf's Brother **counseled***—*

"I think that you will find

9 What caution does Wolf's Brother share with his Native American people?

170 *that it is too small a place for both*

and that it will require more work then—

than change would presently require" **9**

BUT

> THE PEOPLE CLOSED THEIR EARS

175   and would not **reconsider**

When the New Place was ready

all the People rose up as one

> and took those things they found of value

> and looked at last upon their new home

180 NOW CONSIDER HOW IT WAS FOR THEM

This New Place

had cool summers and winter protection

and fast-moving streams

and forests around us

185   filled with deer and squirrel

there was room even for our Three Beloved Sisters

AND THE PEOPLE SAW THAT THIS WAS GOOD

AND DID NOT SEE

WOLF WATCHING FROM THE SHADOWS! **10**

reconsider
to think about whether a past action or decision should be changed

10 What problem has been caused because they didn't listen to Wolf's Brother?

apparent
easy to see or
understand

190 *BUT AS TIME PASSED*

They began to see—

for someone would bring deer or squirrel

and hang him from a tree

and go for something to contain the meat

195 *but would return*

to find nothing hanging from the tree

AND WOLF BEYOND

AT FIRST

This seemed to us an appropriate exchange—

200 *some food for a place to live*

BUT

*It soon became **apparent** that it was more than this—*

for Wolf would sometimes walk between the dwellings

that we had fashioned for ourselves

205 *and the women grew concerned*

for the safety of the little ones

Thinking of this

they devised for a while an agreement with Wolf

whereby the women would gather together

210 *at the edge of our village*

and put out food for Wolf and his brothers

BUT IT WAS SOON APPARENT

> That this meant too much food

> > and also Wolf grew bolder

215
> > > coming in to look for food

> > > > so that it was worse than before

WE HAD NO WISH TO TAME WOLF

AND SO

> Hearing the wailing of the women

220
> the men **devised** a system

> > whereby some ones among them

> > > were always alert to drive off Wolf

AND WOLF WAS SOON HIS OLD UNTAMED SELF

BUT

225
They soon discovered

> that this required so much energy

> > that there was little left for winter preparations

> and the Long Cold began to look longer and colder

> > with each passing day

230 THEN

> The men counseled together

> to choose a different **course** **11**

---

devise
to plan or invent
something

course
the path or direction
that someone or
something moves
along

11 What changes
happened with
Wolf after the
People moved
into his
territory?

THEY SAW

> *That neither providing Wolf with food*

235 > > *nor driving him off*

> > > *gave the People a life that was pleasing*

THEY SAW

> *That Wolf and the People*

> > *could not live comfortably together*

240 > > > *in such a small space*

THEY SAW

> *That it was possible*

> > *to hunt down this Wolf People*

> > > *until they were no more*

245 *BUT THEY ALSO SAW*

> *That this would require much energy over many years*

THEY SAW, TOO,

> *That such a task would change the People:*

> > *they would become Wolf Killers*

250 *A People who took life only to sustain their own*

> > *would become a People who took life*

> > > *rather than move a little*

12 How did the People want to change?

IT DID NOT SEEM TO THEM

THAT THEY WANTED TO BECOME SUCH A PEOPLE **12**

255 *AT LAST*

   One of the Eldest of the People

      spoke what was in every mind:

         "It would seem

            that Wolf's Brother's vision

260   *was sharper than our own*

   To live here indeed requires more work now

      than change would have made necessary

maintain
to continue having
or doing something

Grandfather paused, making his knee a drum on which to **maintain** the rhythm of the chant, and then went on.

265 *NOW THIS WOULD BE A SIMPLE TELLING*

   OF A PEOPLE WHO DECIDED TO MOVE

      ONCE WINTER WAS PAST

EXCEPT

   THAT FROM THIS

270   *THE PEOPLE LEARNED A GREAT LESSON*

IT IS A LESSON

   WE HAVE NEVER FORGOTTEN

FOR

At the end of their Council

275   one of the Eldest rose again and said:

"Let us learn from this

so that not again

need the People build only to move

Let us not again think we will gain energy

280   only to lose more than we gain

We have learned to choose a place

where winter storms are less

rather than rebuild

We have learned to choose a place

285   where water does not stand

rather than sustain sickness

13 What is the
lesson learned?

LET US NOW LEARN TO CONSIDER WOLF!" **13**

AND SO IT WAS

> *That the People devised among themselves*

290 > *a way of asking each other questions*

> *whenever a decision was to be made*

> *on a New Place or a New Way*

> *We sought to perceive the flow of energy*

> *through each new possibility*

295 > *and how much was enough*

> *and how much was too much*

UNTIL AT LAST

> *Someone would rise*

> *and ask the old, old question*

300 > *to remind us of things*

> *we do not yet see clearly enough to remember*

"TELL ME NOW MY BROTHERS

TELL ME NOW MY SISTERS

WHO SPEAKS FOR WOLF?" **14**

> **14** What does the question really mean?

cherish
to treat with love or care; to hold dear

305 And so Grandfather's Song ended . . . and my father's voice grew still.

"Did the boy learn to sing with Wolf?" I asked.

"All may," my father answered.

"And did the People always remember to ask Wolf's
310 Question?"

My father smiled. "They remembered for a long time . . . a long time. And when the wooden ships came, bringing a new People, they looked at them and saw that what we accomplish by much thought
315 and considering the needs of all, they accomplish by building tools and changing the Earth, with much thought of winter and little of tomorrow. We could not teach them to ask Wolf's question. They did not understand he was their brother. We knew how long
320 it had taken us to listen to Wolf's voice. It seemed to us that These Ones could also learn. And so we **cherished** them . . . when we could . . . and held them off . . . when we must . . . and gave them time to learn." 15

15 Who are the new People?

325 "Will they learn, do you think, my father? Will they learn?"

"Sometimes wisdom comes only after great foolishness. We still hope they will learn. I do not know even if our own People still ask their question.
330 I only know that at the last Great Council when we talked about the Small Ones in their wooden ships and decided that their way and our way might exist side by side—and decided, therefore, to let them live . . . I only know that someone rose to remind
335 them of the things we had not yet learned about these Pale Ones."

"He rose and he reminded us of what we had already learned, of how these New Ones believed that only one way was Right and all others Wrong.

340 He wondered out loud whether they would be as patient with us—once they were strong—as we were now with them. He wondered what else might be true for them that we did not yet see. He wondered how all these things—seen and unseen—might

345 affect our lives and the lives of our children's children's children. Then to remind us of the great difficulties that may arise from the simple **omission** of something we forgot to consider, he gazed slowly around the Council Circle and asked the ancient

350 question:

> *"TELL ME NOW MY BROTHERS*
>
> *TELL ME NOW MY SISTERS*
>
> *WHO SPEAKS FOR WOLF?"* **16**

omission
the act of leaving something out or undone

16 Who is *Wolf* referring to now?

THE MYSTERIOUS HUMAN BRAIN

"Man is not truly one, but truly two . . . All human beings, as we meet them, are commingled out of good and evil . . ."

Robert Louis Stevenson, *The Strange Case of Dr. Jekyll and Mr. Hyde*

"I have someone else that takes over when it's time for me to work and when I'm on stage, this alter ego that I've created that kind of protects me and who I really am."

—Beyoncé Knowles, on becoming Sasha Fierce

inhibition

a feeling of fear or embarrassment that keeps you from doing something

1 What is an alter ego?

2 How is Herschel Walker different from many of us?

Alter Egos?

The comic book character Clark Kent, who sees a crime happening, rushes into a phone booth and
5 emerges as Superman. Bruce Banner loses control of his anger and transforms into a green version of himself: the Incredible Hulk. Dr.
10 Jekyll exits his laboratory void of **inhibitions** as the villainous Edward Hyde. All of these fictitious characters have another "self" that
15 they become when the need arises. We hear people talk about them, watch superheroes turn into them, and read about them in
20 literature. These alter egos entertain audiences in the world of fantasy. But are alter egos a part of our real world? **1**

25 The answer is yes. Many of us daydream that we are someone else—someone smarter, richer, or more famous. Some of us, like
30 Beyoncé, take on different personalities around different people and in different situations. Some of us love costume parties.
35 These are typical kinds of "alter egos." They express our imagination and help us explore who we are. But a person whose alter egos are
40 too "real" may have a mental illness called dissociative identity disorder. All-Pro running back Herschel Walker is one of these
45 people. He was diagnosed with this disorder shortly after he retired from the NFL. **2**

"I would say that we wear different hats in different situations. You have a white hat for your home life. You have a red hat for work. You have a blue hat for hanging out with your friends. As an athlete, you've got a green hat for competition. But with DID, your hats get all mixed up, meaning that your hat for competition has now become your home hat, your home hat has become your work hat, your work hat has become some other hat, and so on. So now you're in trouble because your family can't relate to your competition hat, for example. Plus, you're feeling out of control and have no idea what's going on . . . your substitute comes in and takes over when you can't handle the situation."

—Herschel Walker, on having DID

Dissociative Identity Disorder

50 Dissociative identity disorder (DID) is a condition in which a single person has more than one **distinct** identity or self. People with DID switch their identities when under stress.
55 Some psychologists believe the condition to be most common among survivors of traumatic events. The condition seems to begin when a child copes with
60 trauma by convincing him- or herself that it is happening to someone else. The child tries to dissociate him- or herself from the experience. This

65 creates a trigger that causes the child to create alternate personalities called "alters" who take over. The alters can carry over into adulthood. A person
70 can lose control over when the personalities "switch" and may not remember what happens to them while they are switched. In fact, many people with the
75 disorder tell tales of memory loss and blackouts. **3**

Many people often mistakenly confuse DID with schizophrenia. Schizophrenia is a mental
80 disorder in which sufferers have difficulty telling the difference between what is real and what

distinct
separate; different

3 What does DID stand for?

controversial
stirring up disagreement or debate

is not real. (See the chart below for more information on
85 this disorder.) However, there are distinct characteristics of DID that distinguish it from schizophrenia. Sufferers of DID don't often see or hear things
90 that are not real, but instead have serious gaps in memory. In addition, their alters usually have recognizable personality types. They might be protectors,
95 frightened children, or even animals. The average number of alters in a person with DID is 10. Some victims claim to have many more. At one DID
100 conference, a woman by the name of Cassandra claimed to have more than 180 of them. ■4

4 What are the attributes of DID?

The Debate

Formerly known as multiple personality disorder, DID is
105 one of the most **controversial** mental disorders. Mental health professionals have studied this illness for years. They disagree on the causes
110 and its treatments. They even disagree on whether it exists.

Many believers consider the disorder a legitimate defense mechanism of children who
115 have been traumatized. Psychologists explain that traumatized children can create another "self" to endure the suffering in their place.
120 Young children have brains

Schizophrenia: Facts and Figures

What is it?	• a severe brain disorder • should NOT be confused with dissociative identity disorder (DID) • can be treated, but cannot be cured
What are its causes?	• genetic factors • developmental problems in the brain
What are its symptoms?	Usually includes: • delusions • lack of emotion • hearing imaginary sounds • brief, empty replies to questions • disordered thoughts • lack of motivation Can also include: • paranoia • impaired memory, attention, problem-solving
Who gets it?	• 1% of the population • people from all cultures • usually appears in early adulthood, between the ages of 15 and 25

---

that are still growing and underdeveloped personalities. This makes them **prone** to "splitting" their personality
125 into "alters." Alters have their own memories and attitudes. These come into play when an alter controls the body and brain of the person with the
130 disorder. The person may not be aware of the disorder until much later in life. Instead, he or she might only feel a sense of forgetfulness or time lapse. **5**

135 Doubters of the disorder do not believe that multiple personalities can exist within a person. Their thinking goes like this. They agree that most
140 sufferers have probably been abused, which leads them to therapy. But, patients' mental instability makes them vulnerable to suggestions
145 by therapists. The therapists might suggest there are hidden memories. Patients feel as though their behavior is rationalized, or explained, and
150 they embrace the diagnosis. **6**

Other doubters argue that the definition of an alter personality is unclear. Some doctors refer to the symptoms as a form of
155 post-traumatic stress disorder (PTSD) instead of DID.

Most cases of DID have been reported in the United States and Canada. This has led
160 people to question the integrity of the disorder and the influence of **media**. Few reports of multiple personality disorder existed until the book and
165 movie *Sybil* were released in the 1970s. After this account of a woman with 16 alters, based on a true story, became known to the public, diagnoses of the
170 disorder significantly increased. Doubters say this is proof it is an imagined disorder. However, believers say it is proof that therapists were simply
175 misguided and undereducated about the disorder before the release. Having been educated, they knew what to look for and how to diagnose, which created
180 a natural increase in cases. **7**

In the Court of Law

Can someone with DID be held responsible for crimes committed by the alters? Each state in the United
185 States has its own **standard** for determining whether a person was legally insane, and therefore not responsible, at the time his or her crime was
190 committed. A defendant may be found not guilty by reason of insanity if "at the time of committing the act, he was laboring under such a defect
195 of reason from disease of the mind as not to know the nature and quality of the act he was doing, or if he did know it, that he did not know what he was
200 doing was wrong."

prone (to)
tending to do something or doing it naturally

media
TV, radio, newspapers, the Internet, and other forms of communication as a group

standard
something used to judge, measure, or define something else

5 How do believers defend DID?

6 How do doubters of DID defend their position?

7 How did the movie *Sybil* change things?

previously
earlier; before

transport
to move something from one place to another

8 Why is insanity a complicated concept for people diagnosed with DID?

9 Why was Grimsley found guilty?

10 Why was Denny-Shaffer found not guilty?

With DID, however, insanity is a complicated concept. If the alter knows what he or she is doing and knows that it
205 is wrong, is the person guilty or not guilty? Take a look at a couple of DID court cases. **8**

Robin Grimsley learned she might have cancer.
210 This psychological trauma, according to Grimsley, caused her alternate personality, Jennifer, to emerge. Grimsley described Jennifer as impulsive,
215 angry, fearful, and anxious, and as having a drinking problem. On one occasion, Grimsley drove after drinking and subsequently was charged
220 with driving under the influence of alcohol. In her defense, Grimsley said that when Jennifer, her alternate personality, is in control, Robin,
225 her primary personality, is not aware of what is going on and cannot control Jennifer's actions. Though Grimsley had **previously** been diagnosed
230 with DID, the court found her guilty of the crime. According to the court, an individual's criminal responsibility rests on the mental state of the alter in
235 control at the time of the crime. The court concluded that because the alter personality—Jennifer—was not unconscious at the time of the drunken

240 driving, Grimsley as a whole should be held criminally accountable. **9**

Bridget Denny-Shaffer disguised herself as a medical
245 student, entered a hospital nursery, took a newborn baby, and **transported** the baby to another state, telling her ex-boyfriend that she had given
250 birth. Once captured, Denny-Shaffer was charged with kidnapping and transporting the infant across state lines. Her defense was that she was
255 unconscious and not aware of the kidnapping for all or part of those weeks. In fact, it was shown in court that at least two alter personalities, Rina
260 and Mother Superior, were in control. Denny-Shaffer was found not guilty. The court could not prove that the host personality was mentally awar
265 of the goings on, and thus she couldn't be held responsible fo the actions of the alter egos. The host personality—rather than the alter in control—is
270 the person on trial. If the host personality isn't aware of what is happening, then by reason of insanity, the person is not responsible. **10**

275 Denny-Shaffer, like most criminals found not guilty by reason of insanity, was sentenced to time in a mental

institution. According to the American Psychiatric Association, persons found not guilty by reason of insanity are likely to spend the same amount of time or more in a psychiatric institution as they would have in prison if found guilty of the crime. However, mentally ill people are often found guilty and sent to prison because treatments are offered within prison walls. Are the treatments equal? How are people found to be mentally ill treated in the United States? **11**

Sometimes it is not so obvious. More than 65% of those with a mental illness will still lead a normal, productive life.

Society's Treatment of the Mentally Ill

People who suffered from mental illness during the 17th and 18th centuries were treated horribly. Those judged insane were frequently admitted to madhouses, workhouses, poorhouses, and jails. Those thought to be particularly dangerous were put in restraints and sentenced to confinement.

By the end of the 17th century, the prevailing **image** of the mentally ill was that of uncontrollable, wild animals.

image
a picture in the mind

11 What is the typical sentence for many mentally ill criminals?

Top: *More like a jail than a mental hospital, this facility was built in 1784.*

Middle: *The Northern Michigan Asylum was established in 1885 and has been known as the "11th Street Academy." It looks more like a school.*

Bottom: *A modern psychiatric hospital in Helsingor, Denmark*

implement

to put something into action or put it to use

12 How has the treatment of people with mental illness changed over time?

Harsh treatment and restraint
310 with chains was thought to be needed therapy to suppress the animal instincts. Treatment in public asylums was similar to prison life. The most notorious
315 of these was Bedlam in England. It is said that at one time, spectators could pay to watch the patients there as a form of entertainment. Today,
320 the word *bedlam* is a common noun that means "a state of total confusion."

By the end of the 18th century, a moral treatment movement
325 developed. This movement **implemented** more humane and personalized approaches to treatment of the mentally ill. The following century saw
330 a growth in the number and size of insane asylums. Laws were introduced that allowed authorities to deal with those deemed insane. Unfortunately,
335 the institutions became overburdened with large numbers of people, leading to very few therapeutic activities.

13 Why is DID controversial?

The turn of the 20th century
340 saw even more changes. Advocates worked to improve the conditions in asylums, which were now known as hospitals. New treatments used
345 drugs to control symptoms. More and more patients were

released from institutions. The public began to understand that a mental illness is a
350 disease, just like a physical illness. **12**

Remaining Questions

The debate over DID will likely not be resolved anytime soon. People will continue to debate
355 whether a person can have multiple personalities and whether DID is misdiagnosed. Juries and judges will continue to argue whether all persons
360 should be held accountable for their actions, regardless of their mental state. Among the lingering questions, one fact remains. Since 1999, the
365 Department of Justice has found that more than half of the people in the nation's prisons are mentally ill—and far less than half of those
370 receive any mental health treatment.

Should people be imprisoned for crimes committed by alter egos? You decide. **13**

Out of the 10 leading causes of disability in the United States, four are mental disorders—bipolar disorder, schizophrenia, depression, and OCD.

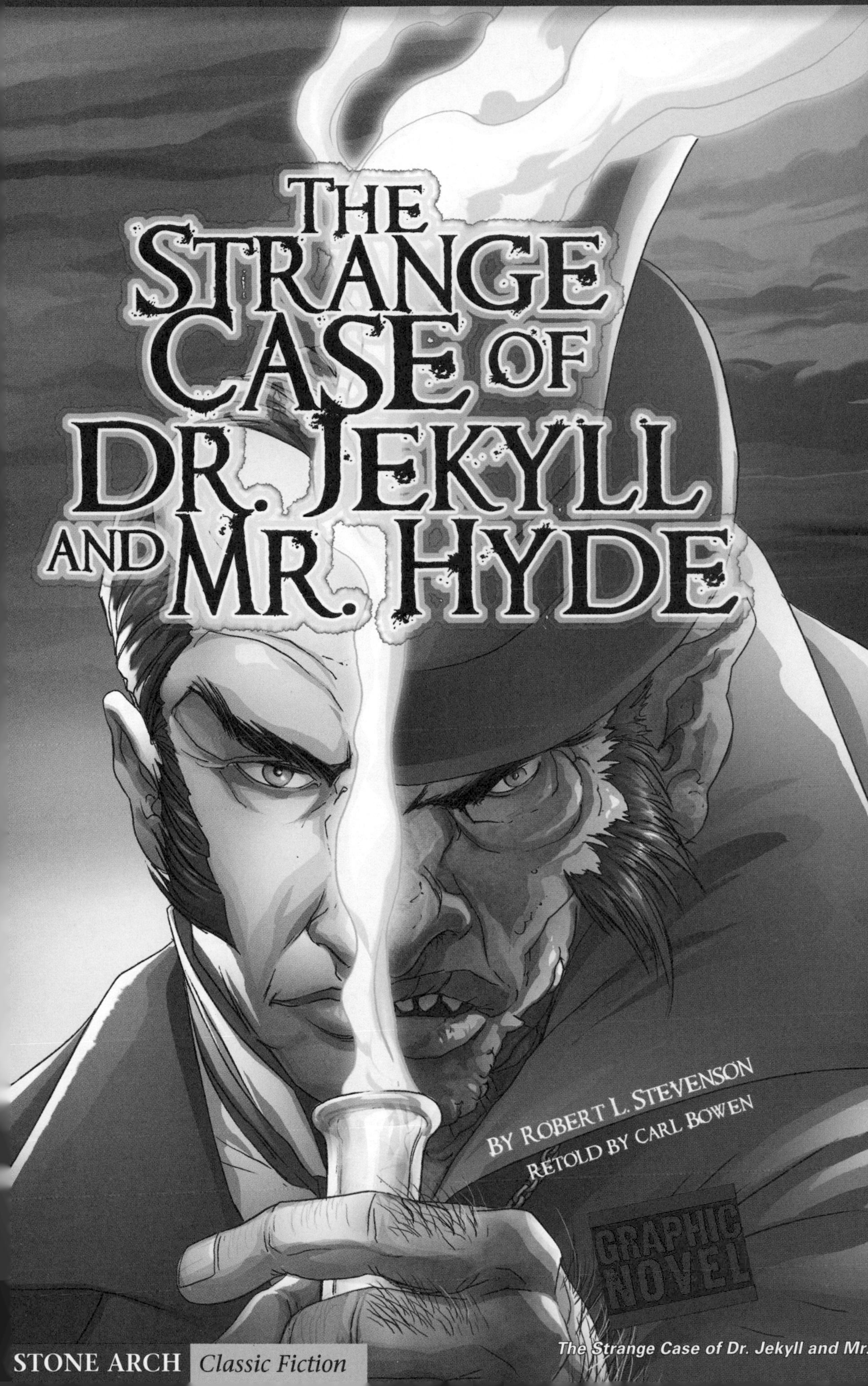

THE STRANGE CASE OF DR. JEKYLL AND MR. HYDE

BY ROBERT L. STEVENSON

RETOLD BY CARL BOWEN

GRAPHIC NOVEL

INTRODUCING . . .

POOLE, THE BUTLER

GABRIEL UTTERSON

DR. HENRY JEKYLL

HASTIE LANYON

EDWARD HYDE

1 Where does the story take place?

London, 1885. Gabriel Utterson walks with his cousin Richard Enfield... **1**

Say, Utterson, you see this property here?

Yes, we walk past it once a week, cousin.

Not long ago, a most remarkable event led me here. I'm surprised I've never told you.

Then tell me now.

CHAPTER 1

A STRANGE VILLAIN

"It happened some months ago, late at night in the Soho neighborhood."

"A young girl collided with a man coming out of a cross street." **2**

2 Why did the man beat the girl?

"Before the girl could even apologize, the man struck her down."

Horrible! You didn't let him get away with it?

Indeed not. While a doctor **attended** the girl, I chased the villain down!

attend
to take care of someone or something

The Strange Case of Dr. Jekyll and Mr. Hyde 441

The awful man then led us to this very property and to that rear door.

He returned with a portion of the sum in gold and wrote a check for the rest.

Did this brute have a key for that door?

Did he give you his name?

Yes. I don't believe he lives here, though.

His name was Edward Hyde.

Hyde? How strange.

The Strange Case of Dr. Jekyll and Mr. Hyde 443

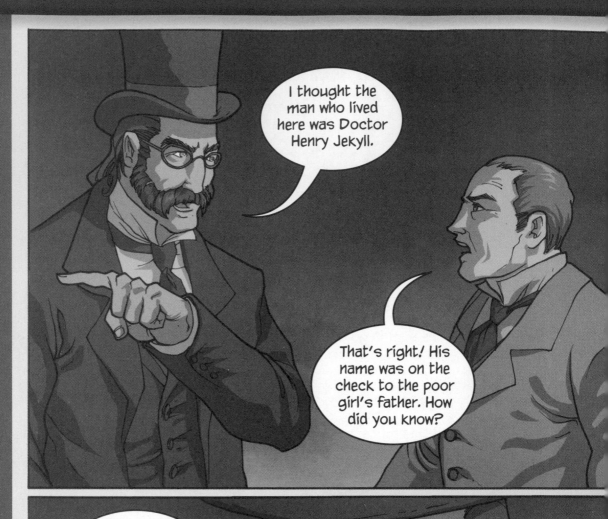

4 What is the connection between Dr. Henry Jekyll and Edward Hyde?

Hours later . . .

All this time and still no sign of—

5 Where does Utterson wait for Edward Hyde?

Wait! Is that him?

Not so fast, Hyde!

What?! Let me go!

CHAPTER 2

MEETING MR. HYDE

The Strange Case of Dr. Jekyll and Mr. Hyde

447

involved
connected with; mixed up with

7 Where is Utterson going to go in the morning?

Early the next day . . .

Good morning, Mister Utterson.

Good morning, Poole. Is Dr. Jekyll in?

Yes sir. Please follow me.

Utterson! What a pleasant surprise. Come in, come in.

I'm glad to find you well. I've been worried.

CHAPTER 3

DR. HENRY JEKYLL

If that will be all, sir.

Yes, thank you, Poole.

Now, what causes you to worry, Utterson?

It's about that man in your will—Edward Hyde. I met him last night.

Is that so?

My cousin, Richard Enfield, has met him as well. He says Hyde came here for help after an **incident** in Soho.

Hyde has his own key to my laboratory in the back.

incident
an event or happening that is noticed or creates a stir

But why? Has he got some hold over you, Henry?

I fear that he means you harm. **8**

8 Why was Utterson worried about Jekyll?

The Strange Case of Dr. Jekyll and Mr. Hyde **453**

You're a true friend, Utterson, but don't worry. I can be rid of Hyde instantly if I choose.

I have a hold over him, you see, not the other way around. 9

9 What hold do you think Jekyll has over Hyde?

I'll take your word for it, Henry, though I still don't trust Hyde.

Of course, Utterson. I understand.

A few months passed without word from Dr. Jekyll or Mr. Hyde. But then . . .

CHAPTER 4

OUT OF CONTROL

Who could be out so late at night?

Aargh!

SMACK!

YES, ME!

YOU!

10 Goodnight, Lanyon! **FROM BOTH OF ME!** HAHAHAHA!!

10 What does "From both of me" mean?

Later, at the morgue . . .

Do you know this man?

His name is Hastie Lanyon, an old friend. What happened to him, Inspector?

He was attacked on the street. A young lady who lives nearby saw the whole thing.

We found this lying in the gutter.

May I see that?

My God, I've seen this before!

11

I believe I know where the murderer lives!

11 Where has Utterson seen the cane before?

The Strange Case of Dr. Jekyll and Mr. Hyde   **459**

The Strange Case of Dr. Jekyll and Mr. Hyde

Weeks later, Dr. Jekyll's butler arrives at Utterson's house . . .

Poole! What brings you here? Is Henry ill?

Mister Utterson, there's something wrong. I've been afraid for about a week. I can bear it no more.

The Doctor has locked himself in his laboratory. I'm afraid for him, sir.

I think there's been foul play. Will you come with me and see for yourself?

Hyde has come back!! We must hurry!

At Dr. Jekyll's house . . .

God grant that there be nothing wrong.

Amen, Poole.

Why are all of Henry's servants still here? 14

They're all afraid, sir.

14 What are the servants afraid of?

The Strange Case of Dr. Jekyll and Mr. Hyde   **465**

15 Who is in the lab?

It's Hyde!

Search for Henry. We might not be too late.

Hyde's killed himself. He must have realized he couldn't escape the police.

But why did he come back here? What's he done with Henry? 16

16 Do you think they will find Henry?

The Strange Case of Dr. Jekyll and Mr. Hyde   469

17 Why does the inspector doubt they will find Henry Jekyll?

"My name is Doctor Henry Jekyll. I was born in London to a wealthy family."

"My loving parents raised me in warmth and safety, wanting for nothing." 18

18 Who is writing the letter Utterson is reading?

"Growing up, I think I enjoyed school more than my friends did."

CHAPTER 5

JEKYLL'S CONFESSION

"I studied hard, got good grades, and didn't waste much time playing."

"My hard work earned me a place at the best college in England."

"There I met Hastie Lanyon, who introduced me to Gabriel Utterson."

"The three of us became great friends."

"During this time, I studied sicknesses of the mind."

"While the body's hurts were easy to fix, the mind was a mystery."

"I studied the mind for many years, asking many questions."

Why are some men smarter than others? Why are some men good and others evil?

"I had no answers for years, until . . ."

That's it. I've got it! Every man has two minds within a single body!

One mind, the high mind, seeks only beauty and goodness in life.

The other, the low mind, is vain and greedy, seeking only what's best for itself. 19

19 What is the difference between the high mind and the low mind? Which mind did Jekyll listen to?

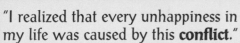

"I realized that every unhappiness in my life was caused by this **conflict**."

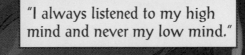

"I always listened to my high mind and never my low mind."

conflict

a clash or struggle between two sides or forces

"In time, I explained this discovery to my friend Lanyon. Like me, he was a man of science. I hoped he might understand."

A neat idea, but not worth anything.

It's not like you can give those minds their own separate bodies.

"He didn't take me seriously."

Goodnight, Henry! From both of me! Ha ha ha! [20]

20 Which quote is a repeat of something said earlier in the story?

"Lanyon was only joking, but what if I could separate the high and low minds from each other?"

"I set out at once to work on this scientific **challenge**."

"The key was a certain rare salt I'd found from halfway around the world."

challenge
a problem or question that takes effort to solve

"I can't be more specific about the **formula** I created. I won't. I can promise you, however, that it worked."

formula
a mixture; a recipe

"I know because I tested it on myself."

The Strange Case of Dr. Jekyll and Mr. Hyde   **477**

"I barely know what happened next."

"I thought I had poisoned myself!"

AHHHHH!

"But instead, I changed." 21

No! It can't be!

Jekyll and Hyde were the same man?!

21 How did Jekyll change physically?

"My formula hadn't worked as I expected. I hadn't been split in two."

"I had created a body for my low mind alone!"

"Since I always ignored my low mind, that body was small and weak."

"The evil things it wanted to do! I'd denied such **urges** all my life!"

urge
a strong need or drive to do something

"My low mind could do every wicked thing I'd never let myself do before."

"But not yet. Not that night."

"I had to make sure the formula worked both ways." **22**

22 Jekyll realized that he couldn't be both people at the same time. Why would that be scary?

The Strange Case of Dr. Jekyll and Mr. Hyde   **481**

"It was just as painful the second time. But I could still feel it having an effect."

"The formula worked, but still not the way I expected. It didn't create a body for my high mind like it had for my low mind."

"I simply became myself again."

"But that was good enough for me."

"Soon, I began using my formula every day. I even changed my name to Edward Hyde because I acted like a completely separate person." **23**

23 How often did Jekyll become Hyde?

"Something Hastie Lanyon would soon find out . . ."

The Strange Case of Dr. Jekyll and Mr. Hyde

"I never forgot how Lanyon had laughed at my idea."

"I wanted nothing more than to prove him wrong."

"I told him all about the formula and what it allowed me to do."

"I expected Lanyon to be amazed. I hoped he'd be proud of me."

"Instead, all I saw in his eyes was horror!" **24**

24 Why was there horror in Lanyon's eyes?

Henry, what have you done?!

The Strange Case of Dr. Jekyll and Mr. Hyde

reaction

what someone feels, says, or does in response to something else

25 What does Jekyll see in the mirror now?

"Lanyon made me leave at once. I'd never seen him so upset."

SLAMM!

"Lanyon's **reaction** made me question everything I'd done."

Had I gone too far? 25

"That night, I decided to set aside my formula."

"I woke the next day. To my relief, my low mind was blessedly quiet."

"But then . . ."

What on earth?

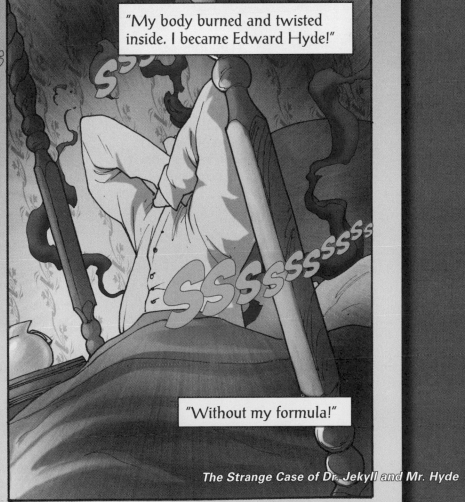

"My body burned and twisted inside. I became Edward Hyde!"

"Without my formula!"

The Strange Case of Dr. Jekyll and Mr. Hyde   **487**

"I rushed to my laboratory quickly, though I don't remember how."

"There, I mixed and drank my formula, half afraid it wouldn't work."

"How had it happened?"

I thought my low mind was at peace!

Now it almost seems to be fighting me for control!

"To my horror, this incident was just the first of many."

"Now, I changed for no reason, and I wasn't fully aware of my actions." **26**

26 After Lanyon's rejection, what began happening to Jekyll?

Where am I? What have I done?!

The Strange Case of Dr. Jekyll and Mr. Hyde **489**

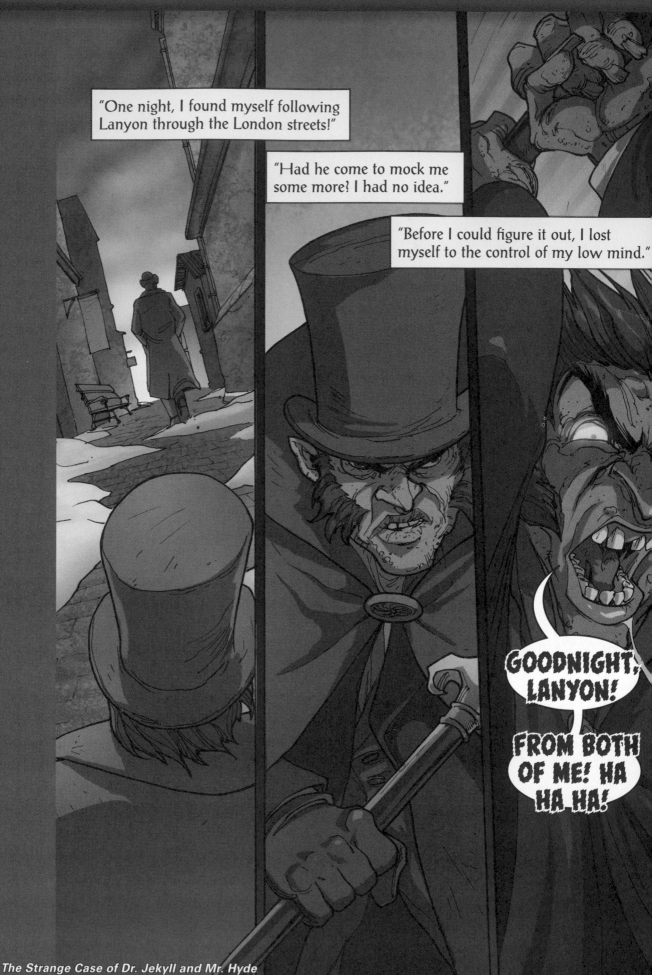

"When I came to my senses, my clothes were stained with blood. My cane was broken."

What have I done!

"I wanted to get home and drink my formula, but I had to get rid of my bloodstained clothes first."

"Although I couldn't remember doing it, I must have killed my friend." **27**

27 How does Jekyll know he killed Lanyon if he doesn't remember doing it?

The Strange Case of Dr. Jekyll and Mr. Hyde   **491**

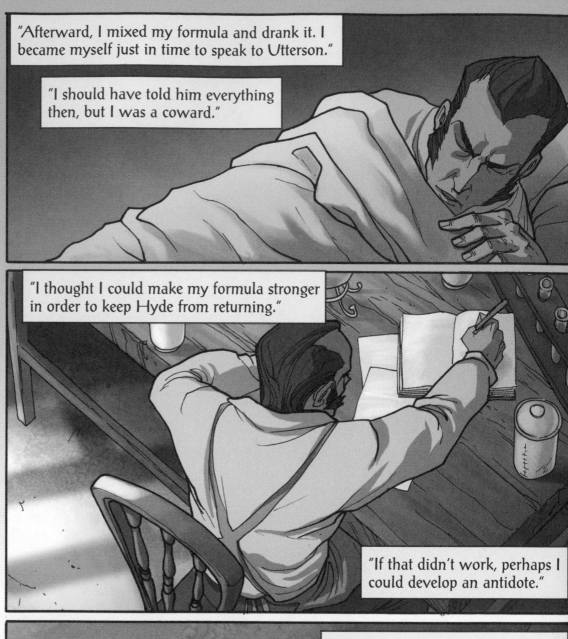

"Afterward, I mixed my formula and drank it. I became myself just in time to speak to Utterson."

"I should have told him everything then, but I was a coward."

"I thought I could make my formula stronger in order to keep Hyde from returning."

"If that didn't work, perhaps I could develop an antidote."

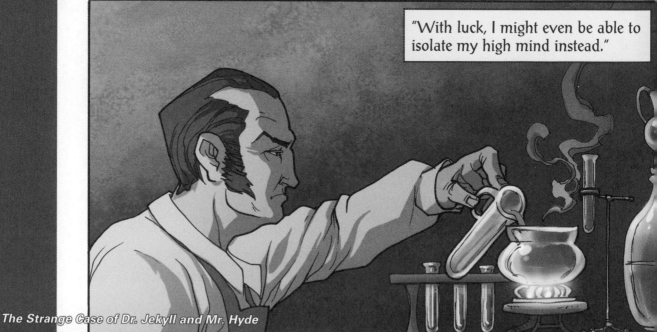

"With luck, I might even be able to isolate my high mind instead."

"But luck was not with me. Hyde found my new notes and destroyed them."

"He burned my original **research** notes too, so I couldn't use them." **28**

research
the act of studying something or gathering information about it

28 Why did Hyde destroy the research notes?

"I found the scraps the next time I took control."

"After all that work, I'd have to start all over again. I didn't bother."

"First, I did the hardest thing a human being has ever done."

"I disposed of the rare salt I **obtained** from halfway around the world."

obtain
to get; to gain

"Without it, my formula doesn't work."

"Second, I wrote a new will that doesn't include Hyde."

"Now, all that's left is to finish writing this confession."

"I understand now that I'm responsible for what Hyde has done."

29 Why did Jekyll dispose of the formula?

"But without my formula, he'll have to face justice for his crimes. This letter will make sure of that." 29

The Strange Case of Dr. Jekyll and Mr. Hyde

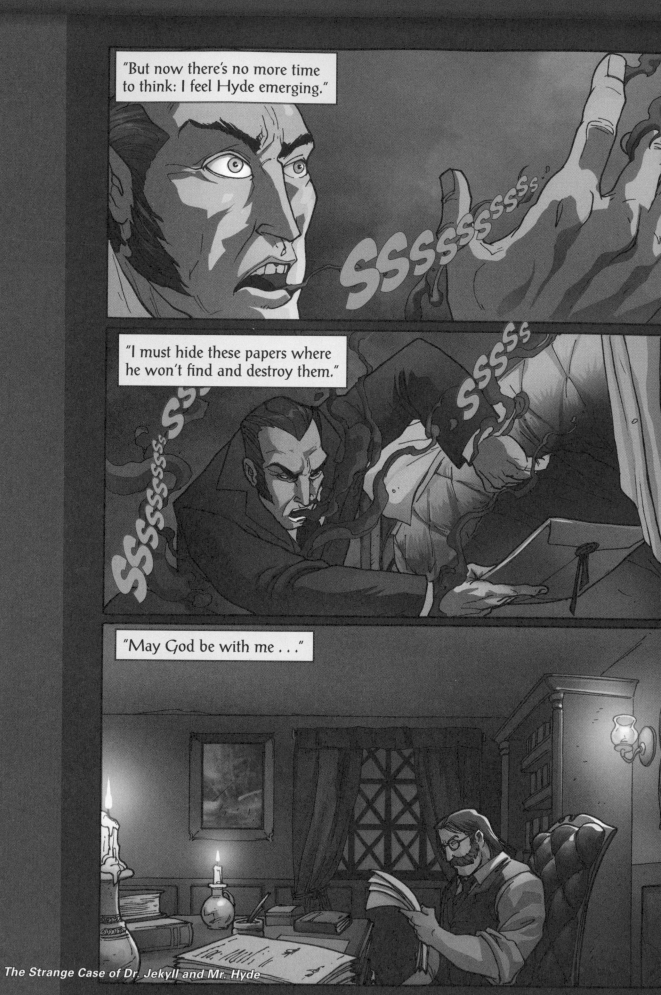

" . . . may God give me strength. Signed, Henry Jekyll."

Poor Henry.

No one else will ever learn the secret of the strange case of Dr. Jekyll and Mr. Hyde. **30**

30 Why does Utterson vow to keep this a secret?

The Strange Case of Dr. Jekyll and Mr. Hyde **497**

NORTH
HIGH SCHOOL

Tradition • Pride • Excellence

1776 North Main Street
Pleasantville, Ohio 43200
614-555-4320

Jan Dogan, Principal

Bennett Baker, Asst. Principal

Marzetta Martinez, Asst. Principal

Peony Kim, Asst. Principal

August 1, 2013

Dear Parents:

Here at North High School, our top **priority** is to provide a safe and disciplined learning environment. Young people who are safe and secure
5 are better students. In response to growing levels of violence in our schools, declining performance on tests, and increasing **truancy**, the school board feels it is necessary to address a major cause of all three—student dress. **1**

10 In 1994, Long Beach, California, became the first large school district to implement a uniform policy. Within one year of adopting the policy, Long Beach reported many successes. The overall crime rate fell by 91%, school suspensions dropped by 90%, sex
15 offenses were reduced by 96%, incidents of vandalism declined 69%, and assaults in the elementary and middle schools decreased by 85%. These results were proof that uniforms were the right fit. Their policy has been replicated throughout the country
20 by districts in New York City, Houston, Dallas, Washington, D.C., New Orleans, Detroit, Atlanta, Boston, Chicago, Miami, Seattle, and St. Louis to name a few. It has been more than 10 years since the proof was publicized, and districts across the country
25 saw the benefit—now it is our time.

Research studies show that school dress affects school success. There appears to be a fundamental relationship between a person's dress and his or her

priority
something that is more important than something else

truancy
being away from school without permission

1 Student dress is being blamed for what three problems?

enforce

to make sure a rule or law is obeyed

enhance

to improve something

distracted

not focused on what you should be focused on

2 What impact did uniforms have on Ohio high schools?

3 What option was considered prior to establishing a uniform policy?

behavior. Virginia Draa, an assistant professor at
30 Youngstown State University, reviewed attendance rates, as well as graduation and proficiency pass rates, at 64 public high schools in Ohio. Her study concluded that those schools with uniform policies improved in attendance, graduation, and suspension rates. **2**

35 Our dress is material. It affects our performance and motivation. People who work out of their home feel their workday is more productive when they are dressed professionally. They feel better about themselves, which makes them feel as though what
40 they are producing is of higher value.

We have had a dress code across the district for many years. However, enforcing the dress code by sending violators to the office has been a problem. They call home and wait for clothes to be brought
45 to school. Sometimes, they get an in-school suspension. All this has only accomplished one thing—less time actively engaged in learning.

Rather than rewriting a dress code that is difficult to **enforce**, the school board has adopted a uniform
50 policy for all grade levels across the district. Even former President Bill Clinton said in a radio address, "If it means teenagers will stop killing each other over designer jackets, then our public schools should be able to require their students
55 to wear school uniforms." The adoption of this school uniform policy will promote school safety, increase learning time, and **enhance** the learning environment—putting North High School on the path to academic excellence. **3**

60 The uniform policy will eliminate a lot of problems we have had in the past with school dress. Students' choice of dress has caused other students to feel threatened, intimidated, and even **distracted**.

Baggy pants, clothing of certain colors, bandannas,
65 and an emphasis on one side of the body (e.g., one
pant leg pulled up) can be interpreted as gang
dress. Dressing as a gang member intimidates
other students and spreads fear. This makes an
environment focused on academic success nearly
70 impossible to achieve.

Pants with large pockets, coats, purses, and
backpacks can hold a weapon or drugs. Students are
unable to feel safe and at ease in their classrooms
when they are worried about the contents of
75 another student's pockets or bags.

Though most offenders disagree on the definition of
"seductive," seductive clothing *is* a great distraction.
Bare midriffs, shoulders, backs, and legs, as well as
overly tight garments, visible underwear, and clothes
80 that draw attention to the bosom or buttocks (i.e.,
V-neck shirts and pants with words on the backside)
cause students to lose their focus and think about
other things.

Clothing advertising cigarettes or alcohol may
85 persuade other students to try these controlled
substances. Television has restricted the advertisement
of cigarettes and alcohol when minors are typically
watching TV, so it doesn't make sense to allow
students to advertise these things in school—a
90 gathering place for minors. Clothing that depicts
violence or foul language may also persuade students
to act in the same manner.

Name-brand and designer labels cause problems
as well. Some students have missed school because
95 they didn't have fashionable clothes to wear or the
one pair of designer jeans was being laundered. If
students are not distracted by the distinction

principle

a belief about what is important or how you should act

resist

to say "no" to something you want but shouldn't have

4 In what ways are clothes a distraction during school?

between the "haves" and the "have nots," they will be able to zero in on what is truly important—
100 learning and growing. **4**

When a child feels safe and unthreatened in school, he or she makes better grades and is a much happier person. Students are excited to come to school when they are dressed well, and they will embrace better
105 moral **principles**. The potential benefits of school uniforms include:

- improving attendance;

- decreasing economic discrimination;

- decreasing violence and theft;

110 • decreasing gang violence;

- improving self-discipline;

- helping parents and students **resist** peer pressure;

- helping students concentrate on their
115 schoolwork; and

- helping staff recognize intruders who come to the school.

Thank you for taking the time to read this letter. I thank you in advance for your cooperation in
120 making our new uniform policy a success. Please read the uniform policy on the following pages, and prepare your child for the upcoming school year.

Sincerely,

5 How does a child need to feel while in school to make good grades and be happy?

Principal Dogan **5**

1776 North Main Street
Pleasantville, Ohio 43200
614-555-4320

Bennett Baker, Asst. Principal

Marzetta Martinez, Asst. Principal

Peony Kim, Asst. Principal

Tradition • Pride • Excellence

Jan Dogan, Principal

Uniform Policy

125 **School Uniforms**

You are required to wear a school uniform at all times while attending school or any school-sponsored activity (unless special permission is given).

130 **A. Basic Uniforms**

<u>Girls:</u> The basic uniform for girls is a long- or short-sleeved gray polo shirt with plain solid-colored brown pants or skorts of cotton fabric. Dresses may be worn but must be solid brown
135 with short or long sleeves and follow the other requirements of this policy. If skorts or a dress is worn, legs must be covered in nude-colored full-length panty hose. Wear brown leather shoes that tie or buckle.

140 <u>Boys:</u> The basic uniform for boys is a long- or short-sleeved gray polo shirt with plain solid-colored brown pants of cotton fabric with a brown leather belt. Wear brown leather shoes that tie or buckle. **6**

145 Clothing must be the **appropriate** size for you, not oversized or undersized. The waist of the garment shall be worn so that the waistband is at the waist and not below the waist. You may not wear baggy/saggy pants.

150 Shirts must cover the midriff, back, and sides at all times; should be fastened with no visible cleavage or undergarments; and may not have a visible manufacturer's logo.

appropriate

fitting; right for a certain time and place

6 What is the difference between acceptable dress for boys and acceptable dress for girls?

restrictive

limiting; keeping someone from having full freedom

consultation

discussion; conversation

7 What body parts can be visible?

155 Skorts and dresses shall be worn no shorter than "mid-thigh." Mid-thigh is determined by placing your student ID at the top of the knee. The garment must touch the ID (using normal posture). **7**

B. **Alternatives**

160 In addition to the above basic uniform, the principal may designate:

1. school-sponsored T-shirts with a crew neck; and

2. more **restrictive** dress code requirements, if
165 approved by the school's administration.

Each school will provide students/parents with a copy of the school's dress code.

C. **Exceptions**

If you enter the school district after the start
170 of the school year, you will have a grace period of ten (10) school days before being required to wear the school uniform.

You may wear special clothing necessary for a school-sponsored activity, as permitted by the
175 principal.

If you are enrolled in a career academy, you may wear the uniform of that program.

8 What are the exceptions to the rule?

The superintendent, in **consultation** with the principal, may waive the school uniform policy
180 on a case-by-case basis for reasons such as, but not limited to, medical necessity or sincerely held religious belief. **8**

D. Outer Garments

185 You may wear coats, jackets, sweatshirts, sweaters, or other appropriate outer garments when necessary due to weather conditions or for other legitimate reasons. The outer garments must be of the appropriate size for you and shall not be overly baggy or violate any other

190 provisions of the dress code.

All backpacks and purses must be see-through. **9**

You may not wear:

1. clothing that is not properly fastened;

2. clothing that is torn or has holes, or pants
195 that are frayed;

3. visible undergarments, sleepwear, or outer garments traditionally designed as undergarments such as boxer shorts or bras;

4. outer garments or accessories (such as
200 backpacks, jewelry, and purses) that have slogans, signs, images, or symbols that:

   • promote drugs, alcohol, tobacco, gang identification, weapons, or inappropriate behavior, or

205 • denigrate or promote discrimination for or against an individual or group.

5. hats, headgear, or other head coverings, except when approved by office staff;

6. body-piercing jewelry, except for earrings
210 on the ears; all other body-piercings must be removed or concealed;

7. jewelry or accessories that may be used as weapons, such as chains, spiked jewelry, or arm bands;

215 8. unnatural hair coloring; (colors other than blonde, brown, black, or auburn)

9. combs, curlers, or hair picks; or

10. sunglasses inside the school building. **10**

9 Why do bags need to be see-through? Could this ever be embarrassing?

10 What accessories CAN be worn?

E. Discipline

220 The principal or designee has the authority to decide whether your clothing complies with school board policy.

If the principal determines that your clothing does not comply with school board policy,
225 your parent/guardian may be asked to bring an appropriate change of clothes to school or you may be asked to leave an after-school activity. You may also receive a disciplinary consequence for violating the school's dress code policy.
230 Repeated violations may result in progressively more serious consequences. **11**

11 What are the consequences for failing to comply with the dress code?

Say YES to Free Dress!

prefer
to like or choose one thing over another

stifle
to keep something from happening

appalling
so bad that it is shocking

survey
a set of questions asked of many different people in order to gather information on a topic

1 What features of our appearance tell a story?

2 Who limits your ability to dress how you please? Does the author agree or disagree with these limitations?

Notice what you are wearing right now. Does your T-shirt have words or pictures on it? Are your jeans, shorts, or shoes
5 in style? Does your jewelry have a special meaning to you?

We may not always be aware of it, but our clothes send strong messages to the people around
10 us. So do our accessories, our hairstyle, and all the "extras" that go with an outfit—devices, ear buds, backpacks, and bags. Your overall clothing message
15 might be "I'm an athlete," "I'm a rebel," or "I want to be a movie star." It might say that you love a particular sports team, that you love high fashion, or that you
20 **prefer** to be comfortable. **1**

Most of us take for granted our freedom to dress however we like. In some cases, however, people do not have this freedom.
25 Many schools have adopted uniforms or strict dress codes. Several nations have made it illegal to wear certain types of religious clothing in public.
30 Parents across the world forbid their children to wear clothes they consider "inappropriate."

These and other measures like them are a tragedy. They trample
35 on a basic human right—the freedom of expression, and in some cases the freedom of religion. They **stifle** growth and creativity. And, they should be
40 overturned. After taking a closer look at a few of these **appalling** bans on self-expression, you'll surely agree. **2**

Same Is Lame

In 2009–2010, about 19 percent
45 of public schools required their students to wear uniforms. Ten years earlier, only 12 percent did. In a **survey** by the U.S. Department of Education,
50 57 percent of schools reported that they had a "strict" dress code. This was a 10 percent **increase** from 10 years earlier.

What explains these frightening
55 increases? Supporters of school uniforms and strict dress codes say that when students are dressed "neatly," they behave better. They also claim that
60 students are less "distracted" by fashion and more focused on learning.

These arguments may sound good. In reality, though, they aren't credible. In fact, they **contradict** the very idea of education itself! School is supposed to be a place of learning, growth, and development. But strict dress codes send mixed messages to kids. On one hand, kids are being told to "learn and grow!" On the other, they are being told to "stay the same!" This sort of contradiction can only lead to confusion in the minds of dress-code kids—who are also the adults of tomorrow. **3**

The sobering truth is this: if young people are taught to conform, or be like everyone else, they will continue to conform in adulthood. How will more sameness solve the world's many problems? We are in desperate need of creative, original thinking. We need new energy and new ideas. We need young people who are taught to be bold and different.

"By instituting a uniform policy," says a leading child psychologist, "schools are taking away kids' **individuality**." In a democracy such as ours— one that values individuality so highly—this type of action should be considered a crime! I take my hat off to those who have tried to cure the problems in education with uniforms, but, it will never work. **4**

In truth, there is little proof to substantiate the benefits of school uniforms. According to the American Civil Liberties Union—an organization developed to defend and preserve the rights and liberties of individuals—there is no link between school uniforms and safety or good grades. Uniforms are simply an infringement on our rights as human beings. Add to that the fact that wearing a prescribed set of clothing every day alleviates free will, and you have a disastrous outcome. Administrators and teachers focus their attention on developing students' decision-making skills and ability to take responsibility for their actions. But both of these skills require real-world practice, something students would receive less of without the freedom to stand in front of their closets and choose what to present to their peers every day.

increase
a growth in size, number, or strength

contradict
to go against; to say the opposite of something

individuality
the state of being different from everyone else

3 What should happen at school?

4 Would the child psychologist agree with the heading, Same Is Lame?

FIRST AMENDMENT

Congress shall make no law respecting an establishment of religion, or prohibiting the free exercise thereof; or abridging the freedom of speech, or of the press; or the right of the people peaceably to assemble, and to petition the Government for a redress of grievances.

EXCERPT FROM THE FIRST AMENDMENT, 1791:

Congress shall make no law respecting an establishment of religion, or prohibiting the free exercise thereof; or abridging the freedom of speech, or of the press; or the right of the people peaceably to assemble, and to petition the Government for a redress of grievances.

ban

to forbid; to formally state that something must not be done, said, or used

valid

logical; based on good, clear thinking

exaggeration

a stretching of the truth; the act of making something seem bigger or more important than it really is

5 How is the United States connected to the laws in France?

6 What needs to be part of the very long journey of acceptance?

Belief Grief

In 2004, France **banned** certain religious clothing in schools and government buildings.
135 Several other nations have passed similar laws. These laws center mainly on religious head coverings worn by Muslim women. Supporters of the laws
140 say that wearing the veils or scarves encourages racism, especially after the events of September 11, 2001. (On that day, Muslim extremists attacked
145 buildings in New York City and Washington, D.C., killing thousands.) Others say that religious clothing in public places challenges the idea that
150 church and state should be separate. **5**

Some of these concerns are **valid**. Religious clothing can bring up negative feelings in
155 those who disagree with a religion's basic ideas. These negative feelings can sometimes lead to violence. And some people believe that religion
160 should have a greater role in government.

But these concerns do not justify laws that ban religious clothing. The laws are quick
165 fixes rather than real solutions. Instead of trying to prevent racism by getting rid of religious clothing, we should try to prevent racism through
170 education. People should take the time to learn about other religions and share their own beliefs in calm and non-threatening ways. Only this

175 will reduce racism and violence for good. And only this will convince people that every religion has a few extremists but is mainly made up of
180 regular folks who want to lead peaceful lives.

The bottom line is this: clothing doesn't create conflict, fear does. And we can't legislate fear
185 away. We have to do the hard work of accepting each other, getting to know each other, and learning from each other. We need to learn how to make our
190 differences a plus rather than a minus. Accepting all kinds of clothing is the necessary first step in this very long journey. **6**

Black Hole of Control

Most parents mean well. They
195 want their kids to grow up, be happy, do good work, and have healthy relationships. They want them to find their way in life and develop their gifts and talents.
200 But they also want their kids to be "normal." They want their kids to reflect positively on their own parenting. Parents think of their children as walking
205 billboards for their own success.

This may be a slight **exaggeration**. But it's true that most parents care what their kids look like on a day-to-day basis.
210 It's also true that many parents have very different standards for dress and overall appearance than their children do.

For example, a 2010 survey
215 showed that nearly 40 percent of young people between the

ages of 18 and 29 have tattoos. By contrast, only 15 percent of people their parents' age have tattoos. These statistics reflect a trend that goes beyond tattoos. What was once considered taboo is quickly becoming the norm. This trend makes it hard for parents to let go of their "kids"—even those aged 18 to 29! **7**

Naturally enough, this need for control expresses itself in parental rules about how a child may or may not dress. Most six-year-olds don't care how they dress. But by the time a child reaches middle school, the mood has shifted. Daily battles about clothes, makeup, and hairstyles become the norm. The louder the parent says "NO," the louder the child says "YES."

In fact, it's a natural reflex for a teen to say "yes" when a parent says "no." In early adolescence, kids begin to separate from their parents. They go on a mission to find out who they are as individuals. The will to do this becomes even stronger as a teen matures. One very obvious and important way of asserting one's identity is by wearing unique—and sometimes startling—clothes and accessories. **8**

Because it is a natural part of growing up, a teenager who wants to wear blue hair, ripped jeans, or a nose ring should be permitted to do so. True, there are some limits to this idea. No child—or adult—should wear clothes that are insulting or indecent. (We all know these types of clothing when we see them.) But if the fashion choice is harmless, it should be allowed. If a child wants to wear purple-striped jeans with an orange-and-black plaid top, his or her parents should say nothing but "Have a nice day!" Then, they should congratulate themselves on raising such a creative, adventuresome kid. Creative self-expression must be in their jeans. **9**

And remember, parents: the best way a child can learn is through making a mistake. If an outfit is a terrible choice, your kids' friends will definitely let them know! **10**

The Skinny

If you've noticed a theme in this argument, it might be "Your clothes reflect who you are." People have been expressing themselves through clothing since the earliest humans realized they had a choice between buffalo skins and bear skins. Today, the choice might be between skinny jeans and wide-legged pants. But the stakes are the same. Any attempt to limit our basic freedom to dress—in a school, in a nation, or in a home—is an attempt to limit our very humanity.

So, go ahead and make a statement. Explore who you are. Experiment with your style. Say "yes" to your own sense of dress. Self-expression is always in fashion. **11**

7 What do tattoos have to do with the way people dress?

8 How do you assert your identity?

9 Who determines whether dress is insulting or indecent?

10 What advice does the author give parents?

11 What is "The Skinny" on the author's point of view? Do you agree or disagree?

from

The Good Earth
by Pearl S. Buck

fruition
completion; a good outcome

It was Wang Lung's marriage day. At first, opening his eyes in the blackness of the curtains about his bed, he could not think why the dawn seemed different from any other. The house was still except
5 for the faint, gasping cough of his old father, whose room was opposite to his own across the middle room. Every morning the old man's cough was the first sound to be heard. Wang Lung usually lay listening to it and moved only when he heard it
10 approaching nearer and when he heard the door of his father's room squeak upon its wooden hinges. **1**

But this morning he did not wait. He sprang up and pushed aside the curtains of his bed. It was a dark, ruddy dawn, and through a small square hole
15 of a window, where the tattered paper fluttered, a glimpse of bronze sky gleamed. He went to the hole and tore the paper away.

"It is spring and I do not need this," he muttered.

He was ashamed to say aloud that he wished the
20 house to look neat on this day. The hole was barely large enough to admit his hand and he thrust it out to feel of the air. A small soft wind blew gently from the east, a wind mild and murmurous and full of rain. It was a good omen. The fields needed
25 rain for **fruition**. There would be no rain this day, but within a few days, if this wind continued, there would be water. It was good. Yesterday he had said to his father that if this brazen, glittering sunshine continued, the wheat could not fill in the ear. Now
30 it was as if Heaven had chosen this day to wish him well. Earth would bear fruit. **2**

He hurried out into the middle room, drawing on his blue outer trousers as he went, and knotting about the fullness at his waist his girdle of blue
35 cotton cloth. He left his upper body bare until he had heated water to bathe himself. He went into

1 Who does Wang Lung live with?

2 What is the weather like on Wang Lung's wedding day? Why is that a problem?

the shed which was the kitchen, leaning against the house, and out of its dusk an ox twisted its head from behind the corner next the door and lowed
40 at him deeply. The kitchen was made of earthen bricks as the house was, great squares of earth dug from their own fields, and thatched with straw from their own wheat. Out of their own earth had his grandfather in his youth **fashioned** also the oven,
45 baked and black with many years of meal preparing. On top of this earthen structure stood a deep, round, iron cauldron. **3**

This cauldron he filled partly full of water, dipping it with a half gourd from an earthen jar that stood
50 near, but he dipped cautiously, for water was precious. Then, after a hesitation, he suddenly lifted the jar and emptied all the water into the cauldron. This day he would bathe his whole body. Not since he was a child upon his mother's knee had anyone
55 looked upon his body. Today one would, and he would have it clean. **4**

He went around the oven to the rear, and selecting a handful of the dry grass and stalks standing in the corner of the kitchen, he arranged it **delicately** in the
60 mouth of the oven, making the most of every leaf. Then from an old flint and iron he caught a flame and thrust it into the straw and there was a blaze.

This was the last morning he would have to light the fire. He had lit it every morning since his mother
65 died six years before. He had lit the fire, boiled water, and poured the water into a bowl and taken it into the room where his father sat upon his bed, coughing and fumbling for his shoes upon the floor. Every morning for these six years the old man had
70 waited for his son to bring in hot water to ease him of his morning coughing. Now father and son could rest. There was a woman coming to the house. Never again would Wang Lung have to rise summer and winter at dawn to light the fire. He could lie in
75 his bed and wait, and he also would have a bowl of water brought to him, and if the earth were fruitful there would be tea leaves in the water. Once in some years it was so. **5**

fashion
to make; to shape

delicately
with a soft touch and great attention to detail

3 How has the earth been good to Wang Lung and his father?

4 What did Wang Lung treat himself to on his wedding day?

5 What is Wang Lung expecting of his new wife?

And if the woman wearied, there would be her
80 children to light the fire, the many children she
would bear to Wang Lung. Wang Lung stopped,
struck by the thought of children running in and
out of their three rooms. Three rooms had always
seemed much to them, a house half empty since his
85 mother died.

Now the grandsons were coming, grandsons upon
grandsons! They would have to put beds along the
walls and in the middle room. The house would be
full of beds. The blaze in the oven died down while
90 Wang Lung thought of all the beds there would
be in the half-empty house, and the water began
to chill in the cauldron. The shadowy figure of
the old man appeared in the doorway, holding his
unbuttoned garments about him. He was coughing
95 and spitting and he gasped, "How is it that there is
not water yet to heat my lungs?" **6**

Wang Lung stared and recalled himself and was
ashamed.

"This fuel is damp," he muttered from behind
100 the stove. "The damp wind—"

The old man continued to cough perseveringly
and would not **cease** until the water boiled. Wang
Lung dipped some into a bowl, and then, after a
moment, he opened a glazed jar that stood upon a
105 ledge of the stove and took from it a dozen or so of
the curled dried leaves and sprinkled them upon
the surface of the water. The old man's eyes opened
greedily and immediately he began to complain.

"Why are you wasteful? Tea is like eating silver." **7**

110 "It is the day," replied Wang Lung with a short
laugh. "Eat and be comforted."

The old man grasped the bowl in his shriveled,
knotty fingers, muttering, uttering little grunts.
He watched the leaves uncurl and spread upon the
115 surface of the water, unable to bear drinking the
precious stuff.

cease
to stop; to come to
an end

precious
very valuable; hard
to get and not to be
wasted

6 What else is
Wang Lung
expecting of his
new wife?

7 How is tea like
eating silver?

recklessly
carelessly; without concern for the harm that might be done

warped
bent out of shape

"It will be cold," said Wang Lung.

"True—true—" said the old man in alarm, and he began to take great gulps of the hot tea. He passed
120 into an animal satisfaction, like a child fixed upon its feeding. But he was not too forgetful to see Wang Lung dipping the water **recklessly** from the cauldron into a deep wooden tub. He lifted his head and stared at his son.

125 "Now there is water enough to bring a crop to fruit," he said suddenly.

Wang Lung continued to dip the water to the last drop. He did not answer.

"Now then!" cried his father loudly.

130 "I have not washed my body all at once since the New Year," said Wang Lung in a low voice. **8**

He was ashamed to say to his father that he wished his body to be clean for a woman to see. He hurried out, carrying the tub to his own room. The door
135 was hung loosely upon a **warped** wooden frame and it did not shut closely, and the old man tottered into the middle room and put his mouth to the opening and bawled, "It will be ill if we start the woman like this—tea in the morning water and all
140 this washing!"

"It is only one day," shouted Wang Lung. And then he added, "I will throw the water on the earth when I am finished and it is not all waste."

The old man was silent at this, and Wang Lung
145 unfastened his girdle and stepped out of his clothing. In the light that streamed in a square block from the hole he wrung a small towel from the steaming water and he scrubbed his dark slender body vigorously. Warm though he had
150 thought the air, when his flesh was wet he was cold, and he moved quickly, passing the towel in and out of the water until from his whole body there went up a delicate cloud of steam. Then he went to a box that had been his mother's and drew from it a
155 fresh suit of blue cotton cloth. He might be a little

8 How long has it been since Wang Lung washed his entire body?

cold this day without the wadding of the winter
garments, but he suddenly could not bear to put
them on against his clean flesh. The covering of
them was torn and filthy and the wadding stuck
160 out of the holes, grey and sodden. He did not want
this woman to see him for the first time with the
wadding sticking out of his clothes. Later she would
have to wash and mend, but not the first day. He
drew over the blue cotton coat and trousers a long
165 robe made of the same material—his one long
robe, which he wore on feast days only, ten days or
so in the year, all told. Then with swift fingers he
unplaited the long braid of hair that hung down his
back, and taking a wooden comb from the drawer
170 of the small, unsteady table, he began to comb out
his hair. **9**

His father drew near again and put his mouth to the
crack of the door.

"Am I to have nothing to eat this day?" he
175 complained. "At my age the bones are water in the
morning until food is given them."

"I am coming," said Wang Lung, braiding his hair
quickly and smoothly and weaving into the strands
a tasseled black silk cord.

180 Then after a moment he removed his long gown
and wound his braid about his head and went out,
carrying the tub of water. He had quite forgotten
the breakfast. He would stir a little water into
cornmeal and give it to his father. For himself he
185 could not eat. He staggered with the tub to the
threshold and poured the water upon the earth
nearest the door, and as he did so he remembered
he had used all the water in the cauldron for his
bathing and he would have to start the fire again.
190 A wave of anger passed over him at his father. **10**

"That old head thinks of nothing except his eating
and his drinking," he muttered into the mouth of
the oven; but aloud he said nothing. It was the last
morning he would have to prepare food for the old
195 man. He put a very little water into the cauldron,

9 What does
Wang Lung
wear on his
wedding day?

10 What did Wang
Lung forget to
do on his
wedding day?

divert

to cause someone or something to get off track or lose focus

drawing it in a bucket from the well near the door, and it boiled quickly and he stirred meal together and took it to the old man. **11**

Wang Lung went into his own room then, and drew
200 about him again the long blue robe and let down the braid of his hair. He passed his hand over his shaven brow and over his cheeks. Perhaps he had better be newly shaven? It was scarcely sunrise yet. He could pass through the Street of the Barbers
205 and be shaved before he went to the house where the woman waited for him. If he had the money he would do it.

He took from his girdle a small greasy pouch of grey cloth and counted the money in it. There were six
210 silver dollars and a double handful of copper coins. He had not yet told his father he had asked friends to sup that night. He had asked his male cousin, the young son of his uncle, and his uncle for his father's sake, and three neighboring farmers who lived in
215 the village with him. He had planned to bring back from the town that morning pork, a small pond fish, and a handful of chestnuts. He might even buy a few of the bamboo sprouts from the south and a little beef to stew with the cabbage he had raised
220 in his own garden. But this only if there were any money left after the bean oil and the soybean sauce had been bought. If he shaved his head he could not, perhaps, buy the beef. Well, he would shave his head, he decided suddenly. **12**

225 He left the old man without speech and went out into the early morning. In spite of the dark red dawn the sun was mounting the horizon clouds and sparkled upon the dew on the rising wheat and barley. The farmer in Wang Lung was **diverted** for
230 an instant and he stooped to examine the budding heads. They were empty as yet and waiting for the rain. He smelled the air and looked anxiously at the sky. Rain was there, dark in the clouds, heavy upon the wind. He would buy a stick of incense and place
235 it in the little temple to the Earth God. On a day like this he would do it.

11 What else does Wang Lung expect of his new wife?

12 How did Wang Lung treat himself on his wedding day?

He wound his way in among the fields upon the narrow path. In the near distance the grey city wall arose. Within that gate in the wall through which
240 he would pass stood the great house where the woman had been a slave girl since her childhood, the House of Hwang. There were those who said, "It is better to live alone than to marry a woman who has been slave in a great house." But when he had
245 said to his father, "Am I never to have a woman?" his father replied, "With weddings costing as they do in these evil days and every woman wanting gold rings and silk clothes before she will take a man, there remain only slaves to be had for the poor." **13**

250 His father had stirred himself, then, and gone to the House of Hwang and asked if there were a slave to spare.

"Not a slave too young, and above all, not a pretty one," he had said.

255 Wang Lung had suffered that she must not be pretty. It would be something to have a pretty wife that other men would congratulate him upon having. His father, seeing his **mutinous** face, had cried out at him, "And what will we do with a pretty
260 woman? We must have a woman who will tend the house and bear children as she works in the fields, and will a pretty woman do these things? She will be forever thinking about clothes to go with her face! No, not a pretty woman in our house. We are
265 farmers. Moreover, who has heard of a pretty slave who was virgin in a wealthy house? All the young lords have had their fill of her. It is better to be first with an ugly woman than the hundredth with a beauty. Do you imagine a pretty woman will think
270 your farmer's hands as pleasing as the soft hands of a rich man's son, and your sun-black face as beautiful as the golden skin of the others who have had her for their pleasure?" **14**

Wang Lung knew his father spoke well.
275 Nevertheless, he had to struggle with his flesh before he could answer. And then he said violently, "At least, I will not have a woman who is pock-marked, or who has a split upper lip."

mutinous
strongly wanting to rebel, or disobey someone in authority

13 What is the background of Wang Lung's bride?

14 What criteria did Wang Lung's father require for his chosen wife?

acknowledgment
a sign or action
that shows you
know something
is true

15 How much did
Wang Lung's
father pay for
his wife?

"We will have to see what is to be had," his
280 father replied.

Well, the woman was not pock-marked nor had she
a split upper lip. This much he knew, but nothing
more. He and his father had bought two silver
rings, washed with gold, and silver earrings, and
285 these his father had taken to the woman's owner
in **acknowledgment** of betrothal. Beyond this, he
knew nothing of the woman who was to be his,
except that on this day he could go and get her. **15**

from

Nectar in a Sieve

by Kamala Markandaya

I kept Ira as long as I could but when she was past
fourteen her marriage could be delayed no longer,
for it is well known with what speed **eligible** young
men are snapped up; as it was, most girls of her
5 age were already married or at least betrothed. The
choice of go-between was not easy to make: Kali
was the nearest to hand and the obvious one, but
she was garrulous and self-opinionated: rejection of
the young man she selected would involve a tedious
10 squabble. Besides, she had sons of her own and
might well consider them suitable husbands, which
I certainly could not, for they owned no land. Old
Granny, on the other hand, would be the ideal go-
between: she was old and experienced, knew very
15 well what to look for and never lacked patience; but
for some years now I had not traded with her and
she might with every **justification** refuse to act for
me. But in the end it was to her I went. **1**

eligible
available and
meets certain
requirements

justification
a good reason or
explanation

1 Use context to
determine the
meaning of
go-between.

grudge

bad feelings toward someone because of something they did in the past

assess

to think something through in order to make a decision or judgment about it

regretfully

in a way that shows you wish something wasn't true or wasn't happening

preliminaries

activities that take place before an event

2 What merit is Ira's mom looking for in her future son-in-law?

3 How did Ira react to the news of her future husband?

"A dowry of one hundred rupees," I said. "A maiden
20 like a flower. Do your best for me and I shall be ever
in your debt. This I ask you," I said, looking straight
at her, "although Biswas takes my produce and for
you there has been nothing."

"I bear you no **grudge**, Rukmani," she replied.
25 "Times are hard and we must do what we can for
ourselves and our children. I will do my best."

Thereafter never a week went by but she brought
news of this boy or that, and she and I and Nathan
spent long hours trying to **assess** their relative
30 merits. At last we found one who seemed to fulfill
our requirements: he was young and well favoured,
the only son of his father from whom he would one
day inherit a good portion of land. **2**

"They will expect a large dowry," I said **regretfully**.
35 "One hundred rupees will not win such a husband,
we have no more."

"She is endowed with beauty," Old Granny said. "It
will make up for a small dowry—in this case."

She was right. Within a month the **preliminaries**
40 were completed, the day was fixed. Ira accepted our
choice with her usual docility; if she fretted at the
thought of leaving us and her brothers she showed
no sign. Only once she asked a little wistfully how
frequently I would be able to visit her, and, although
45 I knew such trips would have to be very rare since
her future home lay some ten villages away, I
assured her not a year would pass without my going
to see her two or three times. **3**

"Besides, you will not want me so often," I said. "This
50 home, your brothers, are all you have known so far,
but when you have your own home and your own
children you will not miss these . . . ."

She nodded slightly, making no comment, yet I
knew how bruised she must be by the imminent
55 parting. My spirit ached with pity for her, I longed
to be able to comfort her, to convince her that in

a few months' time her new home would be the most significant part of her life, the rest only a preparation . . . but before this joy must come the
60 stress of parting, the loneliness of beginning a new life among strangers, the strain of the early days of marriage; and because I knew this the words would not come **4**

Wedding day. Women from the village came to
65 assist. Janaki, Kali, many I hardly knew. We went with Ira to the river and, when she was freshly bathed, put on her the red sari I had worn at my own wedding. Its rich heavy folds made her look more slender than she was, made her look a
70 child . . . . I darkened her eyes with kohl and the years fell away more; she was so pitifully young I could hardly believe she was to be married, today.

The bridegroom arrived; his parents, his relatives, our friends, the priests. The drummer arrived and
75 squatted outside awaiting permission to begin; the fiddler joined him. There should have been other musicians—a flautist, a harmonium player, but we could not afford these. Nathan would have nothing we could not pay for. No debts, he insisted, no debts.
80 But I grudged Ira nothing: had I not saved from the day of her birth so that she should marry well? Now I brought out the stores I had put by month after month—rice and dhal and ghee, jars of oil, betel leaf, areca nuts, chewing tobacco and copra. **5**

85 "I didn't know you had so much," said Nathan in amazement.

"And if you had there would be little enough," I said with a wink at the women, "for men are like children and must grab what they see."

90 I did not wait for his **retort**, hearing only the laughter that greeted his sally, but went out to speak to the drummer. Arjun, my eldest son, was sitting next to the man, cautiously tapping the drum with three fingers as he had been shown.

retort
an angry or smart-aleck reply

4 How is Ira's mom feeling about Ira's impending wedding day?

5 How is Ira's wedding different from a wedding in your culture?

from *Nectar in a Sieve* **523**

hoist

to lift or heave, usually something heavy

95 "There is plenty of food inside," I said to him. "Go and eat while there is still some left."

"I can eat no more," he replied. "I have been feasting all day."

Nevertheless he had made provision for the morrow:
100 I saw in his lap a bundle bulging with food; sugar syrup and butter had soaked through the cloth patchily. **6**

6 Why is Arjun's bundle bulging with food?

"Join your brothers," I said, **hoisting** him up. "The drummer is going to be busy."

105 He ran off, clinging tightly to his bundle. The wedding music began. Bride and groom were sitting uneasily side by side, Ira stiff in the heavy embroidered sari, white flowers in her hair, very pale. They did not look at each other. About them
110 were packed some fourteen or fifteen people—the hut could hold no more. The remainder sat outside on palm leaves the boys had collected.

"What a good match," everybody said. "Such a fine boy, such a beautiful girl, too good to be true." It
115 was indeed. Old Granny went about beaming: it was she who had brought the two parties together; her reputation as a matchmaker would be higher than ever. We none of us could look into the future. **7**

7 What phrase foreshadows bad news for this couple?

So they were married. As the light faded two
120 youths appeared bearing a palanquin for the newly married couple, lowered it at the entrance to the hut for them to step into. Now that it was time to go, Ira looked scared, she hesitated a little before entering: but already a dozen willing hands had
125 lifted her in. The crowd, full of good feeling, replete with food and drunk with the music, vicariously excited, pressed round, eagerly thrusting over their heads garland after garland of flowers; the earth was spattered with petals. In the midst of the crush
130 Nathan and I, Nathan holding out his hands to Ira in blessing, she with dark head bent low to receive it. Then the palanquin was lifted up, the torchbearers closed in, the musicians took their places. We

135 followed on foot behind, relatives, friends, well-wishers and hangers-on. Several children had added themselves to the company; they came after, jigging about in high glee, noisy and excited: a long, ragged tail-end to the **procession**. **8**

140 Past the fields, through the winding streets of the village we went, the bobbing palanquin ahead of us. Until we came at last to where, at a **decorous** distance, the bullock cart waited to take them away.

Then it was all over, the bustle, the laughter, the noise. The wedding guests departed. The throng
145 melted. After a while we walked back together to our hut. Our sons, tired out, were humped together asleep, the youngest clutching a sugary confection in one sticky fist. Bits of food lay everywhere. I swept the floor clean and strewed it with leaves. The
150 walls showed cracks, and clods of mud had fallen where people had bumped against them, but these I left for patching in the morning. The used plantain leaves I stacked in one heap—they would do for the bullocks. The stars were pale in the greying night
155 before I lay down beside my husband. Not to sleep but to think. For the first time since her birth, Ira no longer slept under our roof. **9**

procession

a group of people moving forward as part of a public event

decorous

polite, proper, and respectful

8 What was the mood of the wedding? How was Ira feeling?

9 How was Ira's mom feeling?

All Nature seems at work. Slugs leave their lair—
The bees are stirring—birds are on the wing—
And Winter, slumbering in the open air,
Wears on his smiling face a dream of Spring!
And I, the while, the sole unbusy thing,
Nor honey make, nor pair, nor build, nor sing.

Bloom, O ye amaranths! bloom for whom ye may,
For me ye bloom not! Glide, rich streams, away!
With lips unbrightened, wreathless brow, I stroll:
And would you learn the spells that drowse my soul?
Work without hope draws nectar in a sieve,
And hope without an object cannot live.

"Work Without Hope"
by Samuel Taylor Coleridge, 1825
The poem that inspired Kamala Markandaya's title

from

My Sister's Keeper
PART 1

by Jodi Picoult

If Mr. Webster had decided to put the word *freak* in his dictionary, *Anna Fitzgerald* would be the best definition he could give. It's more than just the way I look: refugee-skinny with absolutely no chest
5 to speak of, hair the color of dirt, connect-the-dot freckles on my cheeks that, let me tell you, do not fade with lemon juice or sunscreen or even, sadly, sandpaper. No, God was obviously in some kind of mood on my birthday, because he added to this
10 fabulous physical combination the bigger picture— the household into which I was born. **1**

My parents tried to make things normal, but that's a relative term. The truth is, I was never really a kid. To be honest, neither were Kate and Jesse. I
15 guess maybe my brother had his moment in the sun for the four years he was alive before Kate got diagnosed, but ever since then, we've been too busy looking over our shoulders to run headlong into growing up. You know how most little kids
20 think they're like cartoon characters—if an anvil drops on their heads they can peel themselves off the sidewalk and keep going? Well, I never once believed that. How could I, when we practically set a place for Death at the dinner table? **2**

1 Name two things that Anna is criticizing.

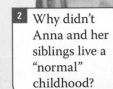

2 Why didn't Anna and her siblings live a "normal" childhood?

acute

serious; severe; sharp

donor

a person who gives something in order to help a person or group

drastically

quickly and to a great degree

3 Why does Anna end up in the hospital with Kate?

25 Kate has **acute** promyelocytic leukemia. Actually, that's not quite true—right now she doesn't have it, but it's hibernating under her skin like a bear, until it decides to roar again. She was diagnosed when she was two; she's sixteen now. *Molecular relapse*
30 and *granulocyte* and *portacath*—these words are part of my vocabulary, even though I'll never find them on any SAT. I'm an allogeneic **donor**—a perfect sibling match. When Kate needs leukocytes or stem cells or bone marrow to fool her body into
35 thinking it's healthy, I'm the one who provides them. Nearly every time Kate's hospitalized, I wind up there, too. **3**

None of which means anything, except that you shouldn't believe what you hear about me, least of
40 all that which I tell you myself.

As I am coming up the stairs, my mother comes out of her room wearing another ball gown. "Ah," she says, turning her back to me. "Just the girl I wanted to see."

45 I zip it up and watch her twirl. My mother could be beautiful, if she were parachuted into someone else's life. She has long dark hair and the fine collarbones of a princess, but the corners of her mouth turn down, like she's swallowed bitter news. She doesn't
50 have much free time, since a calendar is something that can change **drastically** if my sister develops a bruise or a nosebleed, but what she does have she spends at Bluefly.com, ordering ridiculously fancy evening dresses for places she is never going to go.
55 "What do you think?" she asks. **4**

4 Why do you think Anna's mom spends her free time like this?

The gown is all the colors of a sunset, and made out of material that swishes when she moves. It's strapless, what a star might wear sashaying down a red carpet—totally not the dress code for a
60 suburban house in Upper Darby, RI. My mother twists her hair into a knot and holds it in place. On her bed are three other dresses—one slinky and black, one bugle-beaded, one that seems impossibly small. "You look . . ."

65   *Tired.* The word bubbles right under my lips.

My mother goes perfectly still, and I wonder if I've
said it without meaning to. She holds up a hand,
shushing me, her ear cocked to the open doorway.
"Did you hear that?"

70   "Hear what?"

"Kate."

"I didn't hear anything."

But she doesn't take my word for it, because when it
comes to Kate she doesn't take anybody's word for
75   it. She marches upstairs and opens up our bedroom
door to find my sister hysterical on her bed, and
just like that the world **collapses** again. My father, a
closet astronomer, has tried to explain black holes to
me, how they are so heavy they absorb everything,
80   even light, right into their center. Moments like this
are the same kind of vacuum; no matter what you
cling to, you wind up being sucked in. **5**

"Kate!" My mother sinks down to the floor, that
stupid skirt a cloud around her. "Kate, honey,
85   what hurts?"

Kate hugs a pillow to her stomach, and tears keep
streaming down her face. Her pale hair is stuck to
her face in damp streaks; her breathing's too tight.
I stand frozen in the doorway of my own room,
90   waiting for instructions: *Call Daddy. Call 911. Call
Dr. Chance.* My mother goes so far as to shake a
better explanation out of Kate. "It's Preston," she
sobs. "He's leaving Serena for good."

That's when we notice the TV. On the screen, a
95   blond hottie gives a longing look to a woman crying
almost as hard as my sister, and then he slams the

> **collapse**
> to fall down or fall
> apart suddenly

> **5** Why is Anna's
> mom worried?

assume

to believe something is true without first making sure

circumstance

an event or situation; the state of things

6 What is wrong with Kate?

door. "But what hurts?" my mother asks, certain there has to be more to it than this.

"Oh my *God*," Kate says, sniffling. "Do you have
100 any idea how much Serena and Preston have been through? Do you?" **6**

That fist inside me relaxes, now that I know it's all right. Normal, in our house, is like a blanket too short for a bed—sometimes it covers you just fine,
105 and other times it leaves you cold and shaking; and worst of all, you never know which of the two it's going to be. I sit down on the end of Kate's bed. Although I'm only thirteen, I'm taller than her and every now and then people mistakenly **assume** I'm
110 the older sister. At different times this summer she has been crazy for Callahan, Wyatt, and Liam, the male leads on this soap. Now, I guess, it's all about Preston. "There was the kidnapping scare," I volunteer. I actually followed that story line; Kate
115 made me tape the show during her dialysis sessions.

"And the time she almost married his twin by mistake," Kate adds.

"Don't forget when he died in the boat accident. For two months, anyway." My mother joins the
120 conversation, and I remember that she used to watch this soap, too, sitting with Kate in the hospital.

For the first time, Kate seems to notice my mother's outfit. "What are you *wearing*?"

125 "Oh. Something I'm sending back." She stands up in front of me so that I can undo her zipper. This mail-order compulsion, for any other mother, would be a wake-up call for therapy; for my mom, it would probably be considered a healthy break. I wonder if
130 it's putting on someone else's skin for a while that she likes so much, or if it's the option of being able to send back a **circumstance** that just doesn't suit you. She looks at Kate, hard. "You're sure nothing hurts?" **7**

7 What circumstance is Anna referring to?

After my mother leaves, Kate sinks a little. That's
135 the only way to describe it—how fast color drains
from her face, how she disappears against the
pillows. As she gets sicker, she fades a little more,
until I am afraid one day I will wake up and not be
able to see her at all. "Move," Kate orders. "You're
140 blocking the picture."

So I go to sit on my own bed. "It's only the coming
attractions."

"Well, if I die tonight I want to know what I'm
missing." **8**

145 I fluff my pillows up under my head. Kate, as usual,
has swapped so that she has all the funchy ones that
don't feel like rocks under your neck. She's supposed
to deserve this, because she's three years older than
me or because she's sick or because the moon is in
150 Aquarius—there's *always* a reason. I squint at the
television, wishing I could flip through the stations,
knowing I don't have a prayer. "Preston looks like
he's made out of plastic."

"Then why did I hear you whispering his name last
155 night into your pillow?"

"Shut up," I say.

"*You* shut up." Then Kate smiles at me. "He probably
is gay, though. Quite a waste, considering the
Fitzgerald sisters are—" **Wincing**, she breaks off
160 mid-sentence, and I roll toward her.

"Kate?"

She rubs her lower back. "It's nothing."

It's her kidneys. "Want me to get Mom?"

wince

to make a face
in response to
something painful
or unpleasant

8 Why does Kate
want to see the
previews?

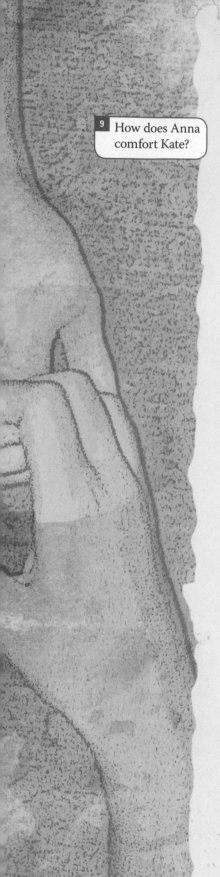

"Not yet." She reaches between our beds, which are
165 just far apart enough for us to touch each other if
we both try. I hold out my hand, too. When we were
little we'd make this bridge and try to see how many
Barbies we could get to balance on it.

9 | How does Anna
comfort Kate?

Lately, I have been having nightmares, where I'm cut
170 into so many pieces that there isn't enough of me to
be put back together.

❖

My father says that a fire will burn itself out, unless
you open a window and give it fuel. I suppose that's
what I'm doing, when you get right down to it;
175 but then again, my dad also says that when flames
are licking at your heels you've got to break a wall
or two if you want to escape. So when Kate falls
asleep from her meds I take the leather binder I
keep between my mattress and box spring and go
180 into the bathroom for privacy. I know Kate's been
snooping—I rigged up a red thread between the
zipper's teeth to let me know who was prying into
my stuff without my permission, but even though
the thread's been torn there's nothing missing
185 inside. I turn on the water in the bathtub so it
sounds like I'm in there for a reason, and sit down
on the floor to count.

If you add in the twenty dollars from the pawnshop,
I have $136.87. It's not going to be enough, but
190 there's got to be a way around that. Jesse didn't
have $2,900 when he bought his beat-up Jeep, and
the bank gave him some kind of loan. Of course,
my parents had to sign the papers, too, and I doubt
they're going to be willing to do that for me, given
195 the circumstances. I count the money a second
time, just in case the bills have miraculously
reproduced, but math is math and the total stays the
same. And then I read the newspaper clippings.

Campbell Alexander. It's a stupid name, in my
200 opinion. It sounds like a bar drink that costs too

much, or a brokerage firm. But you can't deny the man's track record. **10**

To reach my brother's room, you actually have to leave the house, which is exactly the way he likes it.

205 When Jesse turned sixteen he moved into the attic over the garage—a perfect arrangement, since he didn't want my parents to see what he was doing and my parents didn't really want to see. Blocking the stairs to his place are four snow tires, a small

210 wall of cartons, and an oak desk tipped onto its side. Sometimes I think Jesse sets up these **obstacles** himself, just to make getting to him more of a challenge.

I crawl over the mess and up the stairs, which

215 vibrate with the bass from Jesse's stereo. It takes nearly five whole minutes before he hears me knocking. "What?" he snaps, opening the door a crack.

"Can I come in?"

220 He thinks twice, then steps back to let me enter. The room is a sea of dirty clothes and magazines and leftover Chinese take-out cartons; it smells like the sweaty tongue of a hockey skate. The only neat spot is the shelf where Jesse keeps his special

225 collection—a Jaguar's silver mascot, a Mercedes symbol, a Mustang's horse—hood ornaments that he told me he just found lying around, although I'm not dumb enough to believe him.

Don't get me wrong—it isn't that my parents don't

230 care about Jesse or whatever trouble he's gotten himself mixed up in. It's just that they don't really have time to care about it, because it's a problem somewhere lower on the totem pole. **11**

obstacle
an object that is in someone's way

10 What do you think Anna is saving up for?

11 Why don't Anna's parents have time to care about what Jesse is doing?

inferno

a fire blazing out of control

Jesse ignores me, going back to whatever he was
235 doing on the far side of the mess. My attention is
caught by a Crock-Pot—one that disappeared out
of the kitchen a few months ago—which now sits
on top of Jesse's TV with a copper tube threaded
out of its lid and down through a plastic milk jug
240 filled with ice, emptying into a glass Mason jar.
Jesse may be a borderline delinquent, but he's
brilliant. Just as I'm about to touch the contraption,
Jesse turns around. "Hey!" He fairly flies over the
couch to knock my hand away. "You'll screw up the
245 condensing coil."

"Is this what I think it is?"

A nasty grin itches over his face. "Depends on what
you think it is." He jimmies out the Mason jar, so
that liquid drips onto the carpet. "Have a taste."

250 For a still made out of spit and glue, it produces
pretty potent moonshine whiskey. An **inferno** races
so fast through my belly and legs I fall back onto the
couch. "Disgusting," I gasp. **12**

12 What is Jesse like?

Jesse laughs and takes a swig, too, although for
255 him it goes down easier. "So what do you want
from me?"

"How do you know I want something?"

"Because no one comes up here on a social call,"
he says, sitting on the arm of the couch. "And if it
260 was something about Kate, you would've already
told me."

"It *is* about Kate. Sort of." I press the newspaper
clippings into my brother's hand; they'll do a better
job explaining than I ever could. He scans them,
265 then looks me right in the eye. His are the palest
shade of silver, so surprising that sometimes when
he stares at you, you can completely forget what you
were planning to say.

"Don't mess with the system, Anna," he says bitterly.
270 "We've all got our scripts down pat. Kate plays the
Martyr. I'm the Lost Cause. And you, you're the
Peacekeeper."

He thinks he knows me, but that goes both ways—
and when it comes to **friction**, Jesse is an addict. I
275 look right at him. "Says who?" **13**

friction
disagreement or
argument between
people

13 Predict what
Anna wants
from Jesse.

from

My Sister's Keeper
PART 2

by Jodi Picoult

Jesse agrees to wait for me in the parking lot.
It's one of the few times I can recall him doing
anything I tell him to do. I walk around to the front
of the building, which has two gargoyles guarding
280 its entrance.

Campbell Alexander, Esquire's office is on the third
floor. The walls are paneled with wood the color
of a chestnut mare's coat, and when I step onto the
thick Oriental rug on the floor, my sneakers sink an
285 inch. The secretary is wearing black pumps so shiny
I can see my own face in them. I glance down at my
cutoffs and the Keds that I tattooed last week with
Magic Markers when I was bored. **1**

The secretary has perfect skin and perfect eyebrows
290 and honeybee lips, and she's using them to scream
bloody murder at whoever's on the other end of the
phone. "You cannot expect me to tell a judge that.
Just because *you* don't want to hear Kleman rant
and rave doesn't mean that *I* have to . . . no, actually,
295 that raise was for the exceptional job I do and the
crap I put up with on a daily basis, and as

> **1** Where is Anna?
> Why is she
> feeling
> uncomfortable?

lacking

missing something; not having enough of something

interrupt

to say or do something that causes another person to stop doing something

verdict

a decision, a judgment, or a ruling

consume

to take in; to read or process information

2 What is the secretary basing her first impression on?

3 How does Anna get the secretary to change her mind?

a matter of fact, while we're on—" She holds the phone away from her ear; I can make out the buzz of disconnection. "Bastard," she mutters, and then
300 seems to realize I'm standing three feet away. "Can I help you?"

She looks me over from head to toe, rating me on a general scale of first impressions, and finding me severely **lacking**. I lift my chin and pretend
305 to be far more cool than I actually am. "I have an appointment with Mr. Alexander. At four o'clock." **2**

"Your voice," she says. "On the phone, you didn't sound quite so . . ."

Young?

310 She smiles uncomfortably. "We don't try juvenile cases, as a rule. If you'd like I can offer you the names of some practicing attorneys who—"

I take a deep breath. "Actually," I **interrupt**, "you're wrong. Smith v. Whately, Edmunds v. Womens
315 and Infants Hospital, and Jerome v. the Diocese of Providence all involved litigants under the age of eighteen. All three resulted in **verdicts** for Mr. Alexander's clients. And those were just in the past *year.*"

320 The secretary blinks at me. Then a slow smile toasts her face, as if she's decided she just might like me after all. "Come to think of it, why don't you just wait in his office?" she suggests, and she stands up to show me the way. **3**

325 Even if I spend every minute of the rest of my life reading, I do not believe that I will ever manage to **consume** the sheer number of words routed high and low on the walls of Campbell Alexander, Esquire's office. I do the math—if there are 400
330 words or so on every page, and each of those legal

books are 400 pages, and there are twenty on a shelf and six shelves per bookcase—why, you're pushing nineteen million words, and that's only partway across the room.

335 I'm alone in the office long enough to note that his desk is so neat, you could play Chinese football on the blotter; that there is not a single photo of a wife or a kid or even himself; and that in spite of the fact that the room is spotless, there's a mug full of water
340 sitting on the floor.

I find myself making up explanations: it's a swimming pool for an army of ants. It's some kind of **primitive** humidifier. It's a mirage.

I've nearly convinced myself about that last one, and
345 am leaning over to touch it to see if it's real, when the door bursts open. I practically fall out of my chair and that puts me eye to eye with an incoming German shepherd, which spears me with a look and then marches over to the mug and starts to drink. **4**

350 Campbell Alexander comes in, too. He's got black hair and he's at least as tall as my dad—six feet— with a right-angle jaw and eyes that look frozen over. He shrugs out of a suit jacket and hangs it neatly on the back of the door, then yanks a file out
355 of a cabinet before moving to his desk. He never makes eye contact with me, but he starts talking all the same. "I don't want any Girl Scout cookies," Campbell Alexander says. "Although you do get Brownie points for **tenacity**. Ha." He smiles at his
360 own joke.

"I'm not selling anything."

He glances at me curiously, then pushes a button on his phone. "Kerri," he says when the secretary answers. "What is this doing in my office?"

primitive
simple and old-fashioned; an early model of something

tenacity
stubbornness; the quality of not giving up easily

4 What personality traits of Anna are evident in the office?

automatically
without thinking

exalted
of high value or status

(on) behalf
in someone's place or to help someone

experimental
using new methods or ideas that may or may not work

5 How does Alexander receive Anna's offer?

6 What connects Campbell Alexander to Kate?

365 "I'm here to retain you," I say.

The lawyer releases the intercom button. "I don't think so." **5**

"You don't even know if I have a case."

I take a step forward; so does the dog. For the first
370 time I realize it's wearing one of those vests with a red cross on it, like a St. Bernard that might carry rum up a snowy mountain. I **automatically** reach out to pet him. "Don't," Alexander says. "Judge is a service dog."

375 My hand goes back to my side. "But you aren't blind."

"Thank you for pointing that out to me."

"So what's the matter with you?"

The minute I say it, I want to take it back. Haven't I watched Kate field this question from hundreds of
380 rude people?

"I have an iron lung," Campbell Alexander says curtly, "and the dog keeps me from getting too close to magnets. Now, if you'd do me the **exalted** honor of leaving, my secretary can find you the name of
385 someone who—" **6**

But I can't go yet. "Did you really sue God?" I take out all the newspaper clippings, smooth them on the bare desk.

A muscle tics in his cheek, and then he picks
390 up the article lying on top. "I sued the Diocese of Providence, on **behalf** of a kid in one of their orphanages who needed an **experimental** treatment involving fetal tissue, which they felt violated Vatican II. However, it makes a much better
395 headline to say that a nine-year-old is suing God for being stuck with the short end of the straw in life." I just stare at him. "Dylan Jerome," the lawyer

admits, "wanted to sue God for not caring enough about him."

400 A rainbow might as well have cracked down the middle of that big mahogany desk. "Mr. Alexander," I say, "my sister has leukemia." **7**

"I'm sorry to hear that. But even if I were willing to litigate against God again, which I'm not, you can't
405 bring a lawsuit on someone else's behalf."

There is way too much to explain—my own blood seeping into my sister's veins; the nurses holding me down to stick me for white cells Kate might borrow; the doctor saying they didn't get enough the first
410 time around. The bruises and the deep bone ache after I gave up my marrow; the shots that sparked more stem cells in me, so that there'd be extra for my sister. The fact that I'm not sick, but I might as well be. The fact that the only reason I was born
415 was as a harvest crop for Kate. The fact that even now, a major decision about me is being made, and no one's bothered to ask the one person who most deserves it to speak her opinion.

There's way too much to explain, and so I do the
420 best I can. "It's not God. Just my parents," I say. "I want to sue them for the rights to my own body." **8**

7 What gives Anna hope?

8 What is Anna's life like?

Unit 7

Word	Meaning

Unit 8

Word	Meaning

Unit 9

Word	Meaning

Unit 10

Word	Meaning

Unit 11

Word	Meaning

Unit 12

Word	Meaning

Six Traits of Writing: Basic

	Ideas and Development	Organization	Voice and Audience Awareness	Word Choice	Sentence Fluency	Language Conventions
4	Focuses on the topic. Main idea (topic sentence) is clear and well supported with details and elaboration (examples, evidence, and explanations).	Topic sentence clearly states main idea. Ideas are clear and logically organized. Contains concluding sentence.	The words have a strong sense of person and purpose. Brings topic to life.	Words are specific to the content, accurate, and vivid. Word choice enhances meaning and the reader's enjoyment.	Writes complete sentences and varies sentence structure.	There are no grammar errors. There are few or no errors in spelling, capitalization, or punctuation.
3	Mostly focuses on the topic. Sentences supporting the main idea (topic sentence) may be general rather than detailed and specific.	Topic sentence states main idea. Organization mostly clear and logical. May contain concluding sentence.	The words have some sense of person and purpose.	Words are correctly used but may be somewhat general and unspecific.	Writes complete sentences and attempts to use expanded sentences.	There are no major grammar errors. There are few errors in spelling, capitalization, or punctuation.
2	Main idea (topic sentence) is unclear and/or lacks sufficient support.	Structure may not be entirely clear or logical. Paragraph may seem more like a list and/or be hard to follow.	The words have little sense of person and purpose.	Words may be used inaccurately or repetitively.	Writes mostly simple and/or awkwardly constructed sentences. May include some run-ons and fragments.	There are a few grammar errors. There are a few errors in spelling, capitalization, or punctuation.
1	Does not address prompt and/or lacks a topic sentence. Supporting details are absent or do not relate to topic.	No evident structure. Lack of organization seriously interferes with meaning.	The words have no sense of person or purpose. No sense of audience.	Extremely limited range of words. Restricted vocabulary impedes message.	Numerous run-ons and/or fragments interfere with meaning.	There are many grammar and/or spelling errors. There are many errors in capitalization and punctuation.

Six Traits of Writing: Expository

	Ideas and Development	Organization	Voice and Audience Awareness	Word Choice	Sentence Fluency	Language Conventions
4	The thesis is very clear and well focused. Supporting details make the paper very easy to understand and interesting.	Ideas are very clearly organized. All parts of the essay (introduction, body, and conclusion) work together to support the thesis.	The writer's voice is distinctive and very well chosen. The writer knows who his or her audience is.	Words are used correctly and are very well chosen. They create pictures in the reader's mind.	Sentences have an easy flow and rhythm. Transitions are very smooth.	There are no grammar errors. There are few or no errors in spelling, capitalization, or punctuation.
3	The thesis is clear. Supporting details make the paper easy to understand.	Ideas are clearly organized. The paper includes all parts of an essay (introduction, body, and conclusion).	The writer's voice is natural and shows an interest in the topic. The writer knows who his or her audience is.	Words are used correctly. Some words may be a bit general.	Sentences are formed correctly and are varied in structure. Transitions are clear.	There are no major grammar errors. There are few errors in spelling, capitalization, or punctuation.
2	The thesis is not clear. The ideas are somewhat developed, but there are only a few details.	Ideas are fairly well organized. The paper includes all parts of an essay (introduction, body, and conclusion).	The writer's voice is natural, but the writer is not fully engaged in the topic. At times, the writer's viewpoint may be vague.	Most words are used correctly. A few words are too general. Some words are repeated.	Sentences are formed correctly, although they may be similar in structure. Most transitions are clear.	There are a few grammar errors. There are a few errors in spelling, capitalization, or punctuation.
1	The thesis of the paper is unclear or missing. The paper is poorly developed and/or confusing.	Ideas are not clearly organized. The paper may be missing an introduction or a conclusion.	The writer seems uninterested in the topic and unaware of his or her audience.	Most words are used incorrectly, many are too general or frequently repeated.	The sentences do not flow well and lack structure. They are short and choppy or long and confusing.	There are many grammar and/or spelling errors. There are many errors in capitalization and punctuation.

Six Traits of Writing: Fiction

	Ideas and Development	Organization	Voice and Audience Awareness	Word Choice	Sentence Fluency	Language Conventions
4	Clear plot events, as well as a readily identifiable conflict/problem and setting. The climax and resolution are clear. Rich details and sensory description make characters come to life. No irrelevant material.	Beginning grabs reader's attention. Logically sequenced plot. Story transitions link events. Conclusion caps off story and does not leave the reader hanging.	Strong sense of person and purpose behind the words. Brings story to life.	Words are specific, accurate, and vivid. Word choice enhances meaning and reader's enjoyment.	Writes complete sentences with varied sentence patterns and beginnings.	There are no major grammar errors. There are few errors in spelling, capitalization, or punctuation.
3	Identifiable plot events. Conflict/problem may not be entirely clear. The climax or resolution may not be clear. Some details/sensory description. Characters present but may not be fully developed. Setting may be missing. Limited irrelevant material.	Beginning interests reader. Plot somewhat logically sequenced but may lack one story element such as climax or satisfying conclusion. Story transitions link some events.	Some sense of person and purpose behind the words.	Words are correctly used but may be somewhat general and unspecific.	Writes complete sentences with some expansion. Limited variety.	There are a few grammar errors. There are a few errors in spelling, capitalization, or punctuation.
2	Limited plot and/or the conflict/problem is not clear. The setting, climax, and/or resolution may not be apparent. There are insufficient details and description. Characterization is weak. Too repetitious or too much irrelevant material.	Beginning does not capture reader's interest. Plot underdeveloped and two or more story elements (setting, initiating event, climax, resolution) missing. Story transitions missing.	Little sense of person and purpose behind the words.	Word choice limited. Words may be used inaccurately or repetitively.	Writes mostly simple and/or awkwardly constructed sentences. May include some run-ons and fragments.	There are many grammar or spelling errors. There are quite a few errors in capitalization and punctuation.
1	Does not address the prompt or the plot, conflict/problem are not discernible. Description, details, and characterization are missing.	Text has no evident structure. Lack of organization seriously interferes with meaning.	No sense of person or purpose behind the words.	Extremely limited range of words. Restricted vocabulary impedes message.	Numerous run-ons and/or sentence fragments interfere with meaning.	There are many spelling and grammar errors. There are many errors in capitalization and punctuation.

Six Traits of Writing: Persuasion

	Ideas and Development	Organization	Voice and Audience Awareness	Word Choice	Sentence Fluency	Language Conventions
4	Clearly states a position on the issue. Fully develops main ideas with evidence, examples, and explanations that are compelling. No irrelevant information.	Introduction clearly states position. Ideas logically sequenced. Transition sentences link ideas. Conclusion ties essay together and gives reader something to think about. Follows required format.	Strong sense of person and purpose behind the words. Brings issue to life.	Words are specific, accurate, and vivid. Word choice enhances meaning and reader's enjoyment.	Writes complete sentences with varied sentence patterns and beginnings.	There are no major grammar errors. There are few errors in spelling, capitalization, or punctuation.
3	States a position on the issue. Develops main ideas adequately with some evidence, examples, and explanations. Limited irrelevant information.	Introduction states position. Ideas mostly logically sequenced. Some linkage among ideas. Conclusion ties essay together. Follows required format.	Some sense of person and purpose behind the words. Sense of commitment to the issue. Text may be too casual for the purpose.	Words are correctly used but may be somewhat general and unspecific. Limited variety.	Writes complete sentences with some expansion. Limited variety.	There are a few grammar errors. There are a few errors in spelling, capitalization, or punctuation.
2	Does not state a clear position on the issue and/or does not support main ideas with sufficient evidence, examples, and explanations. May be too repetitious or too much irrelevant information.	Introduction may not state a position. Ideas not logically sequenced. Transition sentences missing. Conclusion may be missing. Does not follow required format.	Little sense of person and purpose behind the words. Very little engagement with reader. Text may be too casual for the purpose.	Word choice limited. Words may be used inaccurately or repetitively.	Writes mostly simple and/or awkwardly constructed sentences. May include some run-ons and fragments.	There are many grammar or spelling errors. There are quite a few errors in capitalization and punctuation.
1	Does not address the prompt or does not develop a position. Elaboration lacking or unrelated to the issue.	Text has no evident structure. Lack of organization seriously interferes with meaning.	No sense of person or purpose behind the words. No sense of audience.	Extremely limited range of words. Restricted vocabulary impedes message.	Numerous run-ons and/or sentence fragments interfere with meaning.	There are many spelling and grammar errors. There are many errors in capitalization and punctuation.

Six Traits of Writing: Literary Analysis

	Ideas and Development	Organization	Voice and Audience Awareness	Word Choice	Sentence Fluency	Language Conventions
4	States thesis clearly. Develops main ideas fully with elaborations. Direct quotations from text support ideas. All information pertinent to thesis.	Introduction contains thesis statement and cites title, author of work. Ideas logically sequenced. Transition sentences link ideas. Conclusion offers some evaluation of the work.	Strong sense of person and purpose behind the words. Brings topic to life.	Words are specific, accurate, and vivid. Word choice enhances meaning and reader's enjoyment.	Writes complete sentences with varied sentence patterns and beginnings.	There are no major grammar errors. There are few errors in spelling, capitalization, or punctuation.
3	States thesis clearly. Develops main ideas with some elaboration. May lack direct quotations from text to support ideas. Limited amount of irrelevant information.	Introduction contains thesis statement and cites title, author of work. Ideas mostly logically sequenced. Some linkage of main ideas. Formulaic conclusion may not offer evaluation of the work.	Some sense of person and purpose behind the words. Sense of commitment to the topic. Text may be too casual for purpose.	Words are correctly used but may be somewhat general and unspecific.	Writes complete sentences with some expansion. Limited variety.	There are a few grammar errors. There are a few errors in spelling, capitalization, or punctuation.
2	Does not state thesis clearly and/or minimal development of main ideas. No direct quotations to support ideas. Too repetitious or too much irrelevant information.	Introduction may not have clear thesis. Ideas not logically sequenced. Transitions may be missing. May lack conclusion, or conclusion is formulaic with no evaluation of the work.	Little sense of person and purpose behind the words. Very little engagement with the reader. Text may be too casual for purpose.	Word choice limited. Words may be used inaccurately or repetitively.	Writes mostly simple and/or awkwardly constructed sentences. May include some run-ons and fragments.	There are many grammar or spelling errors. There are quite a few errors in capitalization and punctuation.
1	Does not address the prompt or does not develop a thesis. Elaboration lacking or unrelated to a thesis.	No evident structure. Lack of organization seriously interferes with meaning.	No sense of person or purpose behind the words. No sense of audience.	Extremely limited range of words. Restricted vocabulary impedes message.	Numerous run-ons and/or sentence fragments interfere with meaning.	There are many spelling and grammar errors. There are many errors in capitalization and punctuation.

Copyright Acknowledgements

Photo and Illustration Credits